Trauma and Forgiveness

Consequences and Communities

C. FRED ALFORD

University of Maryland

CAMBRIDGE
UNIVERSITY PRESS

CAMBRIDGE
UNIVERSITY PRESS

University Printing House, Cambridge CB2 8BS, United Kingdom

Published in the United States of America by Cambridge University Press, New York

Cambridge University Press is part of the University of Cambridge.

It furthers the University's mission by disseminating knowledge in the pursuit of education, learning and research at the highest international levels of excellence.

www.cambridge.org
Information on this title: www.cambridge.org/9781107043404

First published 2013

Printed in the United Kingdom by CPI Group Ltd, Croydon CR0 4YY

A catalogue record for this publication is available from the British Library

Library of Congress Cataloguing in Publication data
Alford, C. Fred.
Trauma and forgiveness : consequences and communities / C. Fred Alford.
    pages   cm
ISBN 978-1-107-04340-4 (Hardback)
1. Psychic trauma.   2. Forgiveness.   3. Bereavement–Psychological aspects.
4. Psychology.   I. Title.
BF175.5.P75A44 2014
155.9′3–dc23   2013034563

ISBN 978-1-107-04340-4 Hardback

To Elly, who understands the topic well

Contents

I   Introduction: trauma and forgiveness

As I imagine is the case with most writers, I wrote this introduction after having written the substantive chapters of the manuscript. Shortly before I sat down to write the introduction, a friend asked what my book was about and, when I told him, he immediately assumed that I was writing about the way in which forgiveness helps to overcome hate and heal trauma. This is what I had tacitly assumed when I set out to write this manuscript. What I've learned, and what I hope the reader learns, is that trauma and forgiveness belong to different worlds. Like the Venn diagram most of us learned about in high school or college, the worlds overlap, but they share less than what divides them. In some respects, the key problem is treating each topic with the respect it is due.

This becomes more difficult when forgiveness takes on a magical quality. The risk is greater when forgiveness is understood as a performative act (a deed done with words, as in the statement "I forgive you"). A psychoanalyst quoted later argues that because the real work of coming to terms with the reality of the traumas we have suffered is so difficult and so painful, we turn to forgiveness in the hope that it will heal our pain and rage without our having to go through the hard sorrow-filled work it takes to get there (Smith 2008).

It is difficult to give up the loose, and at times irresponsible, use of forgiveness because the real work that would be required in its place – coming to terms with the grief, the mourning, and the anger – is so terribly difficult and time consuming. Time measured not just in years, but often decades. Precisely because it is so difficult, genuine forgiveness, whether asked for or given, is something to be valued – but not always to be sought or given. Forgiveness is often inappropriate. Forgiveness is frequently unnecessary for the work of life to go on.

The manuscript begins with trauma. It begins with the worst trauma of all, the trauma of Holocaust survivors. My research with Holocaust survivors, conducted almost exclusively through the use of videotaped recordings of interviews with survivors held in the Fortunoff Video Archive for Holocaust Testimonies at Yale University is my data base. My experience watching these interviews is set against the dominant account of trauma in the humanities, at least until recently – that of Cathy Caruth. This account has come to be known as that of the "absent witness." Its basic idea is that those who have suffered severe trauma are unable to testify to their own experience because they were not there when the trauma happened. Their bodies were present, but the trauma was inscribed upon their psyches before their psyches were prepared to receive it, so sudden, awful, and beyond the normal was the trauma. It is the task of those who listen to the witness to tell the stories of the traumatized, lest the only transmission be that of hysteria from one traumatized generation to another.

Even as Caruth and those influenced by her recognize the need to speak on behalf of those who cannot speak for themselves, Caruth is wary, lest putting words to the experience of terrible trauma somehow diminishes or memorializes it in a way that makes it prematurely final. The problem, of course, is what is to be done if the witness cannot speak, and his or her spokesperson cannot speak either, lest he or she turn the experience into stone? And how shall we know?

My experience viewing interviews of Holocaust survivors reveals that this is not the problem. Survivors generally tell complete and coherent stories, narratives with all the qualities of a developed plot. The problem is not that they cannot tell a developed story; the problem is that doing so does little to heal their trauma. There seems to be little or no connection between the ability to tell a mature and developed narrative and the affliction of trauma. Survivors tell coherent narratives in the same way as they live, by doubling: dividing the self into the Holocaust self and the post-Holocaust self. Caruth's account, it turns out, is more suited to explaining and exploring a literary text than the lives of some severely traumatized men and women.

Caruth's account is important in formulating my own. In a sense, her account acts as a foil. In the end, however, my goal is not to criticize Caruth's theory of trauma, but its implication: that the traumatized must be spoken for, as they cannot speak for themselves. In a sense this is true, but not in the sense Caruth intends – in which the result can only be silence. Caruth, in any case, is only my starting point. My goal is to understand trauma as a type of knowledge. Understanding trauma in this way requires a more experience-near formulation of the insult and the injury. It also helps to explain why forgiveness can help illuminate trauma, but is generally not more helpful in healing it.

Chapter 3 turns to the psychoanalyst D. W. Winnicott, who is not generally seen as a trauma theorist. He wrote little explicitly about the topic, though it is implicit throughout his work. For Winnicott, trauma transforms the "true self," as Winnicott calls it, into a way of being that devotes itself to responding to intrusion, never having the capacity to just *be*. In fact, this *is* trauma for Winnicott: the inability to *be*. If all this sounds a little abstract or metaphysical, then the reader will appreciate all the more Winnicott's marvellous ability to bring such terms down to earth, transforming these abstractions into everyday experiences. Chapter 3 also considers the implications of Winnicott's theory of individual trauma for a political theory of trauma.

Trauma is political when it prevents the socially marginalized from appropriating the defensive resources of the culture, resources that mediate between the individual and trauma. Today there are more marginalized people than ever, at least when compared with the wealthy mainstream of Western society. Among the marginalized are people living in persistent poverty, those institutionalized in asylums and prisons, as well as those living on American Indian reservations. Migrant laborers and their children, as well as those pushed to the edges of society, such as the aged, the isolated, and unwelcome strangers in new lands, are also included.

For Caruth, trauma becomes the vehicle of world history, via the hysterical transmission of trauma (understood as post traumatic

stress disorder, or PTSD) down the generations. Winnicott's contribution, and my goal, is to see trauma as more than an individual clinical
disorder, but less than a world historical event. Trauma is political,
but it is political on the scale of groups of individuals, particularly
marginalized groups. Understanding this renders trauma subject to
political analysis and intervention; if, that is, we have the will to look
and to act. This is why it is so important to see trauma with the right
lens: neither too big nor too small. Only then does trauma become
subject to politics. Only then *is* trauma politics.

Chapters 4 and 5 draw on the work of the psychoanalyst
Melanie Klein in order to unravel the knot that is forgiveness. This
may seem surprising, for Klein is better known as a theorist of original
hate. In fact, this is what makes her work so valuable. Whatever
resources for forgiveness one finds in Klein will not come cheaply.

We seem to be living in an era of forgiveness. Forgiveness
is the topic of numerous symposia, hundreds of books, thousands
of professional articles, at least one special edition of a psychoanalytic journal, and the International Forgiveness Institute
(www.forgiveness-institute.org). As a topic of popular psychology
and theology, forgiveness is approached almost entirely in terms of
the benefits it brings to the one who forgives. About the most intelligent statement of this position is that of Ira Byock, who says, "I think
forgiveness is actually a very sophisticated emotional strategy for
caring for ourselves. Because when there is anger and a feeling of
retribution it's really ours and it keeps us stuck. It's hard to move
beyond that sort of anger" (NCC 2001). Dr. Byock works for a hospice,
helping the terminally ill come to terms with their unresolved anger.

The position taken in this manuscript is roughly the opposite of
Byock's, a good man doing good work. Forgiveness is properly about a
normative relationship with the offender and the community, and
forgiveness is a virtue in the classical sense of embodying a human
excellence. As such, forgiveness must meet certain ethical standards
before it should be given. It should not be given primarily in order to
make the self *feel* better, but in order to make the self *be* better, as in

be a better person. Nonetheless, these are complicated issues, and the distinction is never quite so clear in practice as in the normative ideal. The reality of human psychology must be taken into account.

It might seem as if there is a tension between forgiveness as an expression of an ethical relationship and forgiveness as an expression of a human excellence. Seen as a human excellence, forgiveness requires the relationship, but the excellence is not measured by the relationship. Seen as an ethical relationship, the quality or standards of the relationship come first. An interesting consequence of paying attention to the psychology of forgiveness from the British Object Relations perspective is that it sees human excellence in terms of relationships. The result is to mitigate, but not eliminate, this tension between excellence and relationship.

Melanie Klein is known for her concept of reparation, and it would be easy to confuse reparation with forgiveness. They are not the same, and the unfair thing about forgiveness is that reparation is even more important for the victim than the offender. To be sure, the victim need not make reparation to the offender. Rather, the victim, who is often a victim of trauma, must come to see this world as a good enough world to live in, even as it is this same world that is capable of taking everything of value from the victim in a heartbeat. Here is where trauma and forgiveness find their closest connection, here is where the Venn diagram overlaps most fully – not when forgiveness heals trauma, but when the experience of forgiveness, which includes the experience of the impossibility of forgiveness, helps to explain the experience of trauma, and what trauma destroys: faith in the reliability of the world.

Chapter 4 considers Hannah Arendt's well-known explication of forgiveness. Cynthia Ozick calls it "jabberwocky," and while the judgment is harsh, Ozick is not mistaken. Arendt's attempt to save forgiveness for special use in the political realm renders it irrelevant for deeds done under the influence of hate, recklessness, and wilfulness; that is, for most of the actions for which forgiveness is both difficult and important. Arendt also misinterprets the

New Testament on forgiveness. Julia Kristeva and Jacques Derrida also write about forgiveness, and their contributions are assessed.

None of these authors quite seems to grasp the danger posed by forgiveness. The danger is not that it will be seized upon by a few hundred (or few thousand) popular authors who would turn forgiveness into a self-help program: forgive the one who hurt you, and forgive yourself, so you can get on with your life. More dangerous is the idea that one does not need to forgive, because one cannot be harmed by anything that happens to you. This is a crimson thread that runs through Western philosophy, from Socrates to Plato to Aristotle to the Stoics to Nietzsche and beyond. One of the most important things to be learned from forgiveness is how vulnerable we are, and how easily we can be hurt, which is why forgiveness is important and valuable. Recognizing the value of forgiveness, practicing it well as both the one who asks for forgiveness and as the one who grants it, is a cardinal human virtue precisely because it recognizes our terrible fragility.

Chapter 5 develops the Kleinian perspective on forgiveness further, before turning to a section called "Voices of Forgiveness and its Simulacrum." Here it is not theorists, but the people who have struggled mightily with the problems of forgiveness that are considered. Only those people whose actual faces and voices could be seen and heard on video were considered, a practice that excluded a number who have written beautifully about the subject, such as Pumla Gobodo-Madikizela (2003). My goal, as much as it was possible, was to create a situation parallel to that of the testimony of the Holocaust survivors. That turned out to be impossible. A documentary film is so different from a well-conducted videotaped interview with a Holocaust survivor that at some level there is no comparison. Nevertheless, there is something to be said for watching the person speak, often for minutes at a time without interruption (but possibly with editing). The face and body of the speaking subject are simply different, more corporeally real, on video, than words in a text. While I used videos, in virtually every case the quotations are backed up by published text.

The most fascinating thing about the voices section is that none of them quite fits the categories of forgiveness developed in the two chapters on Klein and forgiveness. That's good, not bad. Above all, it's hopeful, for it suggests that real people are more imaginative in finding solutions than theorists. The voices are sometimes troubling. Eva Kor, the first to be heard from, was a "Mengele twin," one of about 100 twins (out of several thousand) who survived the experiments (actually tortures) inflicted upon her and her sister by Josef Mengele. After some preliminary meetings with some of Mengele's surviving colleagues, Kor went to the gates of Auschwitz and read a statement forgiving Mengele. Then she went on to forgive all Nazis. Other Mengele twins were outraged.

Surely Kor misunderstands something fundamental about forgiveness. Yet, when one looks at the life she made for herself, including the founding of a Holocaust museum in Terra Haute, Indiana (not the most likely place), one begins to wonder what it is that this misnamed "forgiveness" has done for her. Also considered are an activist who was sentenced for unintentionally murdering a policeman during the Vietnam War, the policeman's daughter, and finally a woman who abandoned her children. Not all are dramatic cases. All are about forgiveness. And all have a richness about them that overflows the categories developed in the chapter.

Chapter 6 considers what Donald Winnicott's concept of transitional experience might contribute to our understanding of forgiveness. Something of a palinode to the last chapter, this chapter considers whether forgiveness might stem not from the offender's contrition, but from the way the victim has come to reside in the world. Can the victim come to experience the world itself in a new way, as transitional space, as Winnicott calls it, a space charged with subjectivity, while remaining objectively real? This is a different solution than that offered either by Klein or Moses Maimonides (introduced in Chapter 5), but it is no easier. To live in transitional space requires a willingness to let go of the mental holding of ourselves, which is what we do when we are traumatized. Once again, forgiveness leads to a deeper understanding of trauma. Not because forgiveness heals trauma – though it may help – but because the conditions of forgiveness reveal, as their opposite, the conditions (more precisely, the consequences) of trauma: the inability to stop clinging not only to one's wounds, hatred, and bitterness, but also to the world we live in.

"Don't cling, and don't cling to not clinging" is a wonderful Buddhist saying, and it helps make sense of Winnicott's concept of transitional experience. Winnicott's is not just a piece of advice. He reveals that the ability to experience the world in this way requires the support of others. For adults, the ability to experience the world as a transitional place and space requires living in a community of others who care. As with the treatment of trauma, Winnicott transforms forgiveness into an experience that makes little sense in the absence of a supportive community.

Chapter 6 concludes with the longest case study, the voice of Terri Jentz, who was run over and axed by a man intent on her destruction. Fifteen years after the attack, Jentz returned to the scene, and in repeated trips over the next eight years, sought to find her attacker. What she found instead was that many people in the small community where the attack took place knew or strongly suspected who her attacker was, but did not inform the police, who were themselves remarkably lackadaisical in their investigation. Jentz's attempt to create, out of this not-very-promising community, one that could hold her, so that she might let go of some of her rage and fear, and better come to terms with her trauma, is testimony to human creativity. If you don't have a holding community, if one has let you down, then create one to hold you. Jentz did, but it required the responsiveness of members of the community, particularly the nurses who originally cared for her when she was so severely injured, and who were willing to share themselves with her almost twenty years later.

Chapter 7 is a study of Jean Améry, a Holocaust survivor who was tortured as a member of the resistance. *At the Mind's Limits: Contemplations by a Survivor on Auschwitz and its Realities* had as its original main title *Jenseits Von Schuld und Sühne*. "Beyond Guilt and Atonement," is the literal translation, and easily seen as Améry's ironic evocation of Nietzsche's *Beyond Good and Evil*. Améry sought to rehabilitate resentment as an important and valid emotion in the face of outrage. (Though he wrote in German, Améry used the French *ressentiment*, as did Nietzsche.) Against forgiveness, Améry sets resentment as the only valid moral position. More importantly, Améry claims that one must hold to the impossible, that history itself be reversed. Since that is impossible, Améry settles for what is really his version of the categorical imperative: that offenders *wish* as much as victims that history be reversed, that the Holocaust never happened. The wish is sufficient, as long as it is held with equal fervency by executioner and victim alike. For Améry, ethics must stand against history, against time, against reality, or it is not truly ethical.

Strange as it may seem, I argue that Améry is writing about forgiveness.

> When SS-man Wajs stood before the firing squad, he experienced the moral truth of his crimes. At that moment, he was with *me* – and I was no longer alone ... I would like to believe that at the instant of his execution he wanted exactly as much as I to turn back time, to undo what had been done.
>
> *(Améry 1980: 70)*

What Améry wants from utopian reunion in death is what so many want from forgiveness: a reconciliation with their offender. This is what so many people seem to mean when they talk about forgiveness as the restoration of lost wholeness. The longing for lost wholeness is almost as common among secular proponents of forgiveness as it is among the religious. Like so many, Améry isn't just talking about forgiveness, but his desire for what forgiveness brings, relief from the loneliness and isolation of hurt and pain.

Améry's ethic of resentment makes a valid ethical claim, as well as helping us understand that trauma is not just an illness, but a demand that the past not be as it was. Such a demand need not be futile if it is seen as a moral declaration, not an inability to accept the reality of historical time. The same cannot be said of Améry's refusal to accept aging and death. Aging and death are not enemies of life in the same way that the Nazis were. A natural death, that comes in its own time and its own way, is not an enemy of life, but a part of life. Why Améry was unable to make this distinction is considered.

Coming to properly value forgiveness means coming to see it as a virtue – a rare, fine, and difficult achievement. For there are many ways to miss the mark, and few ways to hit it, as Aristotle almost said about the mean (N. Ethics 1106b: 10–35). How often is forgiveness given in order to make the victim feel better? How often is forgiveness withheld, because withholding forgiveness is easier than letting go of one's attachment to hate and anger, as though hate and anger had come to be the only things one can count on in an unstable, shifting world? Finally, how often is forgiveness ignored out of the fantasy of self-sufficiency, as in "how could one as proud and independent as I be hurt by someone like you?"

Forgiveness is not the primary way in which trauma is healed. Forgiveness has its place. Asked for at just the right time in a serious way, forgiveness can make a difference in how the traumatized person learns to let go of a past that haunts his or her present. Nevertheless, the primary way in which forgiveness and trauma are related is epistemological. Expressed less extravagantly, what forgiveness requires helps us understand what trauma takes from us, and what trauma gives in return. Trauma takes away our confidence in the existence of a stable, ordered, and meaningful existence. Trauma gives back knowledge in return. Trauma is knowledge. Trauma is ethical knowledge. The inability to move forward, the tendency so characteristic of the traumatized to repeat the past, the difficulty in moving from then and there to here and now, is also a statement about what we owe the past. That we respectfully remember our own suffering as well as that of others. That we do not accept what happened without protest, a protest that is beneath all words, often expressed in the symbolism of the body.

For the body may also be a symbol, no less abstract for not being a sentence or a book. Unfortunately, sometimes we pay more than we owe. Sometimes we can't stop paying. Then we need help; not to heal the trauma – healing is not a helpful metaphor here – but to express the trauma in such a way that we can possess the knowledge we already have, and so no longer need to be constantly reminded of.

One thinks here of Plato's doctrine of anamnesis or recollection (*Meno* 81b–d, 85d–86b; *Phaedo* 72c–76d). For Plato, we are born knowing all we shall ever learn and more. The problem is to remember what we already know. Applied to trauma, we may say that the special knowledge that is trauma is possessed long before it is understood. First this knowledge possesses us. Trauma is never healed. If we are fortunate, we will find a world and a way in which we can stop holding ourselves so tightly, as Winnicott might put it, and so make the acquaintance of the trauma that possesses us. This does not mean we shall be healed of trauma, freed of trauma, or be in control of our trauma. On the contrary, to be in control of one's trauma is the problem, not the solution. To possess that by which one is possessed means merely (and it is a lot) that one understands in more than incomprehensible bodily sensations and overwhelming emotional experiences the truth of trauma.

Varied as traumatic experience is, this truth is always the same: that not just the order and stability of my world, but the very existence of the ideas of order and stability are mythic, a ratty human veil to hide the dark insight of Carel the mad cleric in Iris Murdoch's (1966) novel, *The Time of the Angels*.

> Suppose the truth were awful, suppose it was just a black pit, or like birds huddled in the dust in a dark cupboard? ... Who could face this? All philosophy has taught a facile optimism, even Plato did so ... Any interpretation of the world is childish. The author of the Book of Job understood it. Job asks for sense and justice. Jehovah replies that there is none. There is only power and the marvel of power; there is only chance and the terror of chance. (172)

There are ways of living with this reality that do not require deadening of the soul, but one cannot live with this knowledge without experiencing what are sometimes misleadingly called flashbacks. The term is misleading not because these experiences are not disturbing, and not because they do not need to be brought under control in many cases, but because the flashback is also a flash of insight into the reality of the world. The problem is how to respect the insight without making life unlivable. Forgiveness may help one do this, because it tells us that we are vulnerable, and that we live in a community in which this vulnerability is recognized and ritualized in a way that supports the experience of living with trauma. This assumes, of course, that such a community actually exists. Too often it doesn't, for it is fragile and easily destroyed by many of the forces that make up the modern world.

Though his thought does not organize this manuscript, though he gets it quite wrong in important respects, Jean Améry shadows, or perhaps a better word is "haunts," much of this manuscript. He argued strenuously against the medicalization of trauma. He is the most articulate spokesman of the claim that trauma is knowledge. Above all, he refused to let the past become the past, contrary to the popular view that acceptance is key to the healing of trauma. Though Améry is addressed in detail only in Chapter 7, he appears briefly in more chapters than not. He serves as our cicerone to the Hell that is trauma. Because this manuscript is about more than trauma, and because Améry's is neither the first nor last word on the topic, he deserves the place he has found here. A guide to unfamiliar territory, a guide who has been there before, but not one we should want to follow to the end.

Theses of this manuscript:

Trauma is knowledge, and the problem of the traumatized is to gain access to this knowledge in a way that is not self-destructive. This almost always requires the company of others. These others may be friends, lovers, relatives, people who like to listen and care, people who are paid to listen and care.

These others are more readily found in holding communities, as Winnicott might call them. That is, communities in which individuals feel economically and socially secure, as well as secure in having found meaning in their lives, in large measure because they have helped to create it. In such holding communities it is more likely to find people to hold the traumatized. Holding is not a group function, even as it is enabled by a functioning group.

Forgiveness is a virtue in something like the classical sense. While "something like" are weasel words, I can do no better. Trauma illuminates why forgiveness is a virtue, and forgiveness illustrates both why and how trauma is knowledge. Their closest relationship is that of the mutual elaboration and explication of the best meaning of each term. This is, of course, a judgment, which will require an argument to back it up. The contribution of forgiveness to the easing of trauma is real, but not profound.

Trauma becomes less intrusive for many reasons other than acts of atonement and forgiveness, and often, acts of atonement and forgiveness make little difference. Trauma and forgiveness illuminate each other. Sometimes atonement and forgiveness help the traumatized person find a way to live with his or her trauma. That is enough.

2 Is the Holocaust traumatic?

Michael Ignatieff comments about the Balkan war, "the past continues to torment because it is *not* past ... Simultaneity, it would seem, is the dream time of vengeance" (Griswold 2007: 192). One might just as easily say that simultaneity is the nightmare of trauma, a nightmare from which the trauma victim will never awake until the past becomes the past tense. About this, most students and theorists of trauma would agree. About the implications, there is much disagreement.

Cathy Caruth, a literary theorist who combines literary criticism with neurobiology (a curious combination), has created a theory of trauma that is at the same time a theory of history. While Caruth is not as well known among those who work with trauma victims as she is among literary critics, her connection with Dori Laub, psychiatrist, psychoanalyst, and co-founder of the Fortunoff Video Archive for Holocaust Testimonies at Yale University, has made her work familiar to a larger number of psychologists and psychoanalysts (Felman and Laub 1992; Laub 1995). My argument begins with the observation that Caruth's account of psychological trauma does not fit some of the most traumatized men and women of the twentieth century: survivors of the Holocaust. Should this lead us to rethink trauma theory, or should we instead decide that the Holocaust is a special case? About the last question, the correct answer is both, but it will take a while to get there.

Narratives of survivors held in the Fortunoff Video Archive for Holocaust Testimonies at Yale University are the primary source from which my examples of trauma in this chapter are drawn. During the period 2007–2012, I viewed almost 200 testimonies, most around two hours long (Alford 2009a; 2009b; 2012). These accounts fit neither

Caruth's theory, nor the usual way we think about PTSD, at least not without qualification.

Already the reader may be asking him or herself if historical trauma, such as the Holocaust, really has anything to do with PTSD, a clinical diagnosis.[1] It is a question that occupies this chapter. For now the simplest thing to say is that it is Caruth herself who assimilates them. Hers is an ambitious account of trauma as a historical relationship among individuals, generations, and societies.

> If PTSD must be understood as a psychological symptom of the unconscious, it is a symptom of history. The traumatized, we might say, carry an impossible history within them, or they become themselves the symptom of a history they cannot entirely possess.
> (Caruth 1995: 5)

Trauma, from this perspective, carries with it the weight of history, and the traumatized are its representatives. Unfortunately, history's representatives, the traumatized, are (in this account) unable to testify in a coherent manner. That means abiding by the normal conventions of narrative, such as telling a story with a beginning, middle, and end, while being able to move back and forth in time, from then to now. The ability to shift tense, so that the trauma is narrated in the past tense, while the telling remains in the present, turns out to be a significant marker of the narrator's ability to remember rather than relive the trauma.

According to Caruth (1996: 4, 91–92), the victim of extreme trauma repeats an unassimilated experience that was unknowable in the first instance. By "repeats," Caruth and others seem to mean that the witness is frozen in time, unable to do more than tell the same story again and again. When he or she does so, the story is relived or re-experienced in an intrusive manner, involving flashbacks, the witness feeling and acting as if he or she is reliving the experience rather than narrating it. Often the present tense is mixed with the past. Frequently these intrusive flashbacks and memories seem to come out of nowhere; for example, in the middle of family dinner, disrupting the ongoing experience of everyday life.

Caruth's appears to be a version of the acting-out versus working-through theory of trauma, and it is. Acting-out refers to the tendency to relive the trauma, to exist in the present as though it were the past. Those who act-out tend to relive occurrences, not just in flashbacks or nightmares, but in stories that are endlessly repeated, often with little variation, generally with no development. Statements of the form "then I was ... but now I am ..." are rare or non-existent. As has been wisely observed, if there is any empirical meaning to Freud's (1920) death drive it may be this: the tendency to repeat or relive traumatic events in a way that is self-destructive, for it freezes the narrator in a hellish time and place he or she desperately desires to escape.

Working-through is expressed by the traumatized person's ability to say to him or herself something like the following: "Something terrible happened to me back then, and I can never be free of its effects. But I exist in the here and now, which is different from the there and then." The relief working-through brings is that of distance and perspective. Working-through is not a cure. It is a way of living with the trauma one has undergone as history, rather than an endlessly repeated present experience. Though acting-out versus working-through sounds Freudian (1914) in origin, as it is, do not be misled. There is nothing Freudian about Caruth's account. This is so even as she holds to the traditional view that absent intervention, the survivor will continue repeating the intrusive memories because they lack the quality of genuine memory, for they have not been fully transformed into symbols. They never were.

Caruth's account is not Freudian not merely because she rejects (or rather has no place for) what Freud (1898; 1909) called *Nachträglichkeit*, in which memory is overlaid with more recent experience; Caruth's account is not Freudian because there is no psychological depth to the experience of trauma. Truama occurs when the traumatic event is experienced a moment too late, before the self was there to mediate it. Unlike Freud, this is not a developmental claim but a temporal one. Extreme trauma is inscribed upon an otherwise-mature subject who was not there, because the experience was so far beyond the normal it could not be prepared for, categorized, or shared. This is not a Freudian account, even if familiar categories like acting-out versus working-through continue to appear. In what is now the most influential account of trauma among students of the humanities, there is no assumption that the victim of trauma is bringing deep, unconscious material to the surface, or that the truth lies buried deep within. On the contrary, the subject is a camera, the event etched into a portion of the memory that cannot be erased or transformed readily into narrative, as its basic elements are not linguistic symbols, but sensations.

Literary theorists such as Caruth have drawn upon a surprising source of support, the neurobiological research of Bessel A. van der Kolk and several of his associates (van der Kolk and van der Hart 1995). For van der Kolk, traumatic memory is recorded in a unique way in the brain: imagistic, iconic, sensory. These are extremely accurate, almost camera-like images that are almost impossible to integrate into the signifying mind, at least not without extensive therapy. Both Caruth and van der Kolk treat pictures and visual images as though they were non-symbolic, standing in opposition to verbal images, when in fact the picture and the word stand very close together (Leys 2000: 249). Good writing uses words to conjure images, and images can almost always be described in words, or what is poetry for? Not just testimony, but the literature on trauma is filled with the victim's speech, much of which has the quality of a story or narrative, as Lawrence Langer's (1991) *Holocaust Testimonies: The Ruins of Memory*, reveals. Shocking is not the absence of narrative, but the content of the narrative; the narrative of atrocity and disbelief it might be called. Caruth, however, is not making distinctions concerning the content of the narrative one encounters among the traumatized. She is claiming that one does not encounter complex narrative in the first place, even as she (Caruth 1996: 142) admires Langer's book, which is filled with dense and complex narrative. In the end, both Caruth and van der Kolk define traumatic memory as a literal impression that forever (or at least without therapeutic intervention, which uses speech) remains isolated from speech.

Nevertheless, one can see the purpose of the odd alliance between Caruth, the literary critic; van der Kolk, the neurobiologist; and Dori Laub, the psychoanalyst. What they share is the belief that trauma creates a wound, a structural deficit, where representation is not. The result is the "crisis of witnessing," in which the surviving witnesses to the most horrific events of the twentieth century cannot narratively represent their experience (Felman and Laub 1992). A distinction can be drawn between "cannot narratively represent" and "impossible to believe what one knows to be true," a difference not developed by Caruth et al. As Eva L. puts it, "I can't believe it happened to me ... How can they believe if I can't believe?" (T-71).[2] Eva L. is referring to the difficulty she encounters trying to explain to others the horrors she has experienced and witnessed. How can she convince others if she can't even convince herself? And why wouldn't she be able to convince herself? Because she has gone through an experience that was unimaginable, as though it took place on another planet, to another person, in another world.

A careless observer might imagine that Eva L. is a perfect example of Freud's early experience with traumatized and hysterical patients. About such patients Freud said that they accept that an event must have happened, for it could not have been any other way, but they do not remember the event. "Patients themselves accept that they thought this or that, they often add: 'But I can't *remember* having thought it'." "It's easy to tell them their thoughts were *unconscious*," continues Freud, but how to make sense of the fact that these thoughts remain unconscious even after there is no need for repression? "Are we to suppose that we are really dealing with thoughts that never came about ... so that the treatment would lie in the accomplishment of a psychical act which did not take place at the time?" (Freud 1898: 300).

The problem of the patient's lack of confidence in the reality of his or her own memory of trauma continues to haunt not just psychoanalysis, "but the entire modern discourse of trauma" (Leys 2000: 103). But it does not haunt Caruth, and for quite different reasons it will not haunt my account. Eva L. does not fail to remember her experience. In fact, she can narrate it in great depth and with full conviction. She simply sometimes can't believe it happened because it is so utterly alien not only to her present experience, but to ordinary human experience for which she might otherwise find a context. The experience is not irretrievable, just unbelievable. This is not to say she doubts its reality, or is unable to articulate the traumatic experience in a sophisticated narrative, one that has all the signs of having worked through the experience, such as making a sharp distinction between "then and there" and "here and now." In fact, the sharpness of this distinction is precisely what troubles Eva.

In Caruth's account, there is no "unbelievable" to be narrated in the first place. Narrative is replaced in trauma by a neuro-camera that can only repeat itself. Actually, that's not quite true. In Caruth's account, the neuro-camera becomes a neuro-transmitter of hysteria, in which the only way the Holocaust is conveyed by those who experienced it is in the mode of horror so deep and terrible that it is at once overwhelming and contaminating. "What is transmitted is 'not the normalizing knowledge of the horror but the horror itself'" (Leys 2000: 268; internal quote from Michaels 1996: 8).

Of course, the mind is not really a camera, and Caruth does not imagine that it is. Nevertheless, her language suggests a literalness to the process of traumatic memory that does little to clarify the experience. According to Caruth, trauma is experienced as the "literal registration of an event ... Modern neurobiologists have in fact suggested that the unerring 'engraving' on the mind, the 'etching into the brain' of an event in trauma may be associated with its elision of its normal encoding in memory" (Caruth 1995: 152–153). Generally employing a language that tends toward the physical reduction, or at least the material elucidation, of emotional experience, Caruth concludes that "trauma is the confrontation with an event that, in its unexpectedness or horror, cannot become, as Janet says, a 'narrative memory' that is integrated into a completed story of the past" (Caruth 1995: 153). That latter claim, the unavailability of trauma to narrative memory, is reasonable, familiar, and in the case of the vast majority of Holocaust witnesses, false. The core problem with Caruth's claim is not, however, that she makes a false claim; an account can be fruitful but false. The core problem with Caruth's claim is that she couches it in a language that tends to mystify, rather than clarify, the experience of trauma. She does so by placing trauma beyond a phenomenological or experience-based account of extreme human experience, an account still within the province of the victim. The result is to render extreme trauma the subject of expert listeners who must, it seems, take on the burden of the original victims.

NO NARRATIVE ABOUT AUSCHWITZ

For Caruth, language testifies to severe trauma when its denotative and connotative functions fail, and what is transmitted is not a narrative of the trauma, but the intense emotions associated with it. An implication of this assumption according to Dori Laub is that we, the readers and listeners, become participants and co-owners of the traumatic event (Felman and Laub 1992: 57). In other words, listening to testimony about extreme trauma becomes a process in which the listener is willing to become traumatized him or herself, in order to feel what words cannot represent. This would imply that the listener of Holocaust testimony must partake of the Holocaust in a second-order fashion (admittedly an unclear term, but Caruth does not elaborate upon the process of trans-mission), for this is the only way the non-representable can be known – by allowing oneself to be infected by the emotional contagion of the trauma, or as Caruth (1995: 11) puts it, "the history of a trauma, in its inherent belatedness, can only take place through the listening of another."

Caruth does not mean that through the listening of another the victim of trauma can hear and understand him or herself, and in this way begin to work through the trauma, or at least this is not her primary meaning. Caruth means that only the listener can experience with conscious awareness the trauma that the original victim could not. The context of Caruth's statement is her wider claim that trauma is the historical link not just between individuals, but between generations. "History is precisely the way we are implicated in each other's traumas" (Caruth 1996: 24). While Caruth assumes that the listener may provide the link between generations, the link is less that of understanding, but of feeling. The trauma of the Holocaust, or Hiroshima, is experienced by subsequent generations as inherited trauma, still felt more than understood (Caruth 1995: 11).

"To what extent does it make sense to conclude that the traumatized view of the world conveys a wisdom that ought to be heard in its own terms?" In part the answer to Kai Erikson's (1995: 198) wise question will depend upon whether trauma victims are, in fact, incapable of telling their own stories. For as Edward Said (1979) has taught us about the intellectual colonization of the Orient, its greatest conceit was in thinking that the West could speak for those who presumably could not speak for themselves.

Caruth would likely agree with Said. For Caruth, as for Berel Lang (2000), we respect the victims of extreme trauma best when we do not try to represent it. It is the gap, the wound, that in its silent unavailability around which we can try to speak about which we should remain silent. The result is to render trauma a silent sacred symbol, the place where narrative is not. Followers of Jacques Lacan (1977) would call this place the real, that about which it is impossible to speak, for the fears, needs, and desires that reside there are so primordial that they cannot be expressed in language. A particularly worrisome exaggeration of this way of thinking is found in Slavoj Žižek's (1989: 50) assertion that the concentration camp is itself but one more instance of the Lacanian real. The real may be a useful, albeit abstract, way of thinking about the psychological trauma that cannot be spoken, the trauma with which Caruth is concerned; however, transforming Auschwitz into but one more example of the real risks placing the Holocaust beyond rational discourse. Of course the Holocaust cannot be represented if Auschwitz cannot be "attached . . . to a concrete image" in the first place (LaCapra 1998: 48;

Žižek 1989: 50). But then it is we who have made unrepresentable what other human beings have created, and still others suffered.

A consequence of this perspective is that the working-through of trauma, that is, coming to experience and express the trauma in the past tense, tends to be equated with a premature closure, a violation of the respect we accord to the silence of the sacred. Caruth puts it this way:

> The danger of speech, of integration into the narration of
> memory, may not lie in what it cannot understand, but in that
> it understands too much ... The possibility of integration into
> memory and the consciousness of history thus raises the
> question, van der Kolk and van der Hart ultimately observe,
> "whether it is not a sacrilege of the traumatic experience to
> play with the reality of the past?"
>
> *(Caruth 1995: 154)*

If it becomes sacrilege to help others put their trauma into words, or to try to understand their trauma as narrative, by which I mean a story with a beginning, middle, and end, with protagonists (in this case, victims and executioners), not just events that happen to people, then what are we to do? Silence may be a way of showing respect, but in the end nothing happens. And if silence is itself not an option, then what? How can we not betray the past by telling it?

In fact, this is a misleading statement of the problem. The testimony of most survivors of the Holocaust is already in well-developed narrative form. They have already committed sacrilege, so to speak. The problem is not that survivors cannot put their experience into narrative; the problem is that doing so, often called working-through, does little to heal them. The problem is not that of experiences that cannot be put into words; it is about words that don't heal, and *not* because they are disconnected from the emotional experience of trauma.

JEAN AMÉRY AND THE DISCIPLINE OF THE WITNESS

Born Hanns Chaim Mayer in Austria in 1912, Améry joined the resistance to the Nazi occupation of Belgium, was arrested, tortured, and sent to the concentration camps Auschwitz, Buchenwald, and Bergen-Belsen. Raised a Roman Catholic by his mother, his father was Jewish and Améry came to identify with a Judaism best represented, he said, by the Auschwitz number tattooed on his left forearm (Améry 1980: 94); that is, with a Judaism of the tormented and oppressed. Jean Améry is an anagram of Mayer, taken by Améry after the war as a way of distancing himself from all things German. A part-time student of philosophy and literature before the war, Améry became a well-known essayist after the war. In ill health, Améry took his own life in 1978, at the age of 66. His suicide came as no surprise. He wrote a well-known book on the topic (Améry 1999).

About the psychological approach to the trauma of the survivor (Améry is specifically addressing the survivor who will not abandon his *ressentiment*, but the argument applies to all survivors who wish to speak for themselves),[3] Améry argues that if testimony is seen as a product of traumatic illness, then its political value is lessened (Améry 1980: 96, 99). As Michel Foucault (1994) wrote about the medicalization of discipline, so Améry understood that to focus on the survivor as the subject of diagnosis and therapy would be to lessen the truth value of his or her experiences as an account of reality. A subjective account to be sure, but the most important subjective account of all, from one who had experienced the reality of the Third Reich in and on his tortured mind and body. For Améry, torture was the essence of the Nazi regime, its victims the most powerful witnesses. Not the medical malfunction of the survivor, but the terrible truth of the reality to which he or she bore witness, is the most important thing the survivor has to tell us.

Améry is, of course, writing from a political perspective, but that is really the point. One has a choice in how to approach the survivor: as witness to the greatest crime in history, or as crippled camera who must be spoken for. Writing about Améry's critique of those who view the survivor primarily as a victim of trauma, Thomas Brudholm (2008: 93) exempts Caruth from Améry's criticism. In fact, she is no more than a special case. If trauma is rendered unspeakable, communicable only to specially trained therapists who have the duty and privilege of translating the original experience into a narrative both victim and others can understand, then the professional discipline (in both senses of the term) of survivors' experiences is complete, by whatever language one wants to call it. For Caruth, the only alternative seems to be the non-comprehending hysterical transmission of trauma from generation to generation.

Améry holds his position as part of his claim that his resentment is a rational response to inhuman treatment, not the reaction of a wounded or traumatized soul who needs treatment before he is politically competent to be heard on his own terms. I agree, but my argument is not based on Améry's assertion. It is based on my experience listening to almost two hundred traumatized Holocaust survivors give narratively coherent accounts of their experiences. However trauma works in the real world, it does not seem to work by destroying the capacity of the witness to competently account for what he or she has witnessed.

"NO ONE CAN UNDERSTAND WHO WASN'T THERE"

A surprising number of witnesses say, in one way or another, implicitly or explicitly, that they "died at Auschwitz." Charlotte Delbo (1995: 267), a survivor who wrote several memoirs about her experience, says right out that "I am not alive. I died in Auschwitz but no one knows it." What could that mean? Especially for men and women who have gone on to marry (or remarry), raise children whom they evidently love and care for, dote on their grandchildren, and participate in their communities, for one hears tell of this in numerous survivor testimonies.

There are of course variants. Max B. says "I should have died at Auschwitz" (T-1125). Earlier he says "plenty of times it wasn't good to survive" (T-94). Several survivors wish they had died with their parents. "We should have died together," me and mother, said Eva L. (T-71). Martin L. expresses a similar sentiment (T-224). Rather than being a reflection of so-called survivor guilt, doubts about survival raise the very real question of whether the pain of living has been worth the price. Holocaust survivors are not the only ones to ask this question, but the frequency with which they ask it so many years after liberation, often amidst what appears to be a full life, is heartbreaking. Primo Levi's evident suicide must be interpreted in this context. Jean Améry's suicide had more complex roots, as will be shown. But perhaps that is always the case.

Relatively few survivors commit suicide (Barak 2005). On the contrary, Elie Wiesel seems correct that the survivor's problem is not Hamlet's problem, "to be or not to be?" The survivor's problem is "to be and not to be" (Wiesel 1982: 54). But how in the world does one do that? How does one learn to live a double life? For that is what we are talking about, and that is how several survivors refer to it. But a strange double life it is, one in which the survivor's Auschwitz double never goes away, and often grows stronger and more insistent over time.

Among the most common phrases uttered by witnesses is the claim that "no one understands who wasn't there" (Sonia P., T-1681; Arthur R., T-2342). One might imagine that such a statement is prologue to criticism of an unknowing or uncaring public. Occasionally it is. More often, such a statement reflects the recognition that the witness has gone through an experience so unbelievable that he or she can hardly believe it. As Eva L. puts it, "I can't believe it happened to me ... How can they believe if I can't believe?" (T-71).

In *The Writing of the Disaster*, Maurice Blanchot (1995) is concerned with the way in which the disaster de-scribes, making writing, and telling, about it almost impossible. By "disaster," Blanchot means those experiences that disrupt our experience of going-on-being with the world, so that we cannot put ourselves and the world back together again (Winnicott 1965f). We cannot tell a story because we have lost the place from which to speak. That place is the present. The disaster de-scribes because it destroys not chronology, but the meaningful experience of time. This is what it means to "die at

Auschwitz," and yet to go on living. One cannot have this experience without having dropped out of chronological time; that is, remaining frozen in time, on the one hand, while continuing to live in ordinary, shared chronological time, on the other, in which events such as Auschwitz are expected to slowly recede into the past. Only they don't. The temporal horizon of many survivors' memories cannot be contained within the conventions of ordinary chronological time.

For Lorna B. (T-94), "I could talk for days about one day in Auschwitz."

Sonia P. (T-1681) says simply, "Impossible to describe, all the happenings, would have to do it for days ... If you take it in detail, I could talk to you for years."

If this is true, if survivors' experience remains incompatible with chronological time, then how can they tell coherent narratives about their experience? For a key aspect of the coherent narrative is its respect for the distinction between "then and there" and "here and now." The answer is doubling. The self that tells the story is not the self entire. Doubling allows coherent narratives to be told by people who, to put it simply, are not as coherent as their story. But then again, few of us are. Our stories are the way we present ourselves in public. More traumatized than most, survivors generally remain capable of presenting a coherent public narrative self.

There are no constants among survivor testimonies, no universal themes. The two that come closest are "no one can understand who wasn't there," and "even today I live a double existence." About the first statement, people in everyday life often say to others things like, "you can't understand because you are a man." Or a mother grieving over the loss of her son or daughter might say, "I wish you could feel my pain for just five minutes; then you might be able to understand what I live with every day." To claim that another who has not undergone a similar experience cannot understand is no barrier to narrative. On the contrary, it is one of the main reasons people tell stories: to create a frame and form for an experience so that another person might understand it. It's not easy.

Even the same words, such as "I was thirsty," mean two different things when you've been working in the garden for a couple of hours and really need a cold drink, and when you have been riding in a locked boxcar with 100 other people for days with nothing to drink but your own urine to wet your lips (Max B., T-94). Or someone else's. Locked in a sealed boxcar to Treblinka with over 130 other people, Benjamin Piskorz says a friend would urinate in his mouth for water, and he would do the same for his friend. "The relief was great, because the urine absorbed the heat of the tongue, and the swelling went down."[4]

The fact that we have all been "thirsty" allows you to understand the thirst of the survivor. But it is at the same time a barrier to understanding, for it suggests a commonality of experience that is false. Few of us will ever understand Max's or Mr. Piskorz's experience of thirst, but like the translation of one language into another, their stories help us imagine what it must be like. This is part of the wisdom of trauma, a wisdom that can be communicated to those with ears to hear, but never shared. It is worth remembering this distinction.

A BRIEF EXCURSUS ON VIDEO TESTIMONY AND METHODOLOGY

Viewing video testimonies is not the same as talking with survivors. The Fortunoff Video Archive has several advantages, however. It contains some of the earliest recorded testimonies, some dating back to the late 1970s, and number in the early 1980s. Today Holocaust testimony is everywhere. Then Holocaust testimony was rare, and many survivors were speaking about their experiences for the first time. Many had never even spoken with their families about the experiences related in their testimonies. Survivors were reluctant to speak, and the American Jewish community, often including family members, often did not want to hear the details of the horror. Later testimonies developed a common language and set of images to characterize the Holocaust experience. Henry Greenspan refers to this as the "ritualization of testimony," which he explains as a consequence of the constricted or ritualized retelling of the Holocaust in the form of oral history. The result, he says, is that "retelling is particularly likely to remain superficial. Without a developing and deepening conversation ... we are most likely to conclude that our presumptions have been confirmed. Hearing what we expect, we are unlikely to hear more" (Greenspan 1998: 33). Though one hears this common language in the Fortunoff testimonies, one is present at its creation.

In 1946, David Boder went to displaced persons camps in France, Switzerland, Italy, and Germany, to interview Holocaust survivors using a huge red Webcor wire recorder, a relatively new invention, along with 200 spools of wire. These are the first recorded interviews with Holocaust survivors, who did not even know what to call themselves, the term "Holocaust" first having been used in the mid-1950s. One survivor refers to herself as a French political prisoner (Alford 2009b). Though there is an immediacy to Boder's interviews compared with the Fortunoff interviews – the earliest of which were done over thirty years later – the emphasis on certain experiences, such as the horror of sealed boxcars packed with humans for days, the selections on the ramp, and the smell of burning flesh that permeated the death camps, were as common and emphatic in these earliest interviews as later ones (Alford 2009b). No matter how stylized, Holocaust narratives did not create the Holocaust. Absent in the Boder testimonies, of course, was any evidence of doubling, for the more elaborate defence mechanisms had not yet had time to develop. Anyone with access to the World Wide Web can hear the Boder testimonies for themselves.[5]

The reader might be concerned that the Fortunoff testimonies were not taken for the purpose of this manuscript; but in a sense they were. The Fortunoff Archive was co-founded by Dori Laub, a psychoanalyst who conceived of the Archive as a place where survivors could talk about their experiences in an unstructured but supportive atmosphere. Though the Archive also contains testimonies taken elsewhere, those taken at the Archive, or through its UCLA affiliate, were taken by men and women trained to ask few questions, allowing the survivor to structure the interview, including the order of presentation. The half dozen best interviewers, including the well-known Holocaust scholar Lawrence Langer, seemed to understand that their first task was to manage their own anxiety, so as not to rush in with questions designed to relieve the interviewer's angst, such as "How did you feel at the moment of your liberation?" Instead, these psychoanalytically informed interviewers allowed the witness to control the interview, while providing emotional support when the past became too much present.

Some interviews are better than others of course, and a good interview depends on whether survivor and interviewer can become a world unto themselves for a couple of hours, something that requires the cooperation of both. In the end, every interview is about trauma: how it is experienced, how it can be narrated, lived with, recalled. The beauty of the Fortunoff interviews is that they don't ask about trauma, they don't ask anything of the witness except that he or she tell his or her story. It's a good format to work with.

DOUBLING

Robert Kraft (2002: 2) argues that doubling is the near-universal theme of those who give Holocaust testimony.

> Almost all witnesses state that they live a double existence.
> There is a Balkanization of memory, where Holocaust memories
> and normal memories are assigned to two, sometimes hostile
> territories ... Consider a few phrases that witnesses use: "a double
> existence," "another world," "a schizophrenic division,"
> "two worlds," "two different planets," "double lives."

Important but difficult to understand is not so much the frequency with which witnesses refer to "doubling," for that is an observational given, but whether they are all referring to the same process, and what that process or processes might be. For some, the process is almost like that of watching another testify. "I made a videotape for my daughter. She said 'mommy, you must be so sad.' But when I see it, it's like it happened to another person ... At moments you get mushy, but at moments you think you're telling someone else's story" (Sonia P., T-1681).

Reuben experiences doubling in a less literal fashion. A concentration camp survivor, he speaks of himself as "like a *gilgul*," a ghost, a soul that comes back without a body to wander the world uneasily, lost. "Reuben's death" is how Henry Greenspan (1998: 66) refers to Reuben's life. Yet, of all Greenspan's "recounters" (his preferred term), Reuben lived out his days surrounded by the most abundant life: wife, six children, and a big dog with puppies wandering in and out of the room in which Greenspan interviews Reuben for hours. Additionally, Reuben is constantly being called to the phone, often, it seems, to settle a community dispute, a role for which he appears well suited but which is entirely informal. What to make of a ghost who seems so alive, or at least so surrounded by life? Greenspan says simply, "The ongoing death that Reuben describes, therefore, should not blind us to the substance of his ongoing life" (67). For Reuben, doubling is a double-helix, the strands of life and death wrapped around each other in a complex pattern that in the end favors life over death, without ever forgetting, or allowing the witness to forget, that every moment of life is twinned with a moment of death.

And vice versa. By focusing solely on the living deaths of those who died at Auschwitz, we "miss the vitality of their ongoing lives, memories and legacies that have nothing to do with the destruction but which allow survivors to recount at all" (Greenspan 1998: 169). This is what I seek to understand – what is broken and what remains, and how these two parts of survivors' lives live on close, but not always intimate, terms.

Asked how she lives with Auschwitz, Charlotte Delbo (2001: 2–3) replies,

> Auschwitz is there, unalterable, precise, but enveloped in the skin of memory, an impermeable skin that isolates it from my present

self. Unlike the snake's skin, the skin of memory does not renew itself ... Alas, I often fear lest it grow thin, crack, and the camp get hold of me again ... I live within a twofold being. The Auschwitz double doesn't bother me, doesn't interfere with my life. As though it weren't I at all. Without this split I would not have been able to revive.

Doubling allows life to continue, but it is always threatened by the intrusion of "the self who died at Auschwitz," as Delbo puts it. Only, perhaps even the self who died at Auschwitz is wishful thinking, as though the self were dead and buried. Even worse is the self who survived Auschwitz and comes back to haunt the self who would dare to live a normal life. More than this I cannot say, for doubling is not so much an abstract concept as an empirical observation.

"Splitting" is a vexed concept in psychoanalysis. However, it is widely agreed that splitting is a defensive process in which the ego divides itself in order to correspond with an experience that cannot be integrated. Melanie Klein (1946) developed the concept further, but it is present in one of Freud's (1938) late theoretical contributions, "Splitting of the Ego in the Process of Defense." The concept of doubling resembles splitting insofar as it is a division of the self in order to come to terms with two incompatible experiences of the world: the Auschwitz self, and the post-Auschwitz self. In general, however, the term "doubling" is not used here in a strict psychoanalytic sense as a synonym for splitting. Rather, doubling is an experiential term, a summary of all the different terms and ways survivors describe their post-Auschwitz experience of themselves. It is Delbo's non-technical, experiential use of the term "splitting" that corresponds most closely to its relationship to "doubling" in this essay.

What is so puzzling about doubling is that everybody does it. Survivors don't double more than the rest of us; they double both less and more. The self is always dual, as almost every thoughtful writer from Plato on has recognized (*Republic*, 435a–443b). The cognitive psychologist Ulric Neisser (1994: 8) states flatly, "Memory is always dual." He means that the individual experiences the present self being aware of the past self experiencing the world. The ironic quality of the extreme trauma that induces doubling is that it results in what appears to be an absence of the usual distinction (doubling) between what is remembered and the remembering self. As seen by one who observes the witness testifying, particularly the witness who begins to become traumatized and overwhelmed as he or she recounts the experience, the distinction between the "remembering self now" and the memories of the past self begin to fail. In other words, trauma is expressed through an absence of ordinary doubling.

Traumatic memory has the quality of what Delbo calls "deep memory" (*mémoire profonde*). It is body based, raw, visual, expressed in images, emotion, and physical sensations. These images are all too readily reactivated, and when they are, it is as though the experience was happening all over again. Expressed in simpler language, instead of remembering the traumatic experience, the witness comes to relive it. Or as Bessie K. puts it, "When it comes to me to start talking about it, right away I step into the camp" (T-206). So far, this account of doubling, while not stressing the photographic quality of the memory, is compatible with Caruth's account, indeed with the diagnosis of PTSD.

Where it differs is that many survivors seemed to have extensive *narrative* access to what Delbo calls deep memory, and yet this access does little to heal them. Survivors could recall their experiences in rich and evocative narratives. They did not remain frozen or stuck at the level of imagistic thinking, or simple repetitive story lines. Images became worlds of words, even if present and past occasionally collapsed into each other. Nevertheless, these well-told tales did little to relieve them of their dread. Not just because there is comparability but no commensurability between the Auschwitz experience and ordinary experience, but because the Auschwitz self and the pre- and post-Auschwitz self suffers from the same problem: that of living in different worlds.

In the midst of her interview, Lorna B. brought out some burnt chicken bones from her purse to try to convey the smell of burnt flesh that she had lived with for months at Auschwitz-Birkenau, the smell that haunted her still every time she cooked (or at least burnt) the family meal (T-1126). She was trying, with some success (to hear the gasp of her interviewer), to convey a deep memory, a body-based sensual experience. And yet her success at this communication did little or nothing to relieve her of its burden. Having experienced the unthinkable, many survivors can never quite believe their own story, a story that they generally narrate in a sophisticated fashion. Not the inability to put words to their experience, and not simply an inability to believe their own experience, but an inability to conceive of their own experience as something that could happen to a human being in this world, is their problem.

About those arriving at the railroad station in the ghetto, about to be sent to Auschwitz, Delbo (1995: 4) writes simply, "they expect the worst – not the unthinkable." Common memory can deal with the worst; it has no place for the unthinkable. It is, by the way, almost the same problem that the listener experiences. The survivor knows this, and this knowledge is the ultimate source of his or her doubt. Consider the larger context of a statement of Eva L., a portion of which was quoted previously.

> The older I get, the more questions I ask. Why am I the only one of the whole family to survive? Who would believe if I can't believe it myself? When I was young it was easier, I was busier... I can't believe it happened to me ... People ask me to tell the story, and I refuse. I can't believe a human could go through this ... Every day was a year. How can they believe a human can survive under this if I can't believe it? How can they believe if I can't believe? (T-71)

Auschwitz, for one who has lived inside it, is evidently incomparable. Not merely the pre-Auschwitz self, but the post-Auschwitz self can hardly believe it. In a sense, this was the Nazis' greatest and most perverse victory. They created a regime of death so horrendous that not merely those who were not there, but those who were, can hardly believe it. Or as Eva L. puts it, "if I could come here and have a family and live a normal life, more or less, then how could it have happened?" (T-71).

DOUBLING AS THE LOSS OF VALUE

In doubling, deep memory is cast adrift from ordinary or common memory (*mémoire ordinaire*) because ordinary memory lacks concepts and categories to explain a world that is no longer meaningful in human terms (Delbo 2001: 2–3). "*Warum?*" (Why?) asks Primo Levi (1996: 29) of a prison guard who has just snatched an icicle out of his hand as he was about to suck on it to relieve his terrible thirst. "*Hier gibt es kein warum*" answered the death camp guard. (Here there is no why, no reason.) When the entire world has no "*Warum?*" (no why), when the only answer is sadism, starvation, and death, then the self of everyday life possesses no resources to contain the experience, no moral framework by which to evaluate it, no chronological framework within which to say "this too shall end," no emotional framework with which to shield itself from unremitting terror and loss. Then pre- and post-Auschwitz self lack a sufficient vocabulary of value to communicate with the Auschwitz self. At issue is not soma versus psyche, or inscribed psyche versus narrative psyche, at issue is value.

The experience of the absurd, which Albert Camus (1955: 45) defines in terms of the gulf between humanity's demand for meaning and nature's unreasoning silence, takes on a new and strictly human meaning. Humans demand a meaning comprehensible to the pre- (and post-) Auschwitz self. The world of death that was Auschwitz replies with a meaning no longer comprehensible in the discourse of ordinary human life and death, in which death is measured by individuals, not piles of nameless corpses. Or as Leon put it:

> People hadn't become ciphers yet. They were still, up to that moment, human beings. With a name, with a personality. And when they were gone, their image was retained. But the mass disappearing into the gas chambers–, they're just a mass of people

going–, like into a slaughterhouse. There was a difference.
A qualitative and quantitative difference.

(Greenspan 1998: 159)

Doubling is the consequence of the clash of values, though that makes it sound too elevated, too abstract. At issue is the clash between the values of life and death, Eros and Thantos, the will to live and the will to destroy. Doubling results when a world oriented to the values of life is conquered and overrun by a world in which the values of death reign. In order to know something, you have to have something to compare it to (Plato, *Meno* 80d-81e). If the new is entirely unrelated to the old, if there is no category belonging to the old world that resembles that of the new, then the new world will lack reality, for it is impossible to find a place for it in the story (narrative frame) of one's life.

DOUBLING AS PERPETUAL MOURNING

The persistence of doubling is explained not only by the survivor's inability to translate between two separate realities, two worlds, the persistence of doubling is also an expression of perpetual mourning, a loss that cannot be worked through, a loss that is as real, vivid, and painful as it was fifty years ago, in some cases.

Jean Améry (1980: 45–48) writes that the experience of persecution was, at the very bottom, that of extreme loneliness. A profound insight, it is not alien to the concept of doubling as perpetual mourning, in which terrible experiences are experienced as the loss of all human connection. It is this loss that is experienced as death, as if there were no difference between one's own death and the death of everyone and everything one ever valued and believed in. Perhaps there isn't any difference. Or rather, the difference is that from this death, one can go on living, including the lives of variety and richness, lives such as Reuben's, or Primo Levi's. Yet, almost every survivor who goes on to live such second lives talks about a special sadness and loneliness that overcomes them at family gatherings. Indeed, for some survivors, such gatherings are terrifying, threatening to engulf them in endless sorrow. As Eva L. puts it, "So hungry for family." She means, I think, "I'm so hungry for family," but the sentiment is so primordial it is expressed as hunger in the absence of an "I" (Eva L., T-71).

Why? Not because Eva – and this holds true for many survivors – fails to feel a full measure of love and affection for and from their current families, but because life is no recompense for their losses. The more surrounded they are with living life, the more they are reminded of dead life, the lives that have been lost, and the lost souls they have become as a result, Reuben's "gilgul." It is as if every death has loosened their attachment to this world more than every life has strengthened it. Just a little perhaps, but the cumulative effect is grave.

This is why, I believe, "I should have died at Auschwitz" so often takes the form of "we should have died at Auschwitz," meaning that the witness should have died there with his or her parents or other relatives. At least in retrospect, dying together with one's original family, one's original loved ones would have been the most complete life, the most complete death (Max B., T-1125; Eva L., T-71; Martin L., T-224). Only, let us not forget that most who express this thought made, at the time, at least some small effort, and often an enormous effort, not to die, but to live. Only, who could reckon the costs of a life forever twinned with death?

Here is how the suffering of survivors differs from most who suffer from PTSD. As we think of it today, the person most likely to suffer from PTSD is a woman who has been beaten and raped, or a soldier who has seen horrifying casualties on the battlefield, buddies blown to pieces. For many survivors, the most traumatic experience is the loss of everyone who meant anything to them. Many came from small towns and extended families. For not a few, there was no place and no one to go back to, and no one to go forth with.

Certainly many survivors suffer from PTSD. Their tendency to relive rather than recall is evidence for that, even as it turns out one can relive and tell a story about it (recall) at the same time. But PTSD seems a pale diagnosis for one whose entire world has been depopulated not "merely" of almost every person whom the survivor holds dear, but of the connections that constitute the fleshy human web that keeps us from falling endlessly. For it is these connections that give the world its value. This is why phenomenological or experiential categories, such as living after having died, or living a double life, or a ghost-like existence, are so important. In some strange and not quite arithmetical sense, these losses are additive.

In *The Nazi Doctors: Medical Killing and the Psychology of Genocide*, Robert Jay Lifton (1986: 418–429) characterizes the doctors' key defense mechanism as doubling, the division of the self into two functioning wholes, each part acting as though it were virtually an entire self. Almost in passing, Lifton argues that doubling possesses an adaptive potential that may be life saving "for a victim of brutality such as an Auschwitz inmate, who must also undergo a form of doubling in order to survive. Clearly the 'opposing self' can be life enhancing" (Lifton 1986: 420). Trouble is, the way in which Lifton develops the concept of doubling reveals that it is not some neutral defense mechanism employed by innocent and guilty men alike in order to adapt to extreme circumstances. Lifton's doubling serves death. The doubling I refer to serves life. The only thing the two uses of the term share is a name.

The doubling engaged in by the Nazi doctors worked something like this: confronted daily with death on an unimaginable scale, the doctors came to fear death almost as much as the inmates did. In order to master their fear of death, the Nazi doctors gave themselves over to death, becoming angels of death, servants of the *Todestrieb*, as though they could master death by inflicting it upon others. (Forget for a moment that the Nazi doctors were instruments of the death that terrified them.) Subjected to the starkest form of abjection, a world filled with corpses, the Nazi doctors sought purification through the infliction of death, the mimetic psychology of all purification ritual, as René Girard (1977) has argued.

Mine is not just a summary of Lifton's argument. It is an interpretation, one entirely consistent with Lifton's thesis. If so, then it makes absolutely no sense for Lifton to suggest, even in passing, that doubling, as he describes it, is a defense that may be employed by survivors of Auschwitz, as well as by the doctors who experimented upon and killed their victims. For the Nazi doctors, doubling was a defense that operated primarily during the years they served in the concentration camps, a way of giving themselves over to the *Todestrieb* in order that they might psychologically survive the world of death they were thrust into and made their own. For survivors, doubling is not so much a defense to be explained as a way of living after having died at Auschwitz. For survivors, doubling serves Eros, allowing them to live with what are essentially unbearable experiences. Both experiences happen to be called "doubling." Both concern Auschwitz. There the similarity ends.

CONCLUSION: TRAUMA AS KNOWLEDGE

Trauma, particularly large-scale historical trauma such as the Holocaust, is an ethical experience. Large-scale historical trauma is a clash of values, not just between life and death (though that would be more than enough), but between what one knows and what one can believe. Trauma is the inability to imagine the story one is narrating; not for reasons suggested by Sándor Ferenczi, one of the founding fathers of trauma theory. For Ferenczi, trauma is dissociative, with the result that representation and affect belong to mutually incomprehensible worlds. This is why knowledge doesn't integrate. Representation belongs to a different emotional world than affect. Not only does knowledge – including that gained in psychoanalysis – not heal, but the attempt to bring knowledge to emotional experience only reinforces the split between knowledge and feeling (Ferenczi 1988: 39, 203). One can see how Ferenczi's view might have influenced Caruth. But it is not relevant to the trauma of survivors. Their narrative experience of trauma is filled – sometimes to overflowing – with sensual and body-based images, the language of affect, as the burned chicken bone story reveals.

The problem of survivors is their inability to believe what they know to be true, what they can say to be true. One might say this inability is the result of doubling. I would say that this inability is the cause. Doubling isn't splitting, at least in Ferenczi's sense of dissociation. It is a way of living with the unbelievable, and the unbearable. Knowledge as disaster, Michel Blanchot (1995: ix) calls it, the disaster of learning things about the world that a human isn't supposed to know. As Julia S. puts it, "You're not supposed to see this; it doesn't go with life. It doesn't go with life. These people come back, and you realize they're all broken, they're all broken. Broken. Broken" (T-934). In fact, most are not broken. Doubling is the alternative to breaking. But it is a painful alternative, for it is never complete, and the survivor must live with a knowledge that does not enrich the self, but depletes it.

Doubling is a way to get on with life. Seen from this perspective, doubling is the salve for the wound that never heals, which in this case is good, for lack of closure allows life to continue – sometimes a full life, sometimes a quite restricted one. That depends upon the survivor and the nature of his or her experience (some went through more traumatic experiences than others; some are presumably more resilient than others). But for a vast majority, doubling allows life to go on. Doubling serves Eros in its largest sense, the drive for life after having lived through a world devoted to death.

Here Ferenczi is helpful, concluding late in his career that forgetting is sometimes the best path. "Now is the time for encouragement to the tasks of life and future happiness, instead of pondering and digging in the past." Ferenczi understands that the result is to "sequester" or "encapsulate" traumatic experience. But this is now the goal (Ferenczi 1988: 181; Ferenczi 1994: 260–261). This isn't doubling, but doubling and Ferenczi's late conclusion have more in common than divides them.

How can someone who lived through such trauma, a trauma that has obviously left its mark, embark on "the tasks of life and future happiness"? The answer is doubling, which explains how a

survivor could be such a competent narrator of his or her own experience, and still be chronically traumatized, but often without the
symptoms of extreme trauma, such as a sense of a foreshortened
future. On the contrary, almost every survivor said that it was the
sense of a future that kept and keeps them going. If not for themselves,
then for the children and grandchildren. In so doing, they would be
doing their part to defeat Hitler's mad dream.[6] Since survivors made
this statement thirty to fifty years after the initial trauma, referring to
the unfolding of their own lives, as well as the lives of their children
and grandchildren, it is reasonable to conclude that this hope was not
only realized, but recognized and appreciated still. Many witnesses
certainly talk as if this were the case.

Though survivors are generally able to tell their story in narrative form, characterized by a beginning, middle, and end, frequently
drawing the distinction between "then and there" and "here and
now," the narrative form fails to offer the relief that narrative so often
seems to promise, beginning with Aristotle's account in the *Poetics*.
Why? Aristotle is particularly concerned with tragedy, famously arguing that the well-constructed plot leads to the *katharsis* of pity and
fear (1149b: 20–30 [c6]). Today many agree that the term *katharsis*
refers not to purging, but to clarification or emotional enlightenment.
Greek derivatives of the term frequently referred to a clear body of
water. By the time the greatest Greek tragedies were produced
(c. 460 to 400 BCE), the metaphorical use of the term to refer to a
clear mind was well established (Nussbaum 1986: 388–391).
The *katharsis* of pity and fear is a clarification of what is truly to be
pitied and feared, a clarification that over time leads to an understanding that brings if not peace, then at least acceptance. Surely the main
reason the Holocaust does not lead to *katharsis* is that it is not
tragedy, but atrocity (Langer 1978: xi–xiv). Tragedy requires identifiable characters, not piles of corpses, as Leon reminds us.

There may, however, be another reason that narrative brings
little relief. Doubling, which saves the survivor, prevents emotional
clarification, if emotional clarification is understood as emotional

integration. This was not Aristotle's understanding of *katharsis*, but a modern twist. However, it does not seem an unwarranted stretch in order to make a point. Doubling, which allows the survivor to get on with his or her life, at the same time stands in the way of an integrated experience of the horror that required doubling in the first place. For most survivors, as well as for other victims of terrible trauma, it seems a fair trade.

Not for Améry (1980), who wishes not to get on with his life, but to hold onto his memories of trauma. Why would anyone choose that? Is it really a matter of choice? For now it seems fair to say that for Améry, trauma is not just an ethical experience, but an ethical stance in the face of a world all too eager to forget. If it is an ethical obligation to remember as though one were there, then is it an ethical obligation to remain traumatized? This question is the topic of Chapter 7.

Finally, what are we to conclude about Caruth's influential theory, as well as about the diagnosis of PTSD in general? Do they apply to "ordinary" trauma, but not to extreme historical traumas such as the Holocaust? Or is it rather that this manuscript adopts a different framework within which to think about trauma? There is no simple answer. Since Caruth places her account of trauma squarely within history ("If PTSD must be understood as a psychological symptom of the unconscious, it is a symptom of history"), it seems as if it ought to be able to explain extreme historical trauma, especially that passed down between the generations. That it doesn't explain the testimony of traumatized Holocaust survivors suggests that her explanation is based more on a literary-neurobiological account of trauma than the study of a large group of traumatized individuals.

Caruth writes as though trauma is transmitted within the group, and between generations, by the mechanism of hysteria, an emotional contagion that is beyond words. If this is not the case, if the historically traumatized are not necessarily as narratively incompetent as Caruth suggests, then how does collective trauma work? The wisest answer is also the simplest: it depends upon the particular

historical case we are talking about; every historical trauma is different. Nevertheless, the principles remain the same.

Individual trauma is a blow to the psyche that breaks through
the victim's defenses with such intrusive force that the individual can
only defend against it retrospectively, after the fact. Caruth is not
completely mistaken. Mistaken is the notion that this intrusive force
has the quality of a photographic inscription, rather than a narratively
meaningful event that resists becoming part of what the survivor
knows. For to know what one feels (and even what one can tell others)
about such experiences is to know something terribly frightening
about one's utter vulnerability to pain, caprice, and loss beyond
imagination. To possess such knowledge is "knowledge as disaster."
To come to terms with such knowledge is forever after to live in a
different world, a world fundamentally hostile to human happiness;
indeed, human existence. In a certain sense, Albert Camus' sense
(1955: 45), the world has become absurd, hostile to human purposes.
The world becomes even more absurd when these hostile forces are
aided and abetted by fellow humans, as though the natural world
contains not enough trauma-inducing wounds of its own.

Yet, Caruth's is a complicated story, as complicated as trauma.
In writing about the well-known 1959 French film, *Hiroshima mon
amour*, by Alain Resnais, Caruth writes about a scene in which a
French woman tells her Japanese lover about her days-long traumatic
embrace of her gravely wounded German lover in recently liberated
Nevers. His corpse grew cold as she lay on top of her lover, and still
she lay with him. She merges with him. "All I could find between this
body and mine were obvious similarities, do you understand?
(*Shouting*) He was my first love" (Caruth 1996: 37–42).

Her Japanese lover slaps her, refusing to understand her inability
to distinguish her body from her lover's. His seems an act of incredible
emotional violence. But somehow, in Caruth's interpretation, which
seems plausible, the slap is the culmination of a complex communication that helps the woman break out of her past, and enter into
current history with the Japanese man (42). It is not a pleasant history;

Hiroshima in the 1950s is hardly a resort. But through their encounter, both the French woman and the Japanese man, who had lost his family in the bombing of Hiroshima, are returned to ongoing history. From that point they will proceed their separate ways.

My point, which is not at odds with Caruth's, is that trauma is a complex individual experience. While her generalizations do not hold for Holocaust survivors, whose extreme traumatic history is indeed a "symptom of history," only a fool would fail to see that various, often quite inventive, means of working-through are discovered by victims of trauma. Caruth is no fool. Inventive means of working-through, often with therapeutic assistance, are more likely to be found by those who have not already constructed a double life in order to survive, which tends to be adaptive but relatively inflexible. The French woman utilized not doubling, but merger with a dead beloved as her defense, a different, more motile psychological constellation.

My objection to Caruth is not to the clinical implications of her approach, which leave room for traditional therapy; my objection is to the theoretical import of a position that holds that victims of extreme historical trauma such as the Holocaust must be spoken for, as they cannot represent themselves. At the same time, Caruth resists speaking for the victims, lest she foreclose their experience. The result, at least in theory, can only be silence; silence about things that must and can be spoken.

NOTES

1 According to the *Diagnostic and Statistical Manual of Mental Disorders IV-Text Revision* (DSM IV-TR) (American Psychiatric Association 2000), PTSD requires that two criteria be fulfilled. First, that "the person experienced, witnessed, or was confronted with an event or events that involved actual or threatened death or serious injury, or a threat to the physical integrity of self or others." Second, "the person's response involved intense fear, helplessness, or horror." Symptoms of PTSD include the following: (1) Intrusive and recurrent recollections of the event, including dreams, and flashbacks. (2) Avoidance and numbing, in which people,

places, activities, and even consciousness are avoided, the latter through drink, drugs, sleep. Feelings of detachment and estrangement from others, as though no one else could possibly understand. A restricted range of affect: all the emotions are turned down, including love, affection, pleasure, as though every powerful emotion were a danger. (3) A sense of a foreshortened future. "What's the point in planning anyway? I don't expect to be around that long." (4) Hyper-arousal: Difficulty falling or staying asleep. Irritability or outbursts of anger. Hyper-vigilance. Exaggerated startle response. These symptoms must last for at least a month for the diagnosis of PTSD to be met.

2 Interviews from the Fortunoff Video Archive are identifiable in the text by the prefix 'T-' followed by the accession number. In each case, the full citation should read _____ [first name and last initial of witness] (T-XXXX), Fortunoff Video Archive for Holocaust Testimonies, Sterling Memorial Library, Yale University. The interviews are not anonymous, but the Archive prefers this method of citation. For more on these testimonies, see Alford (2009a). I am not unaware of the irony that my argument makes use of materials in an archive co-founded by one whose work I criticize, at least by proxy, Dori Laub.

3 Writing in German, Améry intentionally uses the French word *ressentiment* as a challenge to Nietzsche. More on Améry and Nietzsche in Chapter 7, where Améry is taken up in some detail.

4 Benjamin Piskorz was interviewed in 1946 by David Boder. See Alford 2009b.

5 At http://voices.iit.edu. The quotations all come from original wire recordings made by David Boder in 1946, transcribed and translated by him. At the website, one can read the transcript, an English translation (when necessary), and simultaneously hear the interview, now digitalized. A selective and heavily edited, but still useful version of Boder's interviews can be found in Donald Niewyk (ed.), *Fresh Wounds: Early Narratives of Holocaust Survivors* (1998).

6 Overwhelmingly, it was those witnesses young enough to have first, and often second, families who survived the concentration camps.

3   Winnicott and trauma

Trauma undermines our confidence in the stability of the world. Not just the external world, but the inner world. Our trust in the world is violated; frequently our ability to trust in the world is ruined. Trauma is a deeply personal experience, and trauma makes no sense unless it is seen in this way. At the same time, traumatizing experiences do not occur in a political vacuum. They are often the outcome of forces set in motion by human beings. Even when not the outcome of human forces, such as an earthquake, human forces may make trauma worse. In general, people in third-world countries suffer the effects of natural disasters longer and more intensely than those in developed countries. People do not become immune to suffering; they only become numb and dissociated; that is, they become traumatized. To be sure, there is something remarkably vulnerable about human beings, both physically and psychologically, that makes trauma a likely outcome of many events. As H. L. A Hart (1994: 194–198) remarked, if human beings had exoskeletons, many of the laws and institutions that protect us would be unnecessary. The degree to which humans are traumatized depends, in good measure, on the social organization that surrounds us. Unlike an exoskeleton, social organization resembles an endoskeleton, holding the pieces together after the intrusion of the shattering blow.

It is difficult to pay sufficient attention to both the intensely personal nature of trauma and its political dimension. One who tries, and in my opinion fails, is Cathy Caruth, as discussed in the previous chapter. Caruth has rendered trauma political – indeed, world historical – the vehicle by which the meaning of history is transmitted from generation to generation. She pays deep respect to the victims of trauma, reminding us of the duality of the original meaning of the

Greek term martyr (μάρτυς), one who is a witness as well as one who bears witness. Whether this witness is as inarticulate as Caruth believes, and whether we should serve as his or her silent accomplice, remain important questions, not yet fully answered. A more complete answer will approach these questions indirectly, asking whether Caruth has paid too high a price in order to render trauma political: the price of depriving trauma of its inwardness, and witnesses of their wisdom? In order to answer these complicated questions, I turn to one whose concept of trauma is profoundly inward.

In a manner almost the opposite of Caruth, the psychoanalyst D. W. Winnicott approaches trauma by asking whether the individual is able, or can be therapeutically enabled, to live a rich interior life, one not devoted to responding to external events, environmental intrusions.[1] Winnicott's account of what this inner world might look like, and how readily it can be ruined, is rich and evocative. More surprising to some may be what he has to say about the social and political conditions under which trauma is experienced, expressed, and mitigated, the issue Caruth would address. Virtually every aspect of Winnicott's work assumes that behind the mother and baby stand first the father, and then the holding community, within which we will live our entire lives if we meet with even a modicum of good fortune. A British Object Relations theorist, Winnicott's is always already a social theory of trauma. Ruth Leys's study of trauma theory, addressed later in this chapter, will clarify this last remark.

One finds in Winnicott's work the basis of two different accounts of trauma, accounts that are distinct, even as they overlap. Both understand trauma as a threat to the core self. The first sees trauma as dramatic penetration of the core self. The second sees trauma as the subtle erasure of the core self, a process that may take years. Traumatic is both the penetration of the core self, as well as the absence of that entity, the core self, whose penetration causes trauma. Having it both ways, trauma, it seems, always has the upper hand.

About the first sense of trauma, Winnicott brings to our understanding of trauma as PTSD a deeper understanding of the experiences that give rise to its symptoms. Central to this understanding is knowledge of the unbearably real. Unbearable knowledge is similar to what Blanchot (1995: ix) called "knowledge as disaster." The survivor of an environmental disaster captures the meaning of knowledge as disaster well when she says:

> While it could be argued that it's not a bad thing to become more knowledgeable, it is, I think, certainly a bad thing to become knowledgeable in the way that we've become knowledgeable. It's like a person who's an agoraphobic. If you're terrified to go out of the house, you don't live a very good life.
>
> (Erikson 1995: 197)

TRUE AND FALSE SELF NOT ONTOLOGICAL
OR STRUCTURAL

In order for this discussion of trauma to be plausible to the reader, he or she is going to have to accept, or be persuaded, that Winnicott's distinction between a true and false self is useful. Accepting this should be possible even for many postmoderns, who deny the ontology of selfhood. With the term "true self," Winnicott (1965e) refers not to a psychic structure, but to a vital psychosomatic center, bound up with a feeling of bodily aliveness, and experienced by self and others most immediately in the spontaneous gesture. Adam Phillips (1988: 97) argues that the true or core self has no content of its own, becoming a sort of "negative theology" – all the false self isn't. Conversely, the false self is that part of a person that devotes its attention, time, and energy adapting itself to others' (originally mother's) moods and expectations. The false self is reactive, compliant, and lacking in spontaneity. The false self exists to protect the true self from being known and exploited by others.

One is tempted to refer to the false self as inauthentic, but putting it that way recalls Michel Foucault's condemnation of Sartre's philosophy as "terrorism" precisely because it sought authenticity in all things. Or as Foucault put it, "more than one person, doubtless like me, writes in order to have no face." For Foucault, facelessness is freedom because non-identity liberates one from the imprisonment of an "infinitely self-referring gaze" (Miller 1993: 52–54, 19). Facelessness liberates the self from social convention and expectation, allowing one to experiment with different selves, different ways of being, including madness. While Foucault would have surely rejected Winnicott's language of the true self, the function of facelessness is similar to what Winnicott calls the false self, protecting the anonymous one from being superficially known and categorized by others, and so exploited. If one considers that the key to the true self seems to be its sense of vitality, of being fully alive – which requires according to Winnicott having a place to which one can retreat in order to be free of the expectations of others – then the difference between Winnicott and Foucault on this issue is as much linguistic as conceptual though, of course, deep theoretical differences remain.

My argument depends not at all upon a strained comparison between Winnicott and Foucault. I make it only to address the valid objection that the concepts of a false and true self must transform a psychological abstraction into a concrete reality subject to reification. What Winnicott refers to by the terms true and false self are the sources of vitality in living (making no distinction between psychic and somatic sources), the way these sources may be corrupted, and how we try to protect these sources. Trauma is an attack on these sources.

TRAUMA ATTACKS THE MEANING OF BEING

Trauma attacks the meaning of being, the meaning of life. The experience of going-on-being is how the meaning of life is frequently characterized by those who study Winnicott, but that way of putting it could be misleading. For Winnicott, the first task is not to go anywhere. Not going but being comes first. To be, and to be, and to be ... without traumatic interruption; that is, without interruption. Not to feel this experience, not to have this experience, but to be this experience, is the meaning of life, for it involves the mind and body as a unity, as though they were one. Or as Winnicott (1992a) puts it:

> The word psyche ... means the *imaginative elaboration of somatic parts, feelings, and functions*, that is, of physical aliveness ... The live body, with its limits, and with an inside and an outside, is *felt by the individual* to form the core for the imaginative self.
>
> *(244, author's emphasis)*

Winnicott tends to define ideal states (most notably the true self) in terms of their opposites. Being is the opposite of reacting. In being, I am in the moment, rather than experiencing the world in a reactive, self-conscious way. "The alternative to being is reacting, and reacting interrupts being and annihilates. Being and annihilation are the two alternatives." Why does Winnicott put it so strongly? Why would he equate reacting with annihilation? Because he is thinking about what it takes "to develop the sophistications which make it possible" to maintain a sense of the continuity of one's existence, even when being is impinged upon (Winnicott 1965c: 47). Trauma is not sophisticated. Trauma has the capacity to destroy even the most developed sense of the continuity of existence. In this sense, trauma induces madness. "Madness here simply means a breakup of whatever may exist at the time of a *personal continuity of existence*" (Winnicott 1971b: 97, author's emphasis).

Against my argument, it might be claimed that for the most part Winnicott is talking about infants and young children, or at least the "infant/patient," to use Abram's (1996: 325) all-purpose term for adults whose trauma can be traced to early childhood. Trauma can't devastate the normal, average adult in the same way, or at least Winnicott provides no evidence that it can. I suggest that going-on-being has the structure of what Henri Bergson called duration (*durée*), the subjective experience of time. With the concept of duration, Bergson (1998: 2) meant that "we change without ceasing ... there is no essential difference between passing from one state to another and persisting in the same state." All that we were goes with us as we continue in subjective time. Nothing ever gets left behind. Going-on-being is not the past flowing into the present. Going-on-being is a sense of unity of past and present in me now, as though time were measured on a piece of elastic that is being slowly pulled longer and longer, but could at any time snap back on itself, the present become the past in an instant (Bergson 2007: 138), which is precisely what happens under the stress of trauma.

A consequence is that the traumatic disruption of my self now disrupts my self all the way down, all the way back, even if up and down, backward and forward, are misleading metaphors. There is no permanent, developed, stable stratum of the self immune to traumatic disruption, traumatic madness. There are degrees of trauma, but the degrees are not measured by the "depth" of trauma, a misleading metaphor, in any case. The degree of trauma is known only in retrospect, and only subjectively, measured by how long it takes the traumatized individual to return to a feeling of going-on-being; or rather, just being.

To be sure, even the deeply traumatized individual generally does not run around acting mad. The deeply traumatized individual generally learns to use his mind to hold him or her self. The result is a split between psyche and soma, and hence the loss of a certain feeling of vitality and spontaneity. This is no small thing, for it is the unity of psyche and soma that is, as we have seen, the key to the meaning of life for Winnicott, what he calls "the feeling of real" (1971c: 80).

TRAUMA AS PENETRATION OF THE CORE SELF

Winnicott (1965d) came to a view, held even more insistently in his late work, that the core self, the source of vitality and spontaneity, where psyche and soma are one, is and should be isolated, "*permanently non-communicating, permanently unknown, in fact unfound*" (187, author's emphasis). Adam Phillips (1988), who has written wisely and well about Winnicott, isn't quite sure what to make of this aspect of Winnicott's theory. "The individual knows," writes Winnicott, "that [the core self] must never be communicated with or be influenced by external reality" (1965d: 187). To be sure, the individual wishes to communicate, to share himself, but his greatest fear is that of being found, of having no place to be alone undisturbed; that is, to just be. "In the artist of all kinds one can detect an inherent dilemma, which belongs to the co-existence of two trends, the urgent need to communicate and the still more urgent need not to be found" (Winnicott 1965d: 187).

Otherwise expressed, we all live between the isolation and madness of excess subjectivity (being lost so deeply in self we can never be found), and the inner impoverishment and anonymous futility of compliance masquerading as objectivity (Phillips 1988: 122). One of the less discussed functions of transitional space is that it provides a location in which we can be known without being found (Winnicott 1971a). Why is being found so disastrous? Because being found is tantamount to being a social self forced to react to the acts of others. There is a time and a place for this; without this dimension of life, we would not be human. Winnicott worries that for many people, being found means being found out, forced out of hiding with no retreat, having to live constantly in a state of reaction to others, while having no self to return to.

PENETRATION OF THE SELF AND PTSD

Winnicott brings depth to the account of trauma with which many are most familiar, trauma defined by PTSD, whose symptoms were outlined in the previous chapter (Chapter 2, note 1). For example, from a Winnicottian perspective, restricted affect, a prime symptom of PTSD, is not only about dulling all emotion so as to keep the most disturbing emotions at bay, restricted affect also reflects the loss of vitality that comes from the disruption of going-on-being, and consequent use of the mind to manage soma, a type of self-holding. In this respect, PTSD is a loss of the meaning of life.

There is, however, another way to look at PTSD, one not contrary to its DSM IV-TR definition, but elaborative of it (American

Psychiatric Association 2000). PTSD is knowledge of the terrible vulnerability of the self in the world. One's faith in the stability of the world is not easily restored once the world's solidity is shattered so that it is experienced as a somatic as well as cognitive event. Hyper-vigilance and exaggerated startle response are, in a larger sense, quite realistic. Once one realizes that one's world can be broken in a moment, everything changes. All the development we have under- taken since birth, all the use we have made of transitional objects, people and culture, all our actual relationships that support us in a woven web of flesh and love and expectations met over and over again until the world seems stable and predictable, can be shattered in a flash, and we are once again an annihilated baby, fearful of falling forever with no one to hold or catch us.

Consider the trauma of brutal assault, rape, a sudden and terrible accident, mass murder, sudden dislocation, an explosion that kills your buddies and leaves you covered in their blood, repeated exposure to the threat of sudden death, a ravaging illness. Remarkable is how abridged the list is; it could go on for pages. Even this abridged list, filled with unusual but hardly rare occurrences, reveals to those who suffer from these experiences something they knew before, but not in the physical way they know afterward.[2] After the trauma, they know, or rather feel, the vulnerability of the embodied self, the "psyche-soma" as Winnicott referred to it, in a new way. This new feeling-knowledge says in a language that is beneath (underneath) but not beyond words that humans can be shattered like glass, and that for many, the shards can never be put together again to make a whole. Once we have experienced this ourselves, or seen it in others close to us, everything changes, for it renders the world fundamentally unstable, fragile beyond words.

To be sure, some people are more willing and able to recognize this reality than others. Winnicott was getting at this point when he said "a recognition of absolute dependence on the mother and of her capacity for primary maternal preoccupation ... is something which belongs to *extreme sophistication*, and to a stage not always reached by adults" (1992b: 304, author's emphasis). It is worthwhile, and difficult, to recognize our dependence on a being and a force, mother, who was beyond both our control and our knowledge (as a separate fallible being with needs of her own) when we needed her the most. Equally difficult to recognize is that in certain key respects, this dependence never ends, it just changes its locus: from mother to world. As adults, we know more, but we can't always do more. Furthermore, much of what we know about those who would traumatize us is hardly comforting: there is hate as well as almost unimaginable selfishness and carelessness about in the world, to say nothing of the terrifying caprice of nature. How does one live with this knowledge after it embeds itself in one's body and mind?

In "The Concept of Trauma" (1989: 146), Winnicott writes that "trauma in the more popular sense of the term implies a breaking of faith ... Trauma is the destruction of the purity of individual experience by a too sudden or unpredictable intrusion of actual fact." The adult individual believes that he or she knows the parameters of pain and loss, including the illness and death of the self and those we love. "They expect the worst – not the unthinkable," says Delbo. Winnicott (1989: 147) elaborates on this interpretation when he says that the more integrated the individual, the more he or she suffers from being traumatized, evidently because he or she now finds it less easy to use primitive defenses to hide from the truth. It is the truth that traumatizes, in part by revealing to us that we never really knew or understood the world we were up against. Or rather, we knew, but we never felt it in our bones; that is, in a way that divides soma from psyche, and so renders us less vital, less alive, less free to be. This is, of course, another way to describe the doubling referred to in the last chapter, as well as its price.

Writing about trauma in a more phenomenological vein, Kai Erikson (1976: 159, 177–170) sees trauma as an existential crisis, a loss of faith in the very idea of order. Not only does the entire world become unsafe, but this anxiety (*angst*, the term employed by Søren Kierkegaard (1980) and often translated as "dread," seems a better term) extends to the inner world of one's body, which can no longer be relied upon either. Instead, the body becomes a source of threatening pains, tremors, spasms. The body's tender cocoon of skin becomes the location of sores and other afflictions; the body's natural rhythms of wakefulness and sleep are disrupted. Natural processes like digestion are called painfully into question.

Erikson (1976: 240) argues that community is a conspiracy to make the world seem safe enough to live in. Community is a set of group arrangements to camouflage the terrible reality and danger of life. In our own time, this is exemplified by the segregation of the sick and the old in hospitals and nursing homes, coupled with the celebration of youth, including "youthful old age," in the mass media. Without group-reinforced denial, it might be impossible to go on living. Trouble is, group-reinforced denial too often depends upon placing large numbers of people beyond its aegis, their existence representing an unbearable reality. Furthermore, denial itself may become destructive, creating a community of the fit inflicting the feared trauma on out-groups and others. The mechanism would be projective identification, but the mechanism is not as important as the idea: group-reinforced denial is not a passive process, as in "we don't believe we are naked and vulnerable before fate." Group-reinforced denial generally requires as its correlate the existence of others who are naked and vulnerable: my group is powerful because yours is weak, my group is invulnerable because yours is vulnerable.

In Thomas Hobbes' state of nature, the world of the zero-sum game, this is literally true: all my gains in security must come from you, or someone like you. The world of psychological security need not be a zero-sum game, but there is something about the way projective identification works in insecure groups that too often makes it seem as if my group can achieve security only by evacuating its members' insecurity into the minds and bodies of vulnerable others. When Winnicott writes about projective identification, it is generally as a means of emotional connection.

Unlike simple projection, projective identification not only attributes one's own psychic state to others, but acts in such a way as to bring about the attributed state in the other, such as anger, or love. Many psychoanalysts, particularly those influenced by Melanie Klein, believe that projective identification works not only at the level of action, as when I project my anger into you, assume you are angry, and act angrily in return, evoking your anger; rather, projective identification works its way behind the other's ego defenses, creating the psychological state it would evoke. For many analysts, projective identification is the means by which we evacuate unbearable emotions into others (Ogden 1979; Winnicott 1971c: 132–136). Winnicott did not emphasize this dimension of projective identification. It would have been helpful if he had. Evacuative identification is a useful way to explain how and why despised and devalued others begin to play the part; that is, begin to act the victims of chronic trauma.

Hanna Segal (2007: 215), a psychoanalyst closely associated with Klein, is particularly critical of the absence of this dimension of projective identification in Winnicott's work. Most needed, she says, is an appreciation of the way in which attentive mothers help young children come to terms with unbearable emotions by holding bits of unintegrated experience until the child can take them back in more integrated form, a constant back and forth process. Groups, one might say, behave like children of inattentive mothers, a point Segal (1997) takes almost literally in appreciating how and why groups may act more madly than their members. In this, of course, she is echoing Freud (1921), even as their explanations differ.

TRAUMA THEORY WITHOUT A HUMAN SUBJECT

One way of approaching the new culture of trauma, a culture in which the self has no place to be, is through a trauma theory particularly well suited to this new world, one in which the individual, as well as his or her relationships, has no place either, albeit for theoretical rather than practical reasons. Ruth Leys's account of the history of trauma theory, particularly its recent history, is helpful in this regard, both for what she says, and what she doesn't.

Leys (2000) argues that accounts of trauma have historically tended to oscillate between two poles, or ideal types: the mimetic and the anti-mimetic. In the mimetic account, trauma is a totally assimilated, unmediated experience, in which the traumatized person cannot psychologically process the ordeal that he or she has undergone. It is this failure to process that accounts for most of the key symptoms of trauma, such as intrusive dreams, memories that have the quality of flashbacks, and so forth.

In the mimetic account, the traumatic event cannot be relegated to the past, because the traumatic past is unavailable to the memory of the conscious subject (Leys 2000: 7–10, 298). The traumatic event is understood as an experience akin to hypnotic suggestion or identification (what Leys means by mimesis), immersing the victim in the traumatic scene or experience so deeply that the experience was and remains unavailable to the subject as cognitive knowledge. On the contrary, the traumatic experience was so powerful and potent that the subject was overcome by the experience. Taken to its ideal typical conclusion, the previously autonomous subject becomes little more than a series of identifications with his or her traumatic, and hence dissociated, roles. It is, for example, only in the mimetic account that phenomena such as identification with the aggressor are possible. Psychodynamic experience remains active in the mimetic account, trauma working itself into dreams and manifesting itself in acting-out, but this activity remains unavailable to the subject. Pierre Janet and Sándor Ferenczi (in all but his late work) are among those associated with the mimetic account. For Leys, Freud had a foot in both camps (2000: 9–10).

The anti-mimetic account is built on the idea that the one who experienced the trauma experienced it a moment too late, before the self was there to mediate it. Trauma is etched upon an otherwise fully constituted subject who was not there, because it was an experience so far beyond the normal it could not be prepared for, categorized, or shared. Unlike the mimetic account, there is no psychodynamic assumption that the traumatic experience is embedded in and mixed with unconscious experience. On the contrary, the victim is a camera, the event etched in a portion of the memory that cannot be erased or transformed into narrative. This claim about a camera-like etching of an essentially non-verbal, indeed non-verbalizable experience, has found its strongest supporter in Cathy Caruth (1996), who has drawn upon the neurobiological research of Bessel A. van der Kolk and his associates (van der Kolk and van der Hart 1995). Their approach was explicated in the previous chapter.

In theory distinct, in practice, the mimetic and anti-mimetic account share a common assumption: that the traumatized individual, qua individual, does not exist. Trauma acts not on a complex social individual in relationships over time, but on a psyche that responds as though it were hypnotized (mimetic). Or the trauma works on an autonomous psyche as an outside force over which the conscious psyche – what the person generally calls "me," or "I" – has virtually no access, so that the traumatized psyche must be represented by others.

One reason Leys reaches such extreme conclusions is because she is working with ideal types; that is, extreme formulations (although it cannot be denied that there is something about Caruth's account, in particular, that lends itself to extremity). A less obvious reason for the extremity of Leys' conclusions is that she writes as if trauma were the province of Freudians, Lacanians, neurobiologists, and literary critics – a diverse group to be sure, but still quite limited. Notable by his or her absence is any member of the Middle or Independent Group of the British Psychoanalytic Society in the years during and after World War II.[3] Neither ignorant nor unconcerned with trauma, every member of this school sought, like Winnicott, to explain human action in terms of relationships rather than drives. Included in this group were Donald Winnicott, Wilfred Bion, Ronald Fairbairn, and later Michael Balint. Also missing are Americans such as Harry Stack Sullivan and Heinz Kohut, both of whom invented new languages by which they might talk about relationships while preserving the language of drives. Neither do contemporary writers such as Christopher Bollas, Stephen A. Mitchell, Jessica Benjamin and Jonathan Lear find any place in Leys's account, as Schwartz (2002) points out. Also missing are the social psychologists of trauma, such as Kai Erikson (1976; 1994), who focus upon the social relationships that make trauma more or less endurable. If one chooses as one's analysts of trauma people who see trauma as akin to a hypnotic suggestion or an etching tool, rather than a human relationship – albeit one that can destroy the possibility of other relationships – then one should not be surprised that Leys's two theories of trauma both lack a genuine human subject. Human subjects live in a fleshy human web of relationships.

The new culture of trauma is not that described by Cathy Caruth (1995; 1996), in which ineffable experiences of dread are hysterically passed down the generations, between fathers and mothers, sons and daughters, who are unable to put words to the emotions connected to traumatic originary experiences, such as the Holocaust or Hiroshima. From a perspective that takes Winnicott seriously, a traumatic culture is one in which it becomes impossible for its members to appropriate the culture, and so extend the transitional experience in the way Winnicott (1971a) writes about in "The Location of Cultural Experience."

The psychological mechanism or process remains an individual one. Members of the culture (or more likely, subculture, such as a marginalized group) find it difficult or impossible to appropriate the culture. This would be potentially traumatic for any individual, for it provides the individual with fewer psychological resources to fall back on in times of stress. This phenomenon may become a group one if the society makes it more difficult for particular groups of people to do this by depriving them of cultural resources and the opportunities to use them.

The result is that culture loses its quality as a transitional experience; that is, as a "potential space" between self and world, subject and object (Winnicott 1971a: 100). With the term "potential space," Winnicott refers to mental space in which the individual takes aspects of "the inherited tradition ... the common pool of humanity," and makes them his own by imaginatively transforming them. Winnicott is referring to the imaginative acquisition of culture. About an evening at the theater, Winnicott (1986) wrote,

> This is the exciting thing about the curtain in a theatre. When it goes up, each one of us will create the play that is going to be enacted, and afterwards we may even find that the overlap of what we have created ... provides material for a discussion about the play that was enacted. (133)

It is in this potential space that adults continue to play, making this culture their own. "I have used the term cultural experience as an extension of the idea of transitional phenomena and of play" (Winnicott 1971a: 99). If culture is not appropriated, then it is never a living experience that can hold us when we are faced with the trauma of everyday life, from illness, to old age to death, to all the other heartaches that confront us, such as the death of a child, or even the expected death of an older parent.

Winnicott draws a distinction between what he calls "subject- ive objects" and "objective objects." Subjective objects are those things we believe exist for us, mirroring our needs and wishes, con- forming perfectly to our view of the world. At first we see mother this way. Subjective objects confirm our sense of being alive. Objective objects are things that exist external to us, without reference to us and our needs and view of reality. They exist in their own right, irrelevant to our subjectivity. They are "not-me-objects," objectively real, but they don't necessarily feel real and alive to us. "Our teddy bears, our Mozart arias, our religious rituals contain in themselves both the subjective and objective poles and hence function as true symbols" (Ulanov 2001: 16). We invest the tradition, the objective object, with something of the subjective object, and thus bring it to life, without reducing the objective to the subjective, which would be mad.

Put an individual, or a population, under enough stress, and its members lose the ability to invest the world with subjectivity. The result is psychological death, which is equivalent to chronic trauma – trauma that destroys an individual's ability to invest and live in transitional space; that is, to just be. Trauma, understood as a social rather than just individual phenomenon, destroys individuals' ability to create a community that can hold its members so that they might find some buffering from the stress and angst that afflicts us all, but that only some experience as trauma.

THERAPY AS THE LIE

If trauma is knowledge, if trauma is a conspiracy to make the world seem safe enough to live in (Erikson 1976: 240), then there is another slightly different way to think about trauma. Trauma resides in the inability to use social conventions (socially sanctioned lies, such as "just you wait, everything is going to turn out OK") in order to relieve anxiety in the way that most of us do. Robinson Crusoe put the lie this way:

> How infinitely good ... providence is, which has provided in its government of mankind such narrow bounds to his sight and knowledge of things; and though he walks in the midst of so many thousand dangers, the sight of which, if discovered to him, would distract his mind and sink his spirits, he is kept serene and calm, by having the events of things hid from his eyes, and knowing nothing of the dangers which surround him.
>
> *(Defoe 1953: 163)*

For some, the inability to use the lie is imposed by others, as discussed above. For others, it is the trauma itself, regardless of source, that destroys the ability to lie to oneself.

More disturbing but intriguing, successful therapy can be defined as enabling the traumatized person to once again use the socially sanctioned lies the rest of us rely on to get by in everyday life. Successful therapy isn't about bringing the traumatized one into closer contact with reality. The traumatized person has already come too close to reality; that is his or her affliction. The task is to reestablish within the traumatized person the ability to use the beliefs, sayings, clichés, and so forth that the rest of us use to get by. Of course, these new defenses will never fit quite as well as before, but perhaps they will fit well enough for the traumatized one to get through the day ... and night.

Partly true

I don't know that this is how therapy works, whether it works this way for many, or a few. Trouble is, I don't believe that clinicians are in a position to know this either. Increased function, the increased ability to retell rather than relive, the diminution of symptoms, all of these may well be achieved by the socially sanctioned lie. For if that is the way that most of us get through life, if the experience of trauma is the experience of having been forced outside of the penumbra of the lie, then the ability to reestablish the lie would be a genuine therapeutic achievement. It would also account for the continued suffering and suicide (as well as their attraction for the rest of us) of those truth tellers, such as Primo Levi and Jean Améry, who could not take up the lie. The devastation that is trauma should lead us to think about how much we really want to know about reality, how close we want to get, and how therapy cures, when it does.

there are multiple realities

This is one reason Holocaust survivors are interesting. Almost all are unable to utilize the socially sanctioned lie; at least not without doubling. One sign of this, and one sees this in many trauma victims (Erikson 1994: 231), though it is most notable in Holocaust survivors, is how drawn they are to others similarly afflicted as the only ones who can possibly understand (Felman 1992: 43; Helen K., T-58). Only those who have lived without the lie and survived can understand that experience, allowing the one who cannot lie to feel a little less alone. Perhaps it is our lies that bind us: as nations, communities, families. Often benign, perhaps even therapeutic, our lies must look like a fortress to those who cannot, or in some cases simply will not, let themselves inside its sheltering walls.

Fascinating in their stories

CULTURE AS SECOND SKIN

Winnicott was interested in what it was like to be born, and what it took to become a self. His answer was that the shell of the self, the boundary-maintaining function, must at first be taken over by the mother, who acts as the infant and young child's second skin, protecting the young child from too much or too little external stimulation, while anticipating his or her physical needs, in as much as that is possible. If the mother does a good enough job, the kernel of the self, the spontaneous self, can develop on its own. If she doesn't, the mother fosters a child whose self is too much on the surface, managing the environment constantly (Stonebridge 2000: 90–93). It is as though the interior of the self never gets to stay inside where it belongs; instead, it spends its time on the surface, managing the self's interactions with its environment in order to survive. Or as Winnicott (1992c: 99) puts it, "the feeling [is that] the center of gravity of consciousness transfers from the kernel to the shell."

Winnicott wrote about early childhood development. At the same time, he always understood that cultural experience for the adult served a comparable function. This is the point of a transitional object: at first a teddy bear or blankie, transitional objects and transitional space come to encompass the entire range of cultural experience, from religion to art to music to familiar foods and smells. What would happen if adult transitional objects and relationships were to become reified; that is, turned into relationships with things that the imagination could not invest with its power of imaginative transformation, so as to make them its own?

Jean Améry (1980: 46–48) was interested in what happened to the exile, the man or woman without a home, as he himself spent much of his adult life in exile from his native Austria. To be without a home, Améry concluded, is to lack a fundamental security. Security stems from not having to constantly respond to chance occurrences, because we have confidence in our understanding of the culture in which we live, while trusting our ability to interpret the language, gestures, and expressions of the citizens among whom we live. "One feels secure, however, when no chance occurrence is to be expected, nothing completely strange to be feared" (Améry 1980: 47). Even if this is an idealization from a man writing in exile, his point is provocative. "There is no 'new home.' Home is the land of one's childhood and youth" (48).

To be sure, over time the exile can learn the subtleties of the language and culture of his or her new home. However, this will always be a mental acquisition, an "intellectual act." He or she will always have to think about it; it will never be entirely natural. Améry is a fine example of the mental self-holding of the exile, who can never feel simply held again, but who must always live on the surface of his skin in the new culture. The exile can never just be, or so Améry argues, and his life seems to attest. Améry (1980: 44) puts it succinctly, "I was no longer an I and did not live within a We." Were he to belabor the point, he might have said, "Because I no longer lived within a We, I could no longer afford to be fully and spontaneously an I." The point is made, in any case.

Home is Where We Start From (1986b), the title of a collection of Winnicott's essays, reflects the same idea. One can build new homes, in new lands, and eventually come to feel that one belongs there. One can even have what Améry (1980: 41) calls a "transportable home," by which he means a religion or ideology. But one can never replace one's first home, and the security it provided (Améry 1980: 46). If one's first home failed to provide this security, then one will always be wanting, using one's mind to take its place, at the cost of just being.

WHEN TRAUMA BECOMES POLITICAL

In a classic essay, "The Concept of Cumulative Trauma," Masud Khan (1963), a member of the Independent Group of the British Psychoanalytic Society (his training analyst was Winnicott), wrote about the consequences of the mother's failure to provide the infant and developing child with an adequate "protective shield."

The consequences of any one failure are unobservable, perhaps insignificant. The result of continued failure over time is the child's failure to develop his or her own ego, as he or she must spend too much time tending to the mother-child relationship, rather than exploring the larger world. Kai Erikson is helpful in thinking about how cumulative trauma expresses itself in the social and political realm.

Erikson writes:

> *Chronic conditions* as well as *acute events* can induce trauma, and this, too, belongs in our calculations. A chronic disaster is one that gathers force slowly and insidiously, creeping around one's defenses rather than smashing through them. People are unable to mobilize their normal defenses against the threat, sometimes because they have elected consciously or unconsciously to ignore it.
>
> *(1994: 21, author's emphasis)*

In fact, as one reads Erikson's *A New Species of Trouble: The Human Experience of Modern Disasters* (1994), it becomes clear that the "age of trauma" to which Erikson referred in an earlier work is not primarily about almost everybody being a little traumatized, as he suggested then (1976: 258). In 1976, Erikson meant that different eras seem to be characterized by maladies that shed light on the culture of the time. In Freud's day, it was hysteria. Some have argued that ours is the age of narcissism and borderline personality disorder. For Erikson, "it may well be that historians of the future will look back on this period and conclude that the traumatic neuroses were its true clinical signature" (258). However, as one reads through the traumatizing disasters to which Erikson refers in *A New Species of Trouble* (1994), it becomes clear that every one of his examples refers not to the general population, but to the chronic traumatization of special populations, whose numbers add up. These include people living in persistent poverty, or institutionalized in asylums and prisons, or living on American Indian reservations. Migrant laborers and their children, and the socially marginal generally, such as the aged, the isolated, and unwelcome strangers in new lands, aliens and immigrants, are also included. Among these groups, says Erikson, one can hardly avoid seeing the familiar symptoms of trauma: numbness of spirit; a susceptibility to anxiety, rage, and depression, a sense of helplessness; loss of various motor skills; a heightened anxiety about threats from their social and physical environment; preoccupation with death; retreat into dependency; and a diminution of ego function (Erikson 1976: 255–256).

Erikson's comments raise several points of interest. For over a century, trauma was medically defined not as the result of an insult to the body or the psyche, but the insult itself, as in the phrase "blunt force trauma." Only in more recent years has trauma come to be defined as the result of the insult to the mind, the intrusion of an unbearable reality into the emotional life of the individual. This suggests to Erikson that if we define trauma by its result, then we define as a traumatic disaster any event that has the power to induce trauma (Erikson 1976: 254–259).

The second point of interest is the way in which Erikson defines trauma. The odd thing about this definition is that when one begins to look at the lives of the chronically traumatized, many (but not all) of these "symptoms" come to seem peculiarly rational, if by "rational" one means in accord with reality. To be chronically poor, not knowing how you are going to pay next week's rent on your crummy motel room, not knowing where you children's next meal is coming from, where you are going to get the dental care to relieve your son's toothache that has been going on for days, fear of the men you encounter on the streets – are these not enough to foster a sense of chronic anxiety about threats from the environment, a sense of helplessness, rage, and depression, in any of us?[4] Would not many of us use numbness as a coping mechanism in this situation? Sometimes the symptoms of trauma are the reflections of a careless (or worse) society, inflicted on its weakest members.

The third point of interest is that even if we live in an age of trauma, even if we are all afflicted by trauma that creeps around our defenses, sabotaging our souls (that is, our true selves), some suffer from chronic trauma far more dramatically than others. It is they who must come first. The source of their suffering is usually readily identifiable, and at least in principle, readily mitigated; if, that is, wealthy societies such as our own possessed the political will to do so. Chronic poverty and homelessness are not as subtle and intellectually interesting as the "crisis of witnessing," as some working along the same lines as Caruth have called it (Felman and Laub 1992), or even a new age of trauma. Nevertheless, the material sources of chronic trauma inflicted upon the most vulnerable members of our society make a moral demand upon us that should not be overlooked in the search for more interesting and arcane intellectual formulations. We should almost always be most concerned with the wretched of the earth, those who live in physical and moral environments of such great insecurity that chronic trauma becomes a rational, or at least realistic, way of life. This dimension of trauma is not invisible. Most of us simply do not go to the trouble of looking. Thinking about trauma in this comprehensive way is one way of looking. And before we can act, we have to look.

A traumatic culture is a literal impossibility. Only individuals can experience trauma. But some cultures make it more difficult than others for individuals to have access to the experiences that protect them from trauma. These protective experiences not only help individuals invest their world with meaning, but allow people to become a living part of this meaningful world, via their participation in transitional objects and relationships. This is the most useful way of thinking about the politics of trauma.[5] It is a way of thinking that stems from not just Winnicott, but from the British Object Relations tradition, which sees individuals as enmeshed in relationships from the beginning of life. Trauma destroys our confidence not only in the stability of these relationships, but in our belief that we can participate in them without exposing our (true) selves to endless exploitation.

CONCLUSION

Trauma is not a political concept. Indeed, Winnicott renders the inner world that is transformed by trauma in terms so subtle they could hardly withstand political analysis. However, when one considers the social and political conditions under which transitional objects and relationships flourish, as well as the conditions that allow individuals to live within themselves, it becomes possible to subject trauma to a political analysis. That is, it becomes possible to consider what types of social and political arrangements might make it almost impossible for some groups of people to participate in those cultural activities that protect us from trauma, and help heal us from the effects of trauma. Erikson's list of special populations is a good starting point, as long as we approach it in the proper spirit, not merely as a list of groups most vulnerable to trauma, but as a question. Why have relatively wealthy Western societies produced so many such groups, and what are we doing about it?

Caruth's approach, on the other hand, seems to have it wrong from the perspective of both trauma and politics. Trauma loses its inwardness as the individual becomes a psychic camera, at least insofar as the conceptualization of trauma is concerned. Politics, on the other hand, becomes the realm of grand history, trauma transmitted from generation to generation, the hidden motive force of history. Ordinary politics, such as easing the lot of the despised and dispossessed, becomes almost irrelevant as far as trauma is concerned. It is ironic that it is the enormous subtlety of Winnicott's account of trauma that renders it most conducive to mundane political solutions. But, as previously suggested, this may be an implication of British Object Relations theory overall.

In the previous chapter, I argued that Caruth deprives us of the wisdom of trauma. But there is a sense in which Winnicott is not entirely open to this wisdom either. Winnicott is preternaturally sensitive to the failures of the holding environment that lead individuals to devote too much attention to holding themselves, too little to participating in transitional objects and relationships. On the other hand, there is a truth to trauma that Winnicott downplays. The world "was not made for the sake of the human being, and ... has not become more human," is how Herbert Marcuse (1978: 69) expressed this truth. In the end, we will all be lost to the void, and the traumas that many of us experience along the way (albeit of vastly varying magnitudes) all point in this direction, all remind us of this reality. At some level of the psyche, there is only one interpretation of the final act of this play, and about this reality, Winnicott would comfort us with teddy bears and blankies. For adults, there are Mozart arias, religion, and, as Nietzsche (1968a) reminds us, Greek tragedy.

For Nietzsche, Greek tragedy makes it possible to live with knowledge of the void. With Winnicott, one has the sense that it is better not to talk about such things. Silence allows for the possibility of transitional space, but also for the possibility of avoidance. Silence creates, avoids, and destroys. It begs to be used wisely. Winnicott uses silence more wisely than Caruth, but neither practices perfect wisdom. But then again, how could they?

NOTES

1 D. W. Winnicott (1896–1971) was a prominent member of the Independent Group of the British Psychoanalytic Society. The Independent Group allied itself neither with Anna Freud nor Melanie Klein, the two leading figures in the Society during and after World War II. His first analysis was with James Strachey, his second with Joan Riviere, lions of the psychoanalytic community.

2 The DSM-IV-TR criterion for PTSD differs from the previous DSM-III-R criterion, which specified the traumatic event should be of a type that was "outside the range of usual human experience." Since the introduction of DSM-IV, with its looser criteria, one study suggests as much as a 50 percent increase in diagnoses of PTSD. From the perspective taken here, it hardly matters. There is more than enough trauma to go around.

3 The name changes from Middle to Independent depending upon the years in question, but that is only a detail.

4 Several years ago, in the county in which my university is located, a 12-year-old boy died of a tooth that became infected, the infection traveling to his brain. His mother was homeless, the family's Medicaid coverage had lapsed, the state plan did not cover dental care, and no private dentist

would care for him. At: www.washingtonpost.com/wp-dyn/content/article/
2007/03/02/AR2007030200827.html.

5 This formulation of the relationship between trauma and the marginalized
group has the advantage of making it clear that trauma remains an
individual phenomenon. While we may talk and write casually about
traumatized groups, there is in reality no such thing. There are only
traumatized individuals, plus any composition laws that explain how the
individuals behave differently in the presence of other group members, who
in this case are generally demoralized. For those interested in such things,
this means that my argument is compatible with the doctrine of
methodological individualism, a key principle of empiricism. On
methodological individualism as a commitment of empiricism, see
Brodbeck (1958).

4   Melanie Klein and forgiveness: theory

The theory and practice of forgiveness is today a moral disaster area. We live in a world in which everybody seems to be offering forgiveness, and few seem to be asking for it, at least not in a serious fashion. Statements such as "I regret the incident, and am sorry if anyone was offended by my choice of words," are by now almost a cliché. Whatever statements like this are, they are not requests for forgiveness. If we are to take forgiveness seriously, then we must consider forgiveness both as a psychological capability and a normative ideal. Ideally, the psychology and morality of forgiveness reinforce each other. Sometimes they do; sometimes they are in conflict.

Dozens, indeed hundreds, of books on forgiveness, mostly of the psychological self-help variety, line the electronic bookshelves of Amazon.com. Most argue that forgiveness heals the self of the one who forgives, overcoming feelings of hatred, rage, and implacable anger that in the end only erode the self, making the victim more miserable and unhappy. We forgive in order to restore our own sense of self-worth. Any sense of forgiveness as a moral relationship (and achievement) between two people is lost. Eva Kor, who stood before the gates of Auschwitz and publically forgave Josef Mengele for his so-called experiments on her as a child, as well as forgiving the Nazis for the destruction of her entire family, is perhaps the most poignant example of forgiveness as self-empowerment, but she is hardly alone. Her voice is heard in the conclusion of the next chapter.

Consider Simon Wiesenthal's *The Sunflower: On the Possibilities and Limits of Forgiveness*. On the cover of the revised version is the simple statement that summarizes the book well. "You are a prisoner in a concentration camp. A dying Nazi soldier asks for your forgiveness. What would you do?" The Nazi soldier, it should be remarked, had committed terrible atrocities against hundreds of Jews, burning many of them alive in buildings they were herded into, shooting any who tried to escape.

Wiesenthal (1997), who presents this story as though it happened to him, says he silently left the dying man's bedside, and the book turns on the question of whether he should have forgiven the Nazi, who seems genuinely repentant. Wiesenthal's bunkmates rightly point out that he was in no position to forgive, primarily because he was selected simply because he was a Jew, and not because he was a victim of this particular Nazi's crimes. Furthermore, a man under a death sentence is not free to forgive. The remainder of the book is taken up by the answers of dozens of famous theologians, teachers, philosophers, and writers to the question of "What would I have done?" had I been in Wiesenthal's place. Among the respondents are Robert Coles, the Dalai Lama, Jean Améry and Herbert Marcuse, along with forty-two others.[1]

It is widely held that whether to forgive the dying Nazi is divided down the middle between Christians and Jews, with few exceptions. Solomon Schimmel (2002) puts it this way:

> Most of the Jews felt that only the victim of a crime has the right to forgive the perpetrator and that in the absence of repentance as defined in Jewish tradition, which includes remorse, confession, apology, and reparation, there is no *obligation* to forgive. Most of the Christians felt that a third party could forgive a sinner, especially if he has confessed and expressed remorse for his deeds, even if he hasn't made reparation or apologized to his victim, and that Christian love mandates forgiveness by a victim, even where the perpetrator hasn't repented.
>
> *(7–8, author's emphasis)*

As striking as the division between Christians and Jews, the number of thoroughly thoughtless comments on forgiveness from all quarters is at least as notable. One commentator, Robert Brown, referred to a rebel in another war who was given the choice by the court of how to punish his torturer. "My punishment is to forgive you," replied the rebel. Though the context of the rebel's comment is unclear, Brown seems to regard the statement as a moral exemplar, as though to say, "If I forgive you, I will, by demonstrating my superior humanity, force you to confront your miserable self" (Wiesenthal 1997: 123).

An Episcopal priest said we forgive in order to get on with life (148). Theodore Hesburgh, priest and former president of Notre Dame University, said, "If asked to forgive anyone for anything, I would forgive" (163–164). Rabbi Harold Kushner, well-known author of *When Bad Things Happen to Good People*, said he would follow the same advice he gave a parishioner: "I'm asking you to forgive because [your husband] doesn't deserve the power to live in your head and turn you into a bitter, angry woman" (2004: 176). Kushner adds, in a statement at odds with his religion, "I'm not sure there is such a thing as forgiving another person" (174). Only God forgives. Perhaps Kushner is unsure about the existence of forgiveness because he has turned it into a strictly intra-psychic process, a version of self-help therapy.

Several *Sunflower* respondents worried about what Dietrich Bonhoeffer calls "cheap grace." As Bonhoeffer puts it, "Cheap grace is not the kind of forgiveness of sin which frees us from the toils of sin. Cheap grace is the grace we bestow on ourselves. Cheap grace is the preaching of forgiveness without requiring repentance." Grace, Bonhoeffer continues, is the gift of forgiveness that is free and unconditional as a result of following Christ. It should not be turned around to mean that one can be assured of God's grace beforehand, and continue one's bourgeois life as before. Grace may be free, but it is not gratis. It requires the reexamination and recommitment of one's entire life (Bonhoeffer 1963: 47, 54).

If Bonhoeffer is correct, as I believe he is, then what is the relationship between the normative ideal and the psychology of forgiveness? The relationship is one in which we learn that forgiveness is a perilous psychological journey, one in which the victim must repeat, in another register, his or her original experience of vulnerability to the offender. More on this difficult concept shortly.

As the failure of even ostensibly thoughtful people reveals, including many of those who responded to Wiesenthal's challenge in *The Sunflower*, there is something about the concept of forgiveness that is slippery and difficult to grasp. Hannah Arendt, usually a reliable guide, renders forgiveness inapplicable to acts of hatred and malice, an odd and disturbing outcome. "Jabberwocky" is Cynthia Ozick's succinct characterization of Arendt's argument. Arendt "is the great moral philosopher of the age, but even she cannot make a Lazarus of history." Ozick (1989) is writing about the Holocaust, Arendt about the nature of political action per se, but any account of forgiveness that renders forgiveness irrelevant to acts of hatred and malice is derisory, even bizarre.

Arguing that in a world in which every significant action unleashes a series of unpredictable and irreversible consequences, Arendt states that only forgiveness allows us to be free to act. "Forgiving serves to undo the deeds of the past." Without being released from the consequences of one's act, our capacity to act would, as it were, be confined to one single deed from which we could never recover; we would remain the victims of its consequences forever, like the sorcerer's apprentice who lacked the magic to break the spell. Without forgiveness, the burden of acting in history would be too great. Forgiveness allows us to begin the world anew, and in that respect forgiveness is a font of creativity, one of the few reactions that share with action the capacity to surprise. Forgiveness intervenes in the tragic nature of existence and action: that we are bound to hurt others no matter what we do, and no matter what our intentions. Forgiveness makes "it possible for life to go on by constantly releasing men from what they have done knowingly" (Arendt 1958: 237, 240).[2]

Arendt's special use of the term "forgiveness" would be acceptable if it did not lead her to abandon any consideration of forgiveness

for acts of hatred and malice. She reads the Greek testament tenden-
tiously, arguing that in the gospels, the duty to forgive:

> does not apply to the extremity of crime and willed evil ... Crime
> and willed evil are rare, even rarer perhaps than good deeds;
> according to Jesus, they will be taken care of by God in the Last
> Judgment, which plays no role whatsoever in life on earth.
>
> *(Arendt 1958: 239–240)*

Arendt's is a mistaken reading of the gospels. For most Christians, the
Last Judgment is now, every single day, expressed by whether we treat
the poorest and most vulnerable among us as we would treat Christ
(Matthew 25: 37–40). Most, but not all, Christians hold to a proleptic
interpretation of forgiveness, in which the forgiveness we have already
received through Christ's sacrifice is a foretaste of eternity.[3] We are
already forgiven, but the gift is not gratis, for we must act and live as
though we earned it in order to be worthy of what we have been given
through Christ's sacrifice (Jones 1995: 121). This is what Bonhoeffer
(1963: 47–53) was getting at when he said the gift of forgiveness is not
cheap, for we have to live as though we are worthy of the grace we have
already received. Not only is Arendt's a misreading of the gospels, hers is
also a misreading of reality. How could Arendt argue that acts of hatred
and malice, to say nothing of pleasure in hurting and lack of remorse
(a working definition of evil) are rare, either in the gospels or our own day?

In an odd way, Arendt has caused the concept of forgiveness to
vanish. The harm inflicted in everyday life by virtue of what it means
to act in error, what she calls trespass, is automatically forgiven. Or at
least she sets no conditions, such as having acted with prudence and
thoughtfulness. Conversely, not only acts of hatred and evil, but
crime, are lifted out of the domain of human forgiveness altogether.
To be sure, Arendt does not render acts of hatred, evil, and crime
beyond human punishment[4] – just human forgiveness. In so doing,
she neuters the concept.

Much of life takes place between the unavoidable trespasses of
everyday life and the mass torture and murder of millions. Yet, about

this land in between, Arendt has nothing to say. Why Arendt treats forgiveness as she does is unclear. Part of the answer seems to be her desire to save the concept for special duty, as it were, in the realm of political action. Another part of the answer seems to be her desire to keep the realm of action free from the complex personal relationships required for forgiveness. She might have done so by rendering forgiveness a private, or even social, relationship, but she does not. She brings forgiveness into politics, but only by creating a world to which it does not apply, except within the narrow confines of a concept of everyday trespass, designed to liberate action from the confines of infinite responsibility.

And yet perhaps this is not the whole story. Hanna Segal, Klein's most well-known interpreter to the larger psychotherapeutic world (Klein's writing is often obscure, her concepts curious), writes that creativity is impossible in the absence of mourning. "It is only when the loss has been acknowledged and mourning experienced that re-creation can take place" (Segal 1952: 199). Segal's view supports Arendt's, insofar as Arendt suggests that forgiveness is itself a form of creativity, allowing the world, or at least a piece of it, to begin anew. Forgiveness breaks old molds, old patterns, surprising offender and victim alike. On the other hand, Segal understands in a way that Arendt does not, that forgiveness is no easy matter. Real forgiveness for serious offenses is the outcome of an act of mourning, a process that takes time and hard labor, the work of grief. This work, I argue in this chapter and the next, requires the cooperation of both offender and victim. It is, in any case, hardly as easy as Arendt suggests. Forgiveness is in large measure the work of mourning.

PARANOID-SCHIZOID AND DEPRESSIVE POSITIONS

Klein's concept of the depressive position will help make sense of the phenomenology of forgiveness. An ironic, indeed unfair, aspect of coming to terms with the trauma that is inflicted by humans is that not just the offender, but also the victim must make reparation for the damage that has been done. Not for a moment do I suggest that the moral burden of trespass falls upon the victim as well as the offender. There is no moral parity. To say that the victim must also make reparation is to say that forgiveness is a long journey for both parties, in which each has duties to perform, duties that the victim may properly decline. There is no necessity for forgiveness, and many alternatives. Turning to Klein will help us understand why forgiveness is so complicated, difficult, and too easily transformed into an attempt to restore inner peace or a sense of power.

A contemporary of Anna Freud, Sigmund's daughter, Klein is generally seen as the founder of the British School of Object Relations. Instead of focusing on the Oedipal conflict, as Freud did, Klein focused on the child's struggle to come to terms with his or her hatred and rage, which she believed were constitutional, inborn. Particularly threatening to the child is the fact that he or she both loves and hates the same person, originally mother or other primary caretaker. How can the child keep from destroying what is good, a source of nourishment, comfort, and love, when he or she is filled with destructive rage at the same person? For it is this same person who must unavoidably frustrate the child with her absence, imperfect response, and so forth.

Klein's explanation is based on what she calls the paranoid-schizoid position, the first organization of the psychological defenses. Klein calls this early organization of the defenses paranoid-schizoid in order to stress the way in which the young child's fears take the form of phantasies of persecution, as well as the way in which the child defends against persecution by splitting, a schizoid phenomenon, in which the child does not let himself know that he both loves and hates the same person. Klein believes that the paranoid-schizoid position begins almost at birth. It is a normally occurring psychotic state, a formulation for which Klein was often criticized. Some have called Klein a theorist of original sin, an exaggeration that nonetheless makes a point: hate comes first.

With the paranoid-schizoid position, Klein (1928) asserts that the alternative to acknowledging one's sadness at all the hatred and pain in the world – including the hatred and pain one would direct against mother and other beloved caretakers – is to divide the world into good and bad, locating the source of hatred and pain in the external bad object, as she calls it. "If I suffer, then someone bad must be causing it, then I must be under attack," would be an example of this way of thinking. Calling the paranoid-schizoid position a position, not a developmental stage, was important to Klein, suggesting that we never leave the paranoid-schizoid position behind. In times of stress, tension, anxiety, and loss, we are all liable to revert to paranoid-schizoid thinking.

The key problem of mental life for Klein is to separate one's love and hate sufficiently in early life to be able to integrate them later on; otherwise, we shall be forever confused as to what is good and what is bad, and so likely to confuse love and hate our whole lives long. For Klein, there is no deeper and more terrifying confusion than this, for it puts everything we love and care about at risk of being destroyed by our own hate.

For Klein, as for Freud, life is a struggle between Eros and the *Todestrieb*, love against death. Only for Klein there is no Nirvana principle, no connection between the hatred and aggression of the death drive and the peace and absence of stimulation that Freud writes of in *Beyond the Pleasure Principle* (1920: 34–43). For Freud, the *Todestrieb* ultimately seeks to return to the origin of things, a state of oblivion. There is, in other words, a type of satisfaction inherent in the *Todestrieb*, a satisfaction from which life itself is a long detour. For Klein, on the other hand, the *Todestrieb* is sadism, envy, and destruction. Nothing in Klein's account of the *Todestrieb* suggests she shared Freud's idea that death is the *telos* of life (Alford 1989: 25).

This might make it seem as if Klein's account of the death drive would be easier to assimilate into mainstream psychoanalytic thought than Freud's. That may not be the case, for Klein makes it clear that the infant and young child hates, envies, and would destroy its mother if it could, regardless of how responsive and loving mother truly is. To be sure, Klein and Kleinians recognize that the mother's response to the child's aggression, how well she is able to contain the child's hatred and envy, make an enormous difference in how well the child is able to integrate its experiences of loving and hating, and so enter into and remain within the depressive position (Klein 1957). Nevertheless, the thesis that the child's hatred and destructiveness is innate, unrelated, at least at first, to the quality of the child's relationship with its mother and others, leaves even some sympathetic followers cold (Likierman 2001: 177).[5]

Not long after the emergence of the paranoid-schizoid position, the child enters into what Klein calls "the depressive position." With the term "depressive position," Klein refers to a developmental achievement in which one knows that one loves and hates the same person. Klein (1940) calls it "depressive" because she believes that the knowledge of how much we hate those whom we love, as well as how much hate there is in the world, must sadden any person, even a child, though both children and adults are often unaware that it is this that makes them sad. As Klein (1948: 36) puts it, "The feeling that harm done to the loved object is caused by the subject's aggressive impulses I take to be the essence of guilt." Depressive guilt, we might call it, as opposed to the guilt associated with the paranoid-schizoid position, which is primarily experienced as fear of retaliation.

In ideal typical development, the paranoid-schizoid position gives way to the depressive position. As the individual matures, the destructive elements of the self are split off and regained, over and over, until greater integration comes about.

> As a result, the feeling of responsibility becomes stronger, and guilt and depression are more fully experienced. When this happens, the ego is strengthened, omnipotence of destructive impulses is diminished, together with envy, and the capacity for love and gratitude, stifled in the course of the splitting processes, is released.
>
> (Klein 1957: 225)

This is the *telos* of normal development, and it is dependent on the integration of destructive, hateful, sadistic, and envious aspects of the self. We should, however, be on the lookout for false reparation, what Kleinians call "manic denial": the pretense by either offender or victim that a serious injury did not occur, or that it may be easily repaired.

If development goes well (and we are talking, it should be noted, about a process that lasts a lifetime; it is never over and done with), the depressive position will culminate in the desire to make reparation for the harm done to others, both in reality and phantasy. Care and concern, says Klein (1964: 65), express "a profound urge to make sacrifices," to make others happy out of genuine sympathy for them.

Donald Meltzer (1981: 179) calls Klein's a "theological model of the mind." By this he means that our internal objects; that is, our internalized images of others – are our gods, giving meaning and purpose to our lives. We might, however, extend this observation to include the recognition that Klein's basic categories are fundamentally ethical or moral in character. As Michael Rustin (1982: 82–83) observes, "Kleinian theory is impregnated with moral categories, and its developmental concepts ... incorporate moral capabilities (notably concern for the well-being of other persons) into their theoretical definition." It could be argued that such a claim commits the naturalistic fallacy, but this would not be correct. Rather than deriving morality from human nature, she discovers morality in the earliest human relationships. (To be sure, whether this is the right morality cannot be answered by Kleinian analysis alone.) Once one discovers morality, can the need for forgiveness be far behind? From a Kleinian perspective, morality means making reparation.

Reparation should not be confused with restoring a broken wholeness, an ideal that risks the manic quality of denial. Among those who write on forgiveness, the restoration of a broken wholeness is a leading theme. As L. Gregory Jones (1995: xii) puts it:

> forgiveness ought not simply or even primarily to be focused on the absolution of guilt; rather, it ought to be focused on the reconciliation of brokenness, the restoration of communion – with God, with one another, and with the whole Creation.

On the contrary, the depressive position, from which mature forgiveness springs, recognizes that because it never was (except in phantasy), wholeness will always be broken, and that some things can never be repaired. This recognition is what we mourn in the depressive position, and in so doing, cease our schizoid splitting of the world into good and bad, whole and broken. It is in the depressive position that we come to recognize how easy it is to break things, and how difficult, and often impossible it is to restore them, let alone to achieve wholeness. Ironic is that only when we have entered the depressive position, which integrates good and bad objects (primarily experiences of people), that we are prepared to mourn an original wholeness that never was. Psychic integration leads not to a restored wholeness, but the recognition of its loss. In the place of wholeness comes a more nuanced experience of a world more subtlety put together while remaining held apart by difference. This is a good thing, or at least the real thing.

The longing for wholeness takes many forms. Jacques Derrida seems to pursue a version of wholeness, what he calls the "radical purity" of forgiveness. With that term, Derrida (2001: 39) refers to what he believes is an aporia, that true forgiveness can only forgive the unforgivable.

> Must one not maintain that an act of forgiveness worthy of its name, if there ever is such a thing, must forgive the unforgivable, and without condition? And that such unconditionality is also inscribed, like its contrary, namely the condition of repentance, in 'our' heritage? Even if this radical purity can seem excessive, hyperbolic, mad? Because if I say, as I think, that forgiveness is mad, and that it must remain a madness of the impossible, this is certainly not to exclude or disqualify it.

In contrast to the radical or unconditional purity model of forgiveness, Derrida posits "ordinary forgiveness," which is based on the model of economic exchange: you are in my debt; I forgive your debt. Derrida attributes such a view to Hannah Arendt, an attribution that seems simplistic. Whatever is wrong with Arendt's view of forgiveness, it is not primarily this.

The only aporia here is one created by the term "forgiving the unforgivable." Once any act is forgiven, it is by definition forgivable (whether it should be or not). Less obvious is why Derrida would dramatize forgiveness in this way, rendering it a madness of excess. Because purity has become the highest value. And what would pure, unconditional forgiveness mean? Evidently it means an act of forgiveness that Derrida (2001: 55) cannot comprehend, such as a "victim of terrorism, a person whose children have ... had their throats cut, or another whose family was killed in a death oven." True enough, forgiveness for such bestial crimes is difficult to imagine, but that is not really the issue. At issue is not whether we can find someone who forgave what most of us would regard as unforgivable, at issue is whether we are to admire this mad excess, whether any of the normative conditions of forgiveness (discussed shortly) were met, and whether the parties came to any sort of mutual understanding.

Rather than admiring and defining forgiveness as mad excess, we should question this understanding – not just the definition, but the search for unconditional and radical purity that lies behind it. If we learn nothing else from Melanie Klein, we learn that nothing in the depressive position is ever pure, but always a mix of good and bad, joyous and sad, hateful and caring. Only in the paranoid-schizoid position do we find purity, the purity of a split-off, one-dimensional experience of the other. Or as Derrida (2001: 44) puts it, "These two poles, the unconditional and the conditional, are absolutely heterogeneous, and must remain irreducible to one another." Paranoid-schizoid thinking is not absent from intellectual work either, though Derrida qualifies his position in other comments.[6]

If Derrida's work on forgiveness is troubling, that of the psychoanalyst Julia Kristeva is even more so. Here is not the place to take up her work on forgiveness, but only some of her comments on Derrida. His radical position regarding forgiveness should be maintained, Kristeva comments, but only in the private sphere.

> This [forgiving the unforgivable] can only be done in strict privacy,
> notably that of the analytic cure ... This is possible in
> psychoanalysis – even in the case of horrible crimes like murder and
> pedophilia – since this is a place where people who had had such
> experiences demonstrate a possibility for change, albeit sometimes
> temporarily and falsely. We can therefore accompany them in this
> movement of transformation and rebirth.
>
> *(Rice 2002)*

Kristeva wrote a book on Arendt, titled simply *Hannah Arendt* (2001).
The last part of the last chapter, titled "Judgment: Between Forgiveness and Promise," addresses Arendt and forgiveness (230–240).
Kristeva seems to have almost no idea how much her idea of forgiveness differs from Arendt's: for Arendt, forgiveness is public, for
Kristeva it is private; for Arendt forgiveness is for ordinary transgressions, for Kristeva it is for the unforgivable. Sigrid Weigel (2002)
makes these and other points well.

In Kristeva's account, forgiveness is the task of the analyst, who
has taken over the role of the confessor. The therapist's goal is to lead
the perpetrator to an emotional rebirth, what evangelical Christians
call being "born again," after Christ's exhortation to Nicodemus (John
3: 3–7). Anyone familiar with Kristeva's account of psychoanalysis will
recognize the evangelical tendency in her work. Or as Kristeva puts it,
"Just as it has been said that philosophy is a white theology because it
kept the logic but not God, I say that psychoanalysis is a colored Judeo-
Christianity because it has added impulses and desires" (Rice 2002).

The virtue of Klein's work is that while it too partakes of the
Judeo-Christian tradition, its feet remain firmly planted on the
ground, under which reside Aeschylus' Furies, still untamed, the topic
of a late work of hers (Alford 1990; Klein 1963). For Klein, there is no
rebirth, except in the realm of manic denial. Regret and remorse are
the currency of the depressive position, out of which may come
confidence that one's love is stronger than one's hate, and ultimately
that there is enough goodness in the world to make life worthwhile.

Perhaps the most surprising implication of Klein's reflections on love, hate, and reparation is that reparation is as much the task of the victim as it is the offender. No moral equation is involved. To offend is not the same as to be victim, and the victim is not a psychological mirror image of the victimizer. Because all of us are guilty of hateful phantasies and acts does not mean that those who act upon them are morally equivalent to those who don't. What it means is that forgiveness is, in its own way, as much an act of reparation as the acts of those who offend and ask forgiveness. The difference between the offender's and victim's reparation is that the offender should aim to repair the damage to the victim, as well as his or her relationship to the victim. The victim's reparation is primarily directed toward repairing his or her experience of the world as a good place to live, good enough so that it has room for the offender.

REPARATION AND FORGIVENESS

It would be easy to argue that Kleinian reparation is a form of forgiveness. For several reasons this would be wrong. Shahrzad Siassi (2004) sees forgiveness as the antecedent of reparation. For Siassi, forgiveness developmentally underlies and precedes the development of gratitude and reparation. This is mistaken if we understand forgiveness as a normative value that recognizes that harm has been done, but wishes to maintain a relationship with the one who has offended. That the first offender is almost always mother (or other primary caretaker) is good practice for tolerating the complex ambivalence that forgiveness will require in later life. To say that forgiveness precedes gratitude and reparation must refer to a concept of forgiveness based on splitting of good and bad, more akin to Derrida's search for the purity of impossible forgiveness.

As forgiveness is not simply the outcome of reparation, neither is forgiveness an automatic or necessary outcome of the depressive integration of trauma or injury. Forgiveness is a concept on the boundary of the psychological and the social, one reason psychoanalysts particularly have had such a difficult time with the concept (Frommer

2005; Smith 2008). If we approach forgiveness as a normative ideal, one that must meet certain standards of excellence, then forgiveness cannot and should not be simply the outcome of a psychological process. The psychological process must be subject to moral cultivation so that it may become a virtue. Forgiveness is an act that has value in itself under the proper circumstances. It is not primarily a feeling. It is good when act and feeling go together, but that is unnecessary.

Furthermore, Klein is extreme in her concern for what she calls internal objects, the way in which internal representations of people and ideas live a psychic life of their own. Frequently she is more concerned with how a person's internal objects (ideas) are making reparation to each other than how the person is, or is not, making reparation to others in the world. This is a tendency in Klein, not an all-or-nothing phenomenon, as I have argued elsewhere, but it is enough to prevent us from equating reparation with forgiveness (Alford 1989; Alford 2006). Klein (1964) is herself responsible for some of the confusion, as she tended to blur the distinction between reparation and forgiveness, as well as the conscious and unconscious referents of reparation, particularly in "Love, Guilt, and Reparation," her treatment of the topic directed at a popular audience (Smith 2008).[7]

The most sensible approach would seem to be Frommer's (2005: 36).

> The mind's ability to shift from the paranoid-schizoid to the depressive position may be regarded as a necessary component in dealing with psychic injury. But to conceive of the psychic infrastructure that comprises the depressive position as sufficient to accomplish a task of forgiving is to fail to appreciate the interactive nature of psychic and interpersonal experience in forgiveness-related phenomena. When it comes to forgiveness, the capacity to move beyond the split between good and bad may actually depend on the presence of explicit interpersonal ingredients that provide the necessary leavening agents.

By "leavening agents," Frommer means relationships in which offenders ask for forgiveness, or make atonement in some way, providing external support for an experience of the world not based on the paranoid-schizoid position. Seeing the relationship as a "leavening agent" suggests the degree to which Frommer's primary focus remains the intrapsychic; nevertheless, the point remains the same. To move from the paranoid-schizoid position to the depressive position after severe trauma and loss, and so becoming able to forgive (the movement is not itself forgiveness, nor is the reparation), should one choose to do so, is enhanced by atonement and similar acts by the offender. The holding community may perform a similar supportive function, a point emphasized in Chapter 6.

Psychoanalysts' suspicion of forgiveness goes back to Freud, holding that the unconscious is so filled with ambivalence that there is no room for forgiveness. Only, "no room" puts it too prosaically.

> Freud establishes forgiveness as a purely conscious phenomenon. By extrapolation, we might conclude that in 'the unconscious' there is no such thing as forgiveness; at best there is ambivalence, with love and hate existing side-by-side, which I believe clinical experience bears out.
>
> *(Smith 2008)*

This is Smith's interpretation of Freud, but an examination of the original Freud sources (1913: 62; 1930: 110) bears him out. More importantly, Smith reflects the widespread analytic belief that the unconscious is too dynamic, too ambivalent, too much a battleground between the forces of love and hate, to ever conclude that anyone can simply "forgive" anyone else. "I forgive you, I hate you, I'll never forgive you, of course I forgive you but I still want to kill you ..." A statement like this probably comes closer to the mark of psychic reality, at least for many analysts.

The most significant psychoanalytic contribution to forgiveness is to see it as one possible outcome of grief and mourning over loss. As Salman Akhtar (2002: 200, 206) argues, while the capacity for forgiveness is necessary for psychic growth, this capacity is the result of analytic work leading to an ability to successfully grieve and mourn. Forgiveness is not a pathway by which we learn to grieve and mourn, even as forgiveness and mourning may eventually reinforce each other. The ability to mourn loss comes first. From this ability, the capacity for forgiveness is born. When and how we grant forgiveness is a matter of cultivation and culture. Though their theoretical constructs differ, Akhtar's position is consonant with Klein's work on reparation and the depressive position, both of which are expressions of mourning and loss. Forgiveness is the outcome of successful mourning. Not a necessary outcome, but a possible one.

Judith Butler makes the good point that we fight not only against the finality of loss, but against the transformation to the self that must follow once we accept this loss. Generally this loss is of another person to whom we are deeply attached, but it may be to an idea about ourselves, or about the world. Jean Améry lost confidence in the stability of the world, and the goodness of the people in it. Like many trauma victims, the loss was irremediable. As Butler (2004) puts it:

> On one level, I think I have lost "you" only to discover that
> "I" have gone missing as well. At another level, perhaps what I have
> lost "in" you, that for which I have no ready vocabulary, is a
> relationality that is neither merely myself nor you, but the tie by
> which those terms are differentiated and related. (22)

In mourning, we mourn for the loss of those parts of ourselves that are lost forever (or so it seems, and it is often true) with the loss of the other, for they were located in the interperson.

This, suggests Frommer (2005: 42), is the reason why we long to forgive.

> Perhaps this is why when we struggle to forgive, the recognition of
> what has been done to us and the expression of remorse from the
> person who has done it feel so much like a lifeline; the other's

acknowledgment allows for the possibility that we may preserve the self we have known in relation to them; that we don't need to mourn its passing.

This raises a hope that is also a troubling possibility: that the greatest risk of forgiveness, the reason for its current popularity, and resultant misuse, is that it hints at the possibility that we can "let go" without mourning what we have lost. *Forgiveness becomes mourning manqué, acceptance without grief.*

Frommer's conjecture, that forgiveness might allow us to bypass grief and go straight to acceptance, because forgiveness allows us to maintain a relationship to the one who has hurt us and caused us grief and loss, allowing us to keep that part of ourselves that knows itself only in relationship to that person, is not applicable to all who offer forgiveness that is out of place. It does not neatly fit Eva Kor, for example, whose voice is heard at the conclusion of the next chapter. While not a general theory of popular forgiveness, Frommer's conjecture is one way of accounting for the current fascination with forgiveness.

Popular forgiveness is forgiveness that offers something for nothing, acceptance of loss without mourning and grief. I can keep my attachments and let them go at the same time. All I have to do is forgive the one who has victimized me, and I can "let go" of my hate and loss without mourning the loss of those parts of myself by which I knew myself in relationship to my victimizer. Even more catastrophic, in many cases, is the loss of belief in the goodness of the world, and the trust one had placed in it. Popular forgiveness promises that I can keep this belief too, as long as I take action, forgiving, rather than confronting, the terrible possibility that I have been acted upon, that something of great value has been taken from me, and that I must grieve and mourn the loss of a belief as though it were a person. What has been taken is what has been given, knowledge as disaster. It is only from the willingness to grieve and mourn this knowledge as loss that genuine forgiveness can arise.

RESENTMENT AND REPARATION

A psychoanalytic interpretation of forgiveness is important to my project, as important as a psychoanalytic interpretation of trauma. And yet, as is the case with trauma, a psychoanalytic interpretation is not the goal. The goal is an enriched understanding of forgiveness, one that brings the normative ideal closer to psychological reality, while at the same time realizing that they need not and should not be one. The psychological need to forgive should not trump the normative ideal of forgiveness, laid out in the sections that follow in this chapter and the next. Conversely, one may choose to forgive as an act of will, even if one remains psychologically unprepared to do so. This is not necessarily a bad or inauthentic thing to do. Psychological reality is a reality as important as any other; it is not prescription.

Bishop Joseph Butler, in his frequently cited sermons on forgiveness, said that forgiveness means the letting go of resentment toward a person who has done one an unjustified and inexcusable moral injury (Butler 2009: sermons viii, ix). As elaborated by Jeffrie Murphy (1988: 15–22), resentment is in a certain sense a virtue. Resentment at an unjustified injury to oneself is a reflection of self-respect. If I did not resent my injury, I would be lacking in self-regard. Accordingly, resentment is not a general condemnation of wrongdoing, but an almost visceral response to the very idea that someone would treat me with such disregard and contempt. Resentment, in other words, is a deeply personal reaction to an injury, one alien to a Kantian (universal) perspective.

While Murphy's "Forgiveness and Resentment" (1988) has been the work through which Bishop Butler has most frequently been interpreted in recent years, Murphy's is in some respects a misleading story.[8] Like so many of his contemporaries, Murphy assumes that forgiveness is an inner psychological struggle, in which the lessening of the desire for revenge is the playing out of a psychological drama of reconciliation. Such an interpretation treats Butler, who preached and wrote in the first quarter of the eighteenth century, as though he were writing today. As both Paul Newberry (2001) and Karen Pagani (2010: 14) argue, forgiveness, for Butler, is an act of enlightened self-interest. One forgives in order not to be caught up in a cycle of endless retribution. Though Butler writes about compassion, it has little to do with forgiveness. Forgiveness has more the quality of a Hobbesian bargain in the absence of a sovereign: I will not take revenge and so be free of the fear that others might take revenge on me. The result is a more civilized world. To see Bishop Butler as focusing on the lessening of resentment for its own sake is unhistorical. It assumes that early modern views of forgiveness were like our own, in which the authenticity of the inward change of heart in both offender and victim are key. In fact, Butler is interested in lessening resentment only insofar as doing so allows the victim not to be driven to revenge; it is the action that counts. As Newberry puts it, forgiveness "is not about how we feel but how we treat each other." As for loving our enemies, Butler (2009: sermon ix, para. 19) says, "it cannot be imagined that we are required to love them with any particular kind of affection."

A focus on the psychology of forgiveness, characteristic of contemporary accounts, including my own, enriches our understanding of forgiveness. Nevertheless, there are certain advantages to seeing forgiveness strictly in terms of action. One advantage is that reconciliation is no longer tied to forgiveness. One can forgive the offender, an act, in the absence of the establishment of a new relationship, or the reestablishment of an old. This is sometimes the best policy, especially for serious offenses. Seen from the perspective of Melanie Klein, this makes sense. Reparation for the victim is not about reconciliation. Reparation is an act internal to the self, even as it is often (but not always) enabled by the response of the offender. The pas de deux that is forgiveness is primarily about reciprocal action, even as it creates new possibilities for psychological development.

For the victim, an inner world must be repaired, and grief and loss must be experienced and acknowledged, all achievements of the depressive position. A victim of a serious offense, one in which the victim's world has been unmade, to use Elaine Scarry's (1987) characterization of the experience of the survivor of extreme trauma, must repair his or her confidence in the world and its goodness. The first step seems to be the recognition that life itself is fragile, so fragile that goodness itself sometimes seems to have fled the world. Saint Augustine put it this way in talking about the loss of his dear friend:

> My eyes look for him everywhere, and he was not there. I hated everything because they did not have him, nor could they now tell me "look, he is on the way," as used to be the case when he was alive and absent from me . . . I was surprised that any other mortals were alive . . . I was even more surprised that when he was dead I was alive.
>
> (Confessions, 4.9)

Reparation for the victim involves a restoration of the depressive position in a new and deeper dimension, in which one knows viscerally that goodness coexists in the world with terrible evil, that life is inseparable from the experience of death of oneself and others, and that some losses are so terrible that they threaten to plunge us into a world of darkness; that is, a world without goodness. Reparation, as an expression of the depressive position, means living in and with a world in which not just life, but goodness itself, is in constant danger, not only from one's own hatred and confusion, but that of others. How is one to live in such a world? If we are fortunate as children, we were sheltered from this terrible knowledge. The evil that we feared then came primarily from within, from our own aggression and hatred. Parents who can experience this fear without undue anxiety or aggression of their own can help the young child integrate his or her love and hate, and so enter into the depressive position.

What is the adult to do, an adult who is thrown back into the paranoid-schizoid position by the harsh reality of the world, a world in which others would and have done the victim terrible harm? The answer (and this is what giving up resentment really means) can only be the ability to see the goodness and badness of the world, and eventually of the offender (if this is possible), as inextricably interwoven. There is no safe place, no secure harbor, only the appreciation of life and its goodness in all its forms, from a beautiful sunrise to a welcoming smile, all mixed up with a darkness that never goes away, but may recede into the background or even disappear for longer or shorter periods of time. This is what the depressive position looks like in the adult.

A rosier vision must, it seems, be regarded as manic denial, as Kleinians call it: the pretense that the victim is omnipotent in some way, able to repair even the most serious losses, or the denial that such losses are possible. An example of manic denial would be the Nietzschean view (1968b), according to which there is no need for forgiveness because a truly strong person will never feel resentment in the first place. Secure in his master morality, even those who harm him are incapable of injuring his self-respect. As Jean Améry (1980: 62–81) argues, such a view hardly makes sense in the shadow of Auschwitz. In reality, forgiveness has to do with neither a Panglossian view of the world, nor one in which some are so strong and noble that they need never be in the position to forgive. On the contrary, forgiveness has much to do with the recognition of the evil and hatred that are always with us; evil and hatred that threaten, but need not destroy the good with which they are so intimately interwoven in the lives of humans. The appeal for forgiveness by the offender may make the difference in whether we can experience the world as good, but it is not the cause.

NOTES

1 Two commentators, Robert Coles and Christopher Hollis, consider the possibility that Wiesenthal's story is a fable. As they recognize, it hardly matters for the purpose at hand.

2 Arendt joins forgiveness and promising as the two capacities that make a social world possible, by making it more predictable. I focus only on what

Arendt has to say about forgiveness. The concepts are functionally connected in her work, but do not depend on each other.

3 Living up to our forgiveness is the opposite of what Dietrich Bonhoeffer called "cheap grace," about which many of the Christian respondents in *The Sunflower* rightly worried (Wiesenthal 1997: 133). "When he spoke of grace, Luther always implied as a corollary that it cost him his own life, the life which was now for the first time subjected to the absolute obedience of Christ ... Luther had said that grace alone can save; his followers took up his doctrine and repeated it word for word. But they left out its invariable corollary, the obligation of discipleship" (Bonhoeffer 1963: 47, 53).

4 For Arendt (1958: 241), punishment and forgiveness are complementary. Both "attempt to put an end to something that without interference could go on endlessly."

5 D. W. Winnicott cannot abide Klein's thesis, writing in "Hate and the Counter-transference" that "the mother hates the baby before the baby hates the mother, and before the baby can know his mother hates him" (Winnicott 1992d: 198). If this is so, then we must rethink the death drive, seeing it as a response to real relationships, including the relationship of being hated.

6 Elsewhere Derrida points out that for forgiveness to be effective, real, and historical, it must engage in the world in a way that must dilute its purity. "It is between these two poles, irreconcilable but indissoluble, that decisions are made and responsibilities taken." Jacques Derrida, "Le siècle et le pardon" (1999: 12).

7 I cite from an online version of Smith's essay without page numbers, at: onlinelibrary.wiley.com/doi/10.1111/j.1745–8315.2008.00082.x/full. The references include the original source, the *International Journal of Psychoanalysis* (2008).

8 Murphy reiterates his stance in *Getting Even: Forgiveness and Its Limits* (2003: 12). Though Murphy sees Joseph Butler as arguing that compassion leads to forgiveness, Murphy holds that Butler's account of forgiveness remains too concerned with externals and consequences, insufficiently concerned with the psychological phenomenology of forgiveness. On the other hand, Charles Griswold in *Forgiveness* (2007: 34) claims that Butler makes compassion the foundation of forgiveness, for it is through compassion that we come to a rational recognition of our shared fallibility. Karen Pagani (2010) in "The Uses and Abuses of Joseph Butler ...," demurs,

stating, "Butler goes to great lengths to draw the distinction between the passions and self-interest in his eleventh sermon, entitled 'Upon the Love of Our Neighbor'" (24). I follow Pagani here, which means that I think Murphy's (2003) interpretation of Butler is on the right track, though his conclusion wrong. Griswold is simply mistaken in his interpretation of Butler.

5   Melanie Klein and forgiveness: practice

The ability to grant forgiveness seems to require, at least in most cases, that the original experience of vulnerability to the offender be reenacted in the realm of thought and speech. In the normatively ideal case, the offender asks for forgiveness, and the victim must trust that the request is real, and that the offender will participate in those further acts or steps that may lead to genuine forgiveness. The first step does not involve letting go of one's resentment. On the contrary, the image of "letting go," which appears so frequently in the literature on forgiveness, is misleading. The real task is both easier and more difficult.

The real task is easier in the sense that experiencing the offender as whole is compatible with resentment, even continued anger. The task is more difficult both because it requires the emotional maturity associated with the depressive position, and because the reality of the offender's mixed status as both good and bad must be assessed from the subjective position that is actually available to the victim. For example, while a third party might judge that an offender is contrite, the position of the victim may be (and may have been) so overwhelmingly vulnerable, tormented, and abused that contrition is simply not a relevant category. Consider, in this case, the position of Simon Wiesenthal in *The Sunflower* – indeed any Holocaust survivor – as well as the victims of torture and abuse (this list is not inclusive). Time does not heal all wounds, nor should it be expected to. A continuing paranoid-schizoid attitude toward real persecutors is neither unrealistic nor undesirable. All acts need not be forgiven, a point to which I will return.

Unlike the original experience, this time around the offender is also vulnerable. He or she has asked for forgiveness, and there is often no way of knowing if it will be forthcoming, an experience made more difficult when one understands forgiveness as a process, rather than simply as pronouncement or act. To be sure, forgiveness need not be explicitly asked for. Normatively (a point discussed shortly), forgiveness is a response to a request to be forgiven. Only in rare cases is it proper to offer forgiveness to one who has not asked for, or made other gestures that may be interpreted as a request for forgiveness. These other gestures might include spending time with the victim without trying to justify oneself, regretting one's act to others who are in a position to convey this regret to the victim, or acting in a way contrary to the original offense, as when a drunk driver who has taken a life commits and remains committed to a life of sobriety.

One thing that makes the achievement of the depressive position so difficult is that one must give up a certain omnipotence, above all, the illusion that the goodness of my life depends on me. This may sound obvious, but it runs against a main current in philosophy. The greatness of Socrates, according to Plato, is that his goodness depended upon no one but himself. Indeed, this is the lesson of Plato's *Republic* (442b-445e). Because the tragic poets (Aeschylus, Sophocles, and Euripides) taught a different lesson, Plato would ban them from his ideal polis. Nietzsche always seemed vainglorious, but consider Socrates' famous line, "Anytus and Meletus can kill me, but they can't harm me" (*Apology*, 30c-d). Is that manic denial? In 399 BCE no, but in a post-Holocaust world, in which harm includes the atrocity of degradation and obliteration of entire families, societies, and nations, as well as the attempted obliteration of a people (*genos*), one wonders if anyone can make the same claim while being of sound mind.[1]

Against the position of Plato's Socrates, Martha Nussbaum has argued that even goodness may be taken from us by severe misfortune, including catastrophic losses, such as the death of one's children. Nussbaum (1986) means not merely one's happiness, but one's moral goodness is subject to a reversal of fortune. The ability to experience the goodness of the world, even in the midst of evil, depends not only on one's inner psychic resources and development, but upon the world itself, and how much it would take from us. After serious injury, there is no guarantee that we will be able to ever find enough goodness in the world, let alone in the offender, to forgive, or in some cases, even to survive. Jean Améry's life and death are exemplary.

FORGIVENESS AS A PAS DE DEUX

In order to be morally significant, forgiveness cannot be seen strictly as a psychological process. Even if forgiveness fosters individual emotional growth, and in this sense is compatible with a virtue ethic (an ethic that relies upon, and strengthens, good character),[2] the very nature of forgiveness is such that it is an interpersonal process, a relationship between and among humans. Forgiveness only takes two, but it is often more convincing and lasting when there are others, a community, to witness and support. Whatever else it is, granting forgiveness for purposes of one's own psychological growth is not genuine forgiveness. Psychological growth may be a by-product; it cannot be the goal, or we are not talking about forgiveness.

The steps involved in the moral dimension of forgiveness reflect the steps taken by the psychological process, but the correspondence is inexact; nor should we expect it be otherwise, for the goal is not the same. The most significant parallel is that the psychological and normative dimensions of forgiveness place both parties in a position of vulnerability. In the case of the victim, it is a position of renewed vulnerability. The steps of forgiveness are a pas de deux, in which the action and reaction of each party helps to make the other better – not just psychologically better, but morally better. From this perspective, forgiveness is an aretaic or virtue ethic. Forgiveness is primarily concerned not with duties or rights, but with the development of good character. Good character, in turn, goes all the way down: I forgive because I am a forgiving person (one who possesses the virtue of forgiveness), not because I am aiming to maximize the happiness of others, or because I am following a universal rule or maxim.

More than good character is needed, however. Developed good character is needed, so that I possess wisdom and prudence in the application of forgiveness. Robert C. Roberts (1995) calls this developed good character "forgivingness." Forgivingness is a virtue because "one's anger at the offender is given up without abandoning correct judgment about the severity of the offense and the culpability of the offender" (289). Such an attitude, practiced in a community and witnessed by others, dampens the human tendency to demonize the offender. It may also strengthen community. The virtue of forgivingness is more difficult to cultivate and practice in mass society, and more difficult still in extreme situations, such as a prison or concentration camp. Toward some serious offenses, the virtue of forgivingness is best practiced by withholding forgiveness, especially when it is not preceded by repentance.

Klein tells us that good character (though she does not call it that) consists in the ability to experience the world from the depressive position. Griswold (2007: xiv–xv) states that forgiveness is unique among the virtues, each party holding the other in his or her power. While the Aristotelian virtues of the large-souled man (*megalopsychos*) certainly require others with whom one can be generous and a good companion, for example, these virtues do not require particular others. Forgiveness requires that a particular person cooperate: the offender requires his victim, the victim his offender. There is a mutual dependence in forgiveness that, while not unique, is distinctively poignant in the way it binds offender and victim together.[3] The opportunity for the victim to cultivate the virtue of forgivingness depends upon the willingness of the offender to take the steps of atonement, and vice versa.

PRACTICING FORGIVENESS

The steps of forgiveness, outlined below, are loosely based on *teshuvah*, as they are laid out by Maimonides's *Laws of Forgiveness*, or *Hilkhot Teshuvah*. The term *teshuvah* means return: to God, Torah, and the good. It is similar in meaning to *metanoia* in the Greek Bible, which refers to the changed state of mind brought about by repentance (Mark 1:15). I chose the *Hilkhot Teshuvah* primarily because Jewish teachings approach forgiveness as a ritualized relationship between human beings, rather than focusing on forgiveness as a relationship between humans and God. Jewish teachings are also more specific about the obligation to forgive if the proper steps are taken. "Maimonides is decisive on this subject: 'The offended person is prohibited from being cruel in not offering *mechila*, for this is not the way of the seed of Israel'" (David Blumenthal, nd). That is not the position taken in this chapter. Instead, it is concluded that because there are many satisfactory alternatives to forgiveness, the victim need not offer forgiveness, though he or she may choose to do so.

In fact, Maimonides comes closer to this position than first appears. *Mechila* means "forgoing the other's indebtedness." It is the most common form of forgiveness, and does not require reconciliation with the offender. It is akin to an act of pardon. The act remains, but the debt is forgiven. A second dimension of forgiveness is called *selichá*. It too is not a reconciliation with the offender, but it involves sympathy for the offender, recognizing that the offender is human, frail, and deserving of a certain sympathy. Christianity makes no such distinction. In fact, Christianity is often criticized (including from within the faith, as Bonhoeffer's critique of cheap grace reveals) for emphasizing God's forgiveness over man's. One can sin and sin, it seems, and bypass the stringent ritual steps of forgiveness by going over the head of the victim, begging for forgiveness directly from God. While there may be some truth to this claim, the reader should not forget Christ's charge.

> If therefore you are presenting your offering at the altar, and there remember that your brother has something against you, leave your offering there before the altar, and go your way; first to be reconciled to your brother, and then come and present your offering.
>
> (Matthew 5: 23–24; also Mark 11: 25)

The steps of forgiveness, according to my loose, contemporary interpretation of Maimonides:

1. The offender acknowledges his or her offense in such as way as to demonstrate an understanding of why the offense was so hurtful.
2. The offender expresses remorse and regret to the victim, as well as those close to the victim. Expressions of remorse and regret to the victim's family are especially important when the victim is no longer in a position to acknowledge remorse (for example, when the victim is dead, whether or not he or she has been killed by the offender).
3. Making compensation when possible and relevant. The compensation must be directed to the victim and victim's family. Compensation to substitutes, such as acts of contrition aimed at the poor and destitute, are appropriate, but only if the victim and his or her family agree with the substitute, or if the victim and family are unavailable or unreceptive.
4. Living differently in the future, demonstrating that one is a changed person. A drunk driver who killed someone might give up drinking and join Alcoholics Anonymous, for example. For some interpreters of the Hebrew Bible, this is the step that validates all the others. Sometimes this is referred to as *teshuvah gemurah*, or complete repentance. Repentance is complete when opportunities to reoffend present themselves, and the offender refrains from doing so.

Forgiveness is a demanding human relationship. Forgiveness may be given freely, but that does not mean that it need not be earned. On the contrary, while I have written of forgiveness in terms of a pas de deux, the two parties may not be cooperating so much as following parallel scripts, each requiring the participation of the other, but not genuinely responding to each other, but rather to the situation each has found him or herself in – "shared fate" it has been called. Though the point often seems lost in today's popular psychology of forgiveness, it is worth remembering that forgiveness understood as a normative ideal requires someone to ask for forgiveness, and someone to grant it. Forgiveness requires someone who will act the part of the penitent, and a victim who is willing to offer forgiveness if certain conditions are met. Each depends on the other, but the dependence may be more upon the role played by the other than the person him or herself. This distinction between role and person is important.

An interesting question is raised by the first requirement, acknowledging the offense. Griswold argues that in expressing regret, the offender should be able to demonstrate that he or she understands the damage done by his or her acts, as well as that he or she is no longer the sort of person who would commit such acts (Griswold 2007: 51, 188–189). Paul Ricoeur makes a similar demand, albeit more abstractly, when he states:

> One must know how to tell one's own story as seen by others. That is to say, to let myself be narrated by the other ... This is difficult. Yet that is how notions such as forgiveness, loss and reconciliation are, it seems to me, related. They have a kind of common ground.[4]

Broken into its constituent parts, Griswold's demand is particularly stringent – that the offender be able to produce three narratives: a narrative demonstrating that the offender understands the suffering of his or her victim; another narrative explaining how the offender came to be the sort of person who could commit such an offense; and finally an explanation of how and in what way the offender has changed, becoming a new person in fundamental respects. One might imagine that the purpose of such a demand is to determine if the offender is capable of genuine empathy with his or her victim, as well as whether he or she has truly experienced a change of heart, insofar as humans are able to know this about each other. Certainly this is part of what Griswold is getting at, but it is not a central as one might suppose.

David Konstan (2010: 165) argues that there is something fundamentally paradoxical in the notion "of self-reform that lies at the heart of the modern understanding of forgiveness." If you can't forgive until a person has truly reformed internally, so as to become another person, then the person you forgive is not the person who committed the offense in the first place (165). Konstan is too literal. Human development assumes that people change yet remain the same; the concept of development would be impossible without this assumption. I am not the same person in so many respects as I was as a boy of 10, or a young man of 16, as I am as a man of 65. But there is an ongoing continuity. I am and I am not the same person as I was then. My identity remains the same; what seemed at the time to be core attributes of my identity have changed, and so become part of a new core. One cannot step into the same river twice, but it remains the same river. Doesn't it?

Griswold (2007) writes that in ideal forgiveness, the offender would put himself in the shoes of the victim through an act of "projective imagination," a kind of "vicarious emotion" of the other's suffering at the offender's hands. However, as he develops this line of thought, it becomes apparent that the goal is not primarily to test the authenticity of the offender, but to achieve a forgiveness that meets the "soul's deepest yearnings," by which he refers to "deep reunion, love, and harmony" (193). In writing about forgiveness in these terms, Griswold reveals the desire behind the narrative requirement is perfect understanding, interpreted as transparency of offender and victim to each other. (It is not always clear in Griswold whether the victim should ideally go through an analogous process, or what this would mean.) If so, then neither the offender nor the victim would have to grieve or mourn, for both would have been shriven and made whole. Forgiveness and the pursuit of wholeness are never far removed from each other. They should be. Wholeness is a phantom ideal, one that must be given up before forgiveness can be seriously pursued.

Because asking for forgiveness is so psychologically demanding, one might question whether the offender must be in the depressive position in order to ask sincerely for forgiveness. One imagines that this must be so, that forgiveness asked for from the paranoid-schizoid position must, it seems, be based on fear of retaliation by man or God. Nevertheless, on this point Bishop Butler seems correct.[5] Forgiveness "is not about how we feel but how we treat each other" (Newberry 2001: 233). Which is why forgiveness is a process, and why it is proper to see *teshuvah gemurah*, or complete repentance, as demonstrated by continued changed behavior, especially when confronted with the opportunity to repeat the offense, as the most important sign of sincerity (Maimonides, *Hilkhot Teshuvah* 2.1). Katherine Ann Power, a leftist radical involved in the killing of a policeman in 1970, one of the voices of forgiveness at the conclusion of this chapter, is a good example.

So far, the steps that must be taken by the offender have been discussed. What is required of the victim?

1. What the argot of forgiveness calls "letting go" of anger and resentment is better seen as the coming together of a fragmented and split-off image of the offender as wholly bad. From this experience it becomes possible to acknowledge the humanity of the offender. Here the intersection with the psychology of reparation is significant. To genuinely see the offender as a mixture of bad and good seems to require that the victim be in the depressive position, an especially hard place to be under the stress of victimization, which reactivates the splitting and paranoia associated with the paranoid-schizoid position. Since some offenses are so heinous (rape, murder), there is no reason to expect that acknowledging the humanity of the offender will be easy. In some cases it may be impossible. In other cases it may be undesirable, as when the offender fails to demonstrate humanity. Arendt's (1964) account of Adolf Eichmann is about such a man.

"Letting go" of resentment is not a very good image of the process of integrating good and bad that forgiveness requires. If, however, we understand letting go as abandoning the longing that the offender will ever understand in anything like the victim's terms, then letting go is an appropriate image. Often the victim wants the offender to understand his or her pain, to feel what it was like to be victimized – not necessarily as an expression of revenge, but as an expression of sympathetic understanding, what some German romantic philosophers have called *Verstehen* (Dilthey 1988). It is not going to happen. Part of the pain of forgiveness is that the offender will never truly understand. Not necessarily because the offender is willingly obtuse, but because such understanding rarely, if ever, passes between two people.

Another's pain is one of the most difficult things in the world to understand, except perhaps by analogy to one's own, which is always imperfect. A mother confronted with her child's pain probably comes closest to suffering-with-the-other, but perhaps that is a stereotype. Surely there are particular people who feel each other's pain as intensely. Nevertheless, there is no reason to believe that offender and victim will come any closer; in all likelihood they will not come nearly as close. Coming to terms with the fact that the offender will never understand, but at best have some general idea of the victim's pain, is all that forgiveness requires, and all that can be reasonably asked: that the offender understand the victim as a fellow human who suffers because of what the offender did – that, and a reasonable expectation that the offender will not reoffend. One does not have to go all the way down the road with Bishop Butler to appreciate that about most acts that require forgiveness, not deep understanding but remorse and a demonstrated commitment to changing one's ways are what is required of the offender. Required is a sense of common humanity, not an intimate knowledge of the other's suffering.

2. Acknowledge the apology. In general, this means what is usually called "accepting the apology," except that if we see forgiveness as a process over time, acknowledgment may precede acceptance, in practice if not in words. I may acknowledge the apology, and still require some time to genuinely accept it. Whether this requires further communication with the offender is not a question that can be settled in principle, but on a case-by-case basis.
3. Abandon revenge. As we have seen in the previous chapter, some psychoanalysts hold that this is impossible, at least in the unconscious. Of course, one may abandon revenge while still thinking or fantasizing about it, and Bishop Butler's focus on acts over attitudes is worth remembering.
4. Further reconciliation beyond that implied in the first three steps is optional and contextual. It will depend largely upon the prior relationship of offender and victim. If a drunk driver kills my child, and subsequently expresses genuine regret and remorse, as well as making acts of contrition,

such as a commitment to a life of sobriety, and perhaps testifying about his experience to others, no further reconciliation is needed beyond the first three steps. Just as there was no prior relationship with the offender, so need there be no relationship afterward, except the (not-insignificant) relationship expressed in the first three steps. On the other hand, if the offender is a wayward spouse with whom one intends to remain married, further reconciliation is both necessary and desirable.

In many respects, the journey of the victim who offers forgiveness (at least when forgiveness is taken seriously) is more arduous than that of the offender. Certainly it is more subtle. Letting go of resentment, while acknowledging the humanity of the offender, requires an attitude associated with the depressive position, an attitude that is particularly difficult to maintain in the aftermath of assault and trauma, whether mental, physical, or both. There is, in other words, a context in which it is both useful and proper to talk about forgiveness in terms of "letting go." This context is normally lacking in popular discussions of forgiveness. The next chapter elaborates on the proper context, which is that of transitional space.

Forgiveness is a virtue, and in that regard it is intentional. But in some respects, forgiveness has to be approached indirectly, not as a willed act, but as the outcome of the process I have called a pas de deux. Offender and victim each have a role to play, but it is not strictly a personal relationship. It is a relationship of persons over time, each of whom seeks something that only the other can provide, not merely by a performative speech act (Offender: "I repent." Victim: "You are forgiven"), but by being willing to participate with the still-unknown other (this is true even among intimates who have lost their way) in a ritual that requires both. Out of this ritual may follow forgiveness, not as a by-product, but not as an act of will either. At its best, the ritual steps of forgiveness create an emotional environment from which forgiveness flows. The ritual of forgiveness creates a shared world that has place for both grief and mourning, experiences of loss and powerlessness that the contemporary world leaves little room for us to contemplate.

Sometimes forgiveness does not flow. There are alternatives, though that puts the distinction too sharply. Forgiveness is part of a constellation of related concepts, such as clemency, mercy, and reconciliation. While it is important to clarify the differences between the concepts, it is equally important to recognize that forgiveness can be withheld, and life still goes on – not as before (even forgiveness does not allow for that), but in many cases, the best possible life under the circumstances.

ALTERNATIVES TO FORGIVENESS

Consider Hannah Arendt's (2003: 396) response to Gershom Scholem concerning why Adolf Eichmann did not deserve mercy. "An act of mercy," she says, "does not forgive murder but pardons the murderer as he, as a person, may be more than anything he ever did. This was not true of Eichmann."[6] Not everyone need be forgiven, and there remain alternatives to forgiveness. Forgiveness is one way, a morally virtuous way, of coming to terms with a world in which good and bad are interwoven, even in the same person. Consider, however, some alternatives to forgiveness, a few of which also recognize the intersection of good and bad:

1. Clemency, the moderation or suspension of punishment without forgiveness.
2. Mercy, the moderation or suspension of punishment due to feelings of pity and common humanity with the offender. Arendt's claim that we exhibit mercy because the offender is more than the sum of his acts is not identical, but it comes close. For an offender to be more than the sum of his acts means he or she must share a common humanity with his victim, indeed with humanity. What else is it to be more than the sum of one's acts than to be human among humans? On this basis we show mercy.
3. Reconciliation that is complete enough for the purposes at hand, even if it neither leads to nor follows an act of forgiveness. Consider, for example, a married couple unable to forgive each other's trespasses, but deciding to continue their marriage for the sake of the children.

Lewis Smedes (1998: 345, 347) argues that "reconciliation cannot happen without forgiveness." He takes this position because he believes that "the objective of forgiving is to overcome human estrangement." Though he does not go as far as Griswold in holding that forgiveness meets the soul's deepest yearnings for reunion and harmony, the idea is similar. Forgiveness creates the conditions under which offender and victim become transparent to each other.

Not only is this a questionable ideal when applied to forgiveness for all the reasons mentioned, but it has the practical disadvantage of disallowing (displacing) a more mundane reconciliation between offender and victim, in which the people decide to live with each other (individuals, groups, nations) in the absence of forgiveness. Out of this process forgiveness may follow, as the daily experience of the complex reality of the other tempers the tendency to see the offender as all bad. In any case, reconciliation is not the consequence of forgiveness but its potentially enabling predecessor.

To equate reconciliation with forgiveness seems equally mistaken. If we are honest about the limits of forgiveness, then it need not go as far as reconciliation. While forgiveness requires two parties – what has been referred to as a pas de deux – they need not really dance. They just have to play their respective roles.

4. Acceptance that a relationship must continue for the sake of both parties, even if neither party forgives or reconciles. Often this is applicable to international or group relations.
5. Forgetting, possible only when victimized by minor transgressions.
6. The continuation of one's own life in the absence of any of the above. Forgiveness is a virtue, but like any virtue, it must be applied with prudence. Some people, such as Eichmann, do not deserve forgiveness. Many Holocaust survivors, quite understandably, never forgave their captors, and many are able to get on with their lives. In fact, it is a little too simple to say that survivors refuse forgiveness. They just don't talk about it. Forgiveness is an ethical category that not only does not apply, but it is so far from their minds that its presence is noticeable primarily by its absence. The nearly 5,000 interviews in the Fortunoff Video Archive for

Holocaust Testimonies are heavily and extensively indexed. Only four contain a reference to forgiveness, and two of these refer to the denial of forgiveness.[7] By contrast, slightly over 200 refer to revenge, also not a popular category. The category of trauma contains thousands of entries and subcategories.

What, one might ask, are the psychological repercussions of the failure to forgive? For many Holocaust survivors, mental sequestration and compartmentalization are the alternative, in which terrible traumas are held in a separate, watertight compartment of the mind. This has consequences, particularly in old age, when the barriers are more likely to break down (Botwinick 2000). However, when one considers the alternative – forgiving people who have committed unspeakable crimes, people who seem not to have understood their crimes as crimes, people who have never asked for forgiveness – then honesty seems the best policy, lest forgiveness become simply bad therapy. Seen from another perspective, doubling may not be an alternative to forgiveness at all. They are simply two separate things: one is an adaptive strategy, the other a relationship. Doubling is not an alternative to forgiveness. It just is.

What about the rest of us, those who have not suffered atrocity, but nonetheless have been victims of an offense, and who have the opportunity to forgive? Most helpful is the insight that forgiveness is a virtue, but it is not a necessary virtue. Often it is a supererogatory virtue. People can get along quite well without it. They can even get along with those who have offended against them, once they realize that the alternative to forgiveness is not hatred and revenge, but the range of possibilities just considered. Claire Schroeder, the daughter of the policeman killed by Katherine Ann Power, renders one of these possibilities concrete, as discussed below. This, though, does not answer the question that remains so puzzling: what is it about so many people in this culture at this time (for it has not always been true, as David Konstan (2010) demonstrates), that not only makes forgiveness so attractive, but aggressively confuses it with a strategy of psychological empowerment and emotional liberation?

Martin Frommer's (2005: 42) hint of an answer, combined with the insights of Judith Butler (2003), seems the best bet, even if it is no more than an educated guess, stemming primarily from the structure of forgiveness itself. This guess was discussed in Chapter 4. Forgiveness seems to hold out the illusory promise that we can bypass grief and mourning, and go straight from loss to acceptance. Forgiveness does so because it promises activity, not passivity. By acting to forgive, I can retain control of the relationship (even if only in my mind, but where else?) with the one who hurt me and caused me so much pain, and so avoid having to give up that part of myself that is attached to the offender in a complex of emotions that may involve identification, hatred, love, fascination, awe, and fear. Giving up that part of myself requires that I mourn the loss in order to eventually come to terms with the pain that person has caused me. Coming to terms with the pain is not a matter of more now for less later. Coming to terms with the pain means accepting terrible losses that will never be made whole.

Compare this reality with the tendency to equate forgiveness with wholeness that we have encountered in this chapter, particularly in Roberts (1995), Griswold (2007), and Smedes (1998). They want from forgiveness not only what it cannot provide, but what it must abandon in order to achieve what it realistically can. One might argue that this is a natural consequence of bringing an essentially religious ideal – forgiveness as reunion with God and man – into the secular world. True enough, but the advantage of approaching forgiveness from a psychological perspective, particularly that of Melanie Klein, is to show that the longing for wholeness is not strictly a religious longing. More importantly, a Kleinian perspective demonstrates why it is so important to abandon the ideal of wholeness in order to achieve what forgiveness realistically can. The depressive position, the position of mature ambivalence, understands (or wordlessly intuits) that wholeness is a lost cause, achieved only by splitting the world and its inhabitants into all good and all bad. Most of the voices of forgiveness, considered here and in the next chapter, seem to understand this instinctively.

VOICES OF FORGIVENESS AND ITS SIMULACRUM

The voices in this and the next chapter originally came from videos, in order to better capture the affect, the tone, the person behind the story. The quotations from the video were checked against a published transcript, and the quotations are almost always from the transcript. A few exceptions are indicated in the endnotes. Unlike the Holocaust testimonies drawn on in Chapter 2, these testimonies were not taken in a psychoanalytic spirit, in which the questioner intervenes as little as possible, and the interview may continue for hours. Nevertheless, most voices continued at length, Kor's for over an hour. It is because I wanted to hear the voices, and see the speaker, that I did not use several fascinating first-person written accounts.[8]

EVA KOR

Eva Kor, along with her twin sister, Miriam, was taken to Auschwitz with the rest of her family when she was ten years old. At Auschwitz, she and her twin sister were separated from their parents, whom they never saw again, and sent to a special barracks, where the "Mengele twins" were kept.[9] Both Eva and her twin were subjected to terrible "experiments;" both survived and were liberated by the Russians. Fifty years later, Eva returned to stand before the gates of Auschwitz on the anniversary of its liberation to read a statement that read, in part, "I, Eva Mozes Kor, a twin who survived as a child of Josef Mengele's experiments at Auschwitz 50 years ago, hereby give amnesty to all Nazis who participated directly or indirectly in the murder of my family and millions of others."[10] It is time, she continued, to forgive but not forget. Other Mengele twins, as they call themselves, were appalled and outraged.

About her statement of forgiveness (for that is what she calls it; she does not ordinarily use the word "absolve"), Kor said, "Forgiveness is nothing more and nothing less but an act of self-healing – an act of self-empowerment. And I immediately felt a burden of pain was lifted from my shoulder – that I was no longer a victim of

Auschwitz, that I was no longer a prisoner of my tragic past, that I was finally free" (Profile).

Whatever it is that Kor is talking about, whatever is making Kor feel better, it is not forgiveness. She has made a category mistake. This is not, however, the immediate or considered reaction of survivors and children of survivors. Their reaction falls into two categories. The first is fairly predictable, but no less important for that reason. Eva Kor has no right to forgive in the name of the dead, no right to forgive men who have never asked forgiveness, never shown regret.

The second reaction, though less common, is not uncommon. It is a desire to keep the pain, for it is a connection to those who have been lost. Says Anita Epstein in an article in *Haaretz*:

> While I did not suffer from the ineffable horror of the concentration camps as Wiesel, my mother, my murdered family members and so many others did, I know what he [Wiesel] means. I, too, want to hold onto my pain. It helps ensure that the past is always present in me. It is an important part of what keeps me close to those I lost and to the world that died with them.
>
> *(Epstein 2010)*

Terrible as it is, the loss of those we love is not the worst thing in the world. Even worse is the loss of the attachments, the memories, represented by the pain of loss. For then we have nothing, not even our memories of our loved ones. Melanie Klein's depressive position is built on this insight. Conversely, it is the ability of atrocity to turn the loss of individuals into the destruction of masses of faceless, nameless people that makes the Holocaust particularly terrible.

It would be easy to say that Eva Kor is granting forgiveness from the paranoid-schizoid position, in which forgiveness becomes a weapon of the divided self. Only it is not that simple. In an interview with a fellow Mengele twin, Joanna Laks says to Eva, "I can't give forgiveness because what would my parents [who were murdered at Auschwitz] say?"

Eva responds: "Do your parents have to give you permission?"

Eva follows this comment up with the observation, "Does she think that living without pain would betray the memory of her loved ones?" To this question, Epstein might well answer yes.

And yet even this is not the full story, for in an interview with Anita Epstein for *Haaretz*, Eva says, "The day I forgave the Nazis, privately I forgave my parents whom I hated all my life for not having saved me from Auschwitz. Children expect their parents to protect them, mine couldn't. And then I forgave myself for hating my parents. Forgiveness is really nothing more than an act of self-healing and self-empowerment."

It is not entirely clear what is going on inside Eva Kor. At a small conference with other Jews, a woman asked in genuine puzzlement, "What is forgiveness [for you]? A separating of yourself, or a joining of yourself with another?" It's a good question, because Kor has been defining forgiveness as self-healing and empowerment, and the questioner is wondering what is going on inside Kor in relationship to others. The questioner has not a clue. I wish I had more.

Kor's answer is that "forgiveness has nothing to do with the perpetrator." One is reminded of Goethe's line, "If I love you, what business is it of yours?" Experiences and emotions that seem so intensely relational, so utterly dependent on the other, are often only dependent on the place of the other in one's own psychic economy, one's imagination. Sometimes forgiveness just happens, and it has very little to do with the other, as the next chapter will suggest about living in transitional space. On the other hand, wherever Kor is located, it is not in transitional space. About forgiving Mengele, Kor says, "I realized then that I even had the power to forgive the god of Auschwitz – this angel of death. And I said, 'Yes, I do. Wow.' And it made me really feel good to realize that I have that power" (Profile).

There can be little doubt that Eva Kor is confusing forgiveness with another category of experience, such as finding a way to empower herself after having been in a position of such terrible dependence as a child, abandoned (as ten-year-old Eva experienced it) by her parents, subjected to the torments of a terrible sadist, charged (by herself) with the care of her twin, to whom she eventually donated a kidney (her twin's kidneys were probably damaged by Mengele's tortures). Filled with the terrible dependence of the weak upon the strong, Eva is herself one of the strong. It is, I think, no accident that it is Eva, holding her twin's hand, leading the parade of Mengele twins out of Auschwitz in their little striped "uniforms" on the day of liberation (the newsreel footage in "Forgiving Dr. Mengele" is clear and deeply moving). To see her is to see a force of nature.

For Eva, "forgiveness to me means that whatever was done to me, it's no longer causing me such pain that I cannot be the person that I want to be" (Profile).

Eva gives this as an answer to a question from a college student at a university in Pennsylvania. She speaks to many such groups, not only in Terra Haute, Indiana, where she lives, but throughout the United States. She has great empathy for the suffering of ordinary American students. There is no sense in which she says, in effect, "You think you have it bad, well, let me tell you about Auschwitz." On the contrary, she uses her experience of surviving Auschwitz to inspire the students with hope that they can deal with their ordinary pain.

At the end of her lecture and question and answer session, there appears to be a hugs session, in which students line up to be hugged by this burly but not unattractive older woman with wide shoulders, powerful arms and big breasts. To each she whispers words of encouragement, as in, "I know it's difficult to grow up," as she wipes away one young woman's tears. There is nothing else this can be called but a laying on of hands, or in this case, hugs. Later, when the auditorium is empty, she says, "The word really is healing rather than just forgiveness."

All the conceptual clarification in the world, a clarification that reveals that Kor is not really talking about forgiveness, does nothing to diminish her achievements, achievements that hardly stop at putting herself back together after living through hell as a child, but in teaching a younger generation a lesson. About the topic of this lesson I remain unsure; I do not believe it is primarily about forgiveness. Perhaps it is about survival. All the psychological clarification in the world – even a clarification that suggests Kor is not truly operating from the depressive position – makes little difference as far as valuing her achievement is concerned.

One sees the limit of her achievement in an unsurprising but unexpected place: in her utter inability to deal with the stories of Palestinian suffering with which she is confronted when she travels to Gaza with an Israeli peace activist group. Perhaps one could think about this as the limit of the defense she has built for herself. Others might call it the limits of her life, limits shared by millions more who have suffered far less.

During one of her trips to Israel, Eva is taken by some Israeli peace activists to Gaza, where she meets with a small group of Palestinian professors of education who want to tell their story. The Palestinians tell Eva they wish the Jews had learned from the Holocaust to appreciate their catastrophe too. The Palestinians appear sad, burdened with grief. After listening to one or two accounts, Eva folds her arms and says she wishes she were back at her hotel, sleeping. "I can't comment. I don't want to hear eight or nine stories of suffering" (there were six Palestinians). The Palestinians are insulted. It was very important to them to tell their stories. Most had traveled only a few miles, but theirs was a journey of two to three hours, for they were detained at several checkpoints, all to come and talk with Kor. One Palestinian pleads, "I'll listen to your story as many times as you want to tell it, but I need to tell my story too." But Kor has shut down. Her body language says it all, as she turns in her chair so that her back is angled toward the group sitting around the table. This normally talkative woman becomes silent.

After the meeting Eva says, "I felt threatened, I was at their mercy ... what if they kidnap me?" Later she says, "My meeting with the Palestinians was disappointing. Forgiveness can't happen while people are getting angry." It is worth noting that none of the

Palestinians, at least on video, appeared angry; all appeared disappointed, burdened, depressed.

Talking to her family the next day, Eva says, "To be in this mixed-up world, one has to be tough." Evidently she can't listen when she is feeling threatened. She can hear pain, but not when she feels under attack, even when this pain is mediated by Israeli peace activists, who explain their own journey from the Holocaust, a journey from not listening because they were too busy building a secure state of their own to feeling the moral necessity of listening. For Eva, Gaza is closer to Auschwitz than Auschwitz.

One is tempted to say that Kor is offering forgiveness from the paranoid/schizoid position, one in which the world is measured in terms of power and security. From this perspective, her forgiveness would have the quality of mock denial, that forgiveness is more than forgiveness, that it has almost magical healing powers, not to mention the power to reverse the positions of offender and victim. Some of Kor's comments lead in this direction. Her fearful ("I was at their mercy") inability to listen to people she felt threatened by, the Palestinians, reinforces this interpretation.

But this is hardly the whole story. Her self-healing seems genuine. Her reaching out to thousands of young people with her story of healing and redemption is a genuine act of reparation, as is her founding, funding, and building of a small Holocaust museum in Terra Haute, Indiana, not the most likely place. Twice. The second time after the museum was destroyed by arsonists. Her children seem reasonably well-adjusted, sharing their mother's projects, while having lives of their own, though all this is difficult to tell from a distance. Her husband is described by one of his children as a typical survivor, supporting his wife, but lacking her intense involvement. Her husband echoes this assessment. Until her retirement, Eva Kor sold real estate. She says she loved it, and that she can't and doesn't think about Auschwitz every day. Perhaps she misunderstands forgiveness, but she understands something else quite well.

For Eva Kor, forgiveness allows her to gain control of the relationship with Mengele and other Nazis, who must have seemed like gods from Hell to a ten year old girl. She need not expose, and grieve the loss of, that ten year old girl, who gave up so much to survive. And yet, such an interpretation sounds just a little too clever. If for no other reason than she has done so much so well, including finding ways to make reparation, understood as acting in such a way as to make hers a world worth living in. For she has done that. And if the paranoid-schizoid position remains alive and well in her relationship to the Palestinians, let us hope that for another generation this too is tempered.

KATHERINE ANN POWER AND CLAIRE SCHROEDER

Katherine Ann Power, a student at Brandeis University during the height of the Vietnam War protests, joined a small group of radical activists who robbed a Boston bank in order to fund their activities. During the bank robbery, a policeman, Walter Schroeder, was killed. The only participant to evade capture, she lived as a suburban mother and award-winning local chef in Oregon for twenty-three years before surrendering to the police in 1993. She was sentenced to 8–12 years in prison for armed robbery and manslaughter. (Power was not at the bank where Schroeder was killed, but at the wheel of a second get-away car about half a mile away.) About her life after the robbery, Power said, "I spent the next twenty-three years of my life with a divided awareness that on the one hand I was a monster, and on the other hand I was going to live" (Whitney 2011b: 78).[11]

Though she talks about it at length, it is never entirely clear why Power surrendered to the police. She says at one point that it was because her son was growing up in isolation, with no knowledge of or connection to his family. (Power was on the F.B.I.'s most wanted list, and took extreme measures to conceal her identity, including cutting herself off from her relatives.) However, Power suffered from depression, and experienced what she says was a deep sense of shame; above all, that she didn't deserve her good life. After spending fifteen months with a family therapist, coming to terms with the fact that nothing but surrender would ease her guilt, her lawyers negotiated the terms of her surrender (Whitney 2011b: 77–80). Her psychological journey was just beginning.

It is not difficult to imagine that Power felt guilt and remorse. On the other hand, the guilt and remorse that seemed to be pushing and punishing Power met with resistance from within, as she consistently contextualized her acts in terms of the violence of the Vietnam War she was protesting, even during her sentencing, when contrition was called for. Later Power would characterize her attitude at that time as defiant. But a strange defiance it was, mixed with her recognition that "I tore something that can never be untorn ... I wanted forgiveness" (Whitney 2011b: 79–80).

After five years of imprisonment, Power came before the parole board for the first time. It was evident to all that she had changed. Claire Schroeder, one of Walter Schroeder's nine children, was one of Power's harshest critics at the time of her sentencing, pointing out how little remorse, and how much self-justification, she heard that day five years ago. Attending the parole hearing, Schroeder said that while Power now seemed to feel genuine remorse, she said only what everyone is expected to say at their parole hearing.

At this point, Power did something that had never happened at a parole hearing in Massachusetts before. The model prisoner (she received her college degree while in prison) withdrew her application for parole, saying that as long as her atonement was connected to her early release, no one would take it seriously. Speaking later, she said simply, "I had to suffer, and I had to be seen to suffer." Without this public sacrifice, her atonement would be merely personal.

The moral of the story so far: if you want forgiveness, you don't necessarily have to ask for it, and you shouldn't expect it; make atonement. Furthermore, understand that atonement is not a performative speech act one done with words. Atonement is made through deeds, generally a change of one's life that takes many years, and often considerable suffering. In Power's case, it meant years in jail.

In the end, Schroeder never grants forgiveness, and Power no longer needs it in order to feel forgiven (Whitney 2011b: 85–86).

About making atonement, Power's psychologist says, "She had to get past all the 'yes, buts ...', as in, 'yes, I did it, but why doesn't Robert McNamara have to be held accountable as I do?'" "I'm in a prison with prostitutes, but where are the johns?" Power says coming to terms with her act was the hardest work she had ever done, getting through layers of defensiveness, the comfort of not looking at what she had done, to "see how much ... human suffering I caused, the holes in lives I left" (Whitney 2011b: 83–84). Power was raised in a strong Catholic family; the language of penitence that she uses freely comes naturally to her.

She was sitting in her cell, "free writing" as she calls it, when the words came to her: "Forgive us our trespasses, as we forgive those who trespass against us ... And that was it. I forgave those generals for being wherever they were [in history], doing whatever they did."

"I saw a world of forgiveness, in which we are all in the embrace of that forgiveness, that forgivableness. I couldn't get myself there until I got those people I hadn't forgiven there. *And I was through*" (Whitney 2011b: 84). She means that she had broken through, reaching that previously unreachable place of forgiveness. A forgiveness that sounds a lot like living under the horizon of sanctification, a place with room enough to hold us all. Beyond that, it is hard to say.

Power's epiphany took place before her dramatic parole hearing. She was released on probation about a year after turning down parole. About whether she can forgive Power, Claire Schroeder now says, "I admire the fact [that she withdrew her request for parole]. It says something in regards to thought, feeling, and growth" regarding the harm she caused. "I hope she can say she redeemed herself, but I can't forgive her, the act is not forgivable. But that's not to say she can't go on to become the person she hopes to become ... That's a great goal. I wish that for her."

One might say that Claire Schroeder is "really" forgiving Power, but she is not. She is quite clear that only her father could do that, and he's dead. She is still angry and bitter after 38 years (Whitney 2011b: 85–86). But in a sense it doesn't matter, and both Schroeder and Power seem to recognize that it doesn't matter. Power has made atonement, both privately and publically. And Schroeder, who is now a sergeant in the Boston Police Department where her father worked, admires Power, sees how much she has changed, even wishes her well. But she cannot forgive Power. What she has done is unforgivable. "Some things we do reverberate forever," says Schroeder on the 38th anniversary of her father's death.[12]

When Power is asked what she wants from the Schroeder family, she says, "I have no right to expect anything from them. I have no right to ask anything of them. It feels to me like a violation of them as victims to say that they have some further work to do" (Whitney 2011b: 86). Power has it just right. Atonement, through acts, over years, need not lead to forgiveness by anyone. It does seem to lead to a type of reconciliation with oneself (self-forgiveness in pop-psychological jargon), and in this case, to respect from, and even well-wishing from, the victim's adult child. Why isn't that more than enough? Power and Schroeder have even participated in a type of pas de deux, characteristic of forgiveness. Only in this case, there is no forgiveness, and the partners never touch. They get close enough.

LIESBETH GERRITSEN

Liesbeth Gerritsen is her name, and she was married to Daniel Glick, with whom she had two children. They were 11 and 7 when she left her husband and children in Boulder, Colorado, to move to Portland, Oregon, 1,200 miles away, to pursue a PhD in clinical psychology. Unlike Katherine Ann Power, Gerritsen lacks a developed sense of what forgiveness requires. She is included here by way of contrast.[13]

What Gerritsen fails to understand is that the past cannot be undone, that even if her children could trust her when she says today that "I won't abandon you again," it will mean something completely different to an adult boy, and an almost-grown teenage girl. What cannot be undone is not answering 17 messages in one day from her daughter, something that happened repeatedly, according to her daughter Zoe, and which Gerritsen acknowledges with sadness. Says Gerritsen, Zoe "wrote these really dire poems, suicidal I imagine, pictures quite disturbing." But Liesbeth had to steel herself against responding lest she break down and return home (Whitney 2011b: 63).

"Someone in the community [where the children lived] called," said Liesbeth. "She said you are working with people who have a mental illness. You are creating a mental illness in your own daughter. I can't tell you ... the devastation ... I was creating these gaping wounds in my kids" (Whitney 2011b: 64). There can be no doubt that Gerritsen felt and feels pain and conflict about her course of action. Her narrative at this point loses its flow, becoming a series of chopped-off words. Nevertheless, she believes she made the right choice, or rather that she had no choice. "I had to say no in preservation of that other piece of myself that hadn't developed, that was like an infant." It is in this context that she talked about being a mother. "I actually started getting panic attacks, boxed in. I was on the bathroom floor, screaming, crying. I remember thinking maybe dying is better than this" (Whitney 2011b: 60).

The problem is that in making her decision, and suffering mightily for it, she believes not that she deserves forgiveness, not yet, but that she is on the road to forgiveness. Her son Kolya puts it this way: "She thinks she's done her penance." She thinks she has suffered enough. "She thinks she's done her time" (Whitney 2011b: 67).

Kolya's right. Gerritsen says the right things, such as, "I always had some excuse, like I was boxed in. Someone needs to hear from me that I did this thing ... I caused you a lot of pain and I'm sorry and I want to be held accountable ... and I want to make amends if you let me." To her children, "I'd say, will you trust me, will you let me in, and know that I won't abandon you again?" (Whitney 2011b: 68). Compare Gerritsen to Power, who has no expectations of the Schroeder family.

Compare too their different attitudes toward shame. About shame, Gerritsen says she felt "a huge and deep shame, which is different from guilt; the shame of not being able to step up to fulfill one's responsibility is huge" (Whitney 2011b: 65). For Power, even shame is self-serving.

> Even more difficult was letting go of my shame. I hid it for a long time, was immersed in it and paralyzed by it, until I finally came to realize this shame was an indulgence. It allowed me to hide; it was about my comfort and not about the Schroeders' legitimate needs. And while the shame was horrible to experience, it was still about me and not about them. I had to get out of my story and into theirs.
> (Whitney 2011b: 83)

With Gerritsen, we face the limit of forgiveness. Even if her children still love and care about their mother, and evidently they do, what she did was so damaging it can never be made whole. Her son is grown now, her daughter almost grown. Gerritsen cannot reenter their lives in the same way, even if they wanted her to, and they don't, at least not at the time the documentary was made, in 2010. All that can be realistically hoped for is something like the following: that Gerritsen is persistent in her presence in their lives now (evidently she is still struggling), and when her children are married with children of their own, and their mother has a chance to be a grandmother, and does so with some devotion, her children might come to some better understanding that leads to forgiveness – a forgiveness of perspective, time, distance, love, a different type of forgiveness, I think.

In her best pop-psychological fashion, Gerritsen says, "The moment where I can completely forgive myself is the moment I can ask for it" (Whitney 2011b: 68). Actually, Power says something similar, but with a big difference. She says she could forgive herself when she could finally forgive the generals and McNamara, and this humility allowed her to accept fully what she had done with no "buts," no mitigations, and no expectation that others would forgive her. That no longer mattered. For she had made her long journey of penance, and arrived at her destination. Gerritsen is still looking for forgiveness from others, which she seems to understand as somehow undoing the past, in the sense of her children saying, "It's ok, we understand; you did what you had to do" – all the "yes, buts" that Power took years to work through.

Gerritsen's situation is different. Through her grandchildren, if she is lucky enough to have them, she might actually have something of a second chance. One does not get the sense she has even begun to see that her redemption, if it is to occur at all, might fall that far into the future.

Here we see Jean Améry's (1980: 62–81) great truth, even if it need not be located in resentment. It is, as we shall see in Chapter 7, a partial truth, but for that reason, no less urgent. We *want* to reverse the past, to undo history. The dream of forgiveness is that the offender would want to reverse the past, make it as though it never happened, as much as the victim. Gerritsen evidently spends a lot of time imagining how she might have handled things differently, how she might have allowed Zoe to come live with her in Portland, how she might have flown back for Kolya's soccer games (Whitney 2011b: 70). Because we can't reverse the past, forgiveness takes enormous amounts of time, and staggering acts of atonement, lasting over a considerable period, often involving public suffering, primarily depending on whether the deed was public (there is no need that Gerritsen's suffering be public). Katherine Ann Power fulfills this requirement. Claire Schroeder speaks and acts appropriately in not forgiving but wishing well, and Liesbeth Gerritsen does not yet understand forgiveness.

Arendt (1958: 237–240) does not grasp the full import of her own insight that forgiveness is necessary because "some things that we do reverberate forever," as Claire Schroeder puts it. Forgiveness arises from the conjunction of two facts about the human condition, as Arendt might put it: we cannot reverse the past and we all make mistakes. It is precisely *because* this is so that atonement becomes so terribly important, understood not as a performative speech act, but as a long and serious journey, requiring years and much sacrifice, depending, of course, on the seriousness of the harm done, and the intent and carelessness of the actor. Arendt has nothing to say about atonement. She should. As far as forgiveness is concerned, this is the act and the relationship that matters most. More on atonement in the concluding chapter.

NOTES

1 The destruction of the Athenian expedition to Syracuse in 413 was not comparable. Thousands died, but Athens remained socially, politically, and culturally intact, even after the loss of the Peloponnesian War, as the trial of Socrates reveals.

2 Virtue ethics relies upon good character, to which it may contribute. There are two well-known alternatives: one is deontological ethics, the ethics of binding, usually universal, obligations to principles and rules. Immanuel Kant is its most famous spokesman. The other is consequentialism, which focuses on the outcome of the act. Utilitarianism is one version of consequentialism.

3 One cannot practice marital fidelity without a particular partner, though one party may be uniquely faithful.

4 "Memory, History, Forgiveness: A Dialogue Between Paul Ricoeur and Sorin Antohi," at www.janushead.org/8–1/Ricoeur.pdf. Ricoeur's essay on forgiveness is a long epilogue to his *Memory, History, Forgetting* (2004).

5 Bishop Butler does say, as discussed in Chapter 4, that we forgive in order not to precipitate an endless cycle of revenge, which would be a paranoid-schizoid way of thinking. However, there remains a sense of goodwill in Butler's concept of forgiveness, even if it does not extend as far as some imagine, a point also discussed in Chapter 4.

6 Arendt's response regarding Eichmann and mercy may seem obvious now, but it is worth recalling the controversy raised by *Eichmann in Jerusalem* (1964). The book was controversial not only for its application of the term "banality of evil" to Eichmann, but even more so for its claim that the Jewish Councils (*Judenräte*) cooperated too freely with the Nazis, causing more Jewish deaths than there otherwise would have been.

7 The index does not pick up brief or passing references. Thus, some valuable passing references to forgiveness are missed. The case of Edith P. referred to in Chapter 7 is not indexed, but was called to my attention by Joanne Rudof, chief archivist. I have viewed almost 200 interviews, and in none did the topic of forgiveness arise.

8 One such account is Pumla Gobodo-Madikizela's *A Human Being Died that Night: A South African Story of Forgiveness* (2003), about her conversations with Eugene de Kock, the commanding officer of the South African government's death squads in the Apartheid era.

9 Of the approximately 1,500 pairs of twins who passed through Auschwitz, only about 100 survived. "Mengele twin" is a term chosen by the surviving twins to refer to themselves.

10 My experience of Eva Mozes Kor is dominated by a documentary film, "Forgiving Dr. Mengele" (Hercules and Pugh, nd). However, almost all of the quotations, including this one, are from two printed sources. First, a profile of the movie – this is the source of Kor's "amnesty to all Nazis" quote. Second, an essay by a critical but sympathetic child of a survivor, Anita Epstein, published in *Haaretz.com*, June 14, 2010, and available at: www.haaretz.com/jewish-world/can-a-holocaust-survivor-ever-forgive-the-germans-1.296163, hereafter referred to as "Epstein." Another source is www.spiegel.de/international/ 0,1518,389491,00.html. Kor's comments about her encounter with the Palestinians are from the movie. Kor's biography, *Echoes from Auschwitz* (1995), stops in 1952, when she enlists in the Israeli army after spending two years recovering on a kibbutz for children who survived the Holocaust. She spent ten years in the army. After reading Kor's biography, one better understands why she would interpret forgiveness as an act of self-healing, but her forgiveness of Mengele was still in the future.

11 Though I originally experienced the testimony of Power and Claire Schroeder in the documentary movie, "Forgiveness" (Whitney 2011a), the book by the same name, *Forgiveness* (2011b), is a virtual transcript of the documentary movie. A few quotations are in the movie that are not in the book, and the book contains extended versions of several quotations from the movie. Almost all of the relevant biographical circumstances and quotations in the text are from the book, and are cited as such in the text. Though she has a biographer, no biography of Power has yet been published. I have consulted *Katherine Ann Power* (2012), but it is not that biography.

12 Though Power does not talk about it in the documentary movie, she mentions briefly in the text of the interview that she was sexually abused by a Catholic priest from the age of nine to eleven. "I have memories of being suffocated in the starched and ironed folds of his floor-length black

Cossack and also of a penis being shoved down my throat. I never spoke about it to my parents." It was a shattering experience, for "it meant that I couldn't trust God or anyone in authority." But Power doesn't talk about it much, and never in connection with her crime. "I do not want it to be thought that being abused by a priest in my childhood is in any way an excuse for my own crime" (Whitney 2011b: 73).

13 Though I originally experienced the testimony of Gerritsen and her children, Zoe and Kolya, in the documentary movie, "Forgiveness" (Whitney 2011a), the book by the same name, *Forgiveness* (2011b), is a virtual transcript of the documentary movie. A few quotations are in the movie that are not in the book, and the book contains extended versions of several quotations from the movie. Almost all of the relevant biographical circumstances and quotations in the text are from the book, and are cited as such in the text. When Oregon Public Broadcasting showed the documentary featuring Gerritsen in April 2011, *The Oregonian* newspaper received and published a number of very harsh criticisms of her. Any reader can find the website containing these, but I will not cite it here. My comments are restricted to Gerritsen's understanding of forgiveness, not her original decision to leave her family, which she understands as a life-saving necessity, and I am not in a position to question.

6 Winnicott: forgiveness and transitional experience

This chapter might occasionally seem to have the quality of a palinode to the last, for it is less concerned with the actual relationship between offender and victim, the pas de deux of forgiveness. This chapter argues that forgiveness sometimes has more to do with the victim's relationship with his or her larger world, including his or her inner world. The offender is not always so important. In fact, the tension between this chapter and the last is more apparent than real. The last chapter was not so much about the actual relationship between offender and victim as it was about the roles each must play if genuine forgiveness, and not its simulacrum, is to happen. This chapter too is concerned with the role the victim must play in relationship to the larger world, one in which the offender is but one of many who must play a part. The victim's real partner in this particular pas de deux is the holding community, as Winnicott calls it. At the conclusion of this chapter, a rather longer story is told about a victim of a terrible crime, Terri Jentz, who must create the community that can hold her. Doing so requires a measure of self-deception and even a little cut-rate forgiveness on her part. However, as we have seen, real life is often more complex, interesting, and even cleverer than the most elegant theories.

The last chapter pointed out that there are many alternatives to forgiveness, so that Berel Lang (1994: 115) is quite mistaken to suggest that a world without forgiveness is fit only for angels or beasts. Neither moral perfection nor endless revenge are the sole alternatives to forgiveness. Alternatives range from pardon, clemency, and mercy, to plain acceptance of what happened. In the last case, life continues; nothing is forgotten, nothing is forgiven. Anger and resentment remain, but these emotions are not all powerful or all consuming;

gradually other aspects of life slip into the foreground. Forgiveness never happens, but its importance, even its relevance, becomes less pressing. One suspects this is the most common resolution of all. More ambiguous resolutions, such as that between Katherine Ann Power and Claire Schroeder, also deserve our attention. To claim forgiveness as the only alternative to revenge forces too much of civilized life into the category of forgiveness, rendering forgiveness incoherent.

It is only in recent years that psychoanalysts have turned their attention to forgiveness. The most acute among them are properly suspicious of forgiveness.[1] Smith (2008) puts it this way:

> The adhesiveness of [the concept of forgiveness] may be because the work of accepting the reality of the traumas we have suffered – and which we have caused others to suffer – is so difficult and so fraught with failure that we embrace the promise that forgiveness will heal our pain, rage, and guilt. The leap of forgiveness is a solution that has become part of our psychic lives.

The alternative to the leap of forgiveness is the slow work of mourning our losses, complicated by the fact that the loss is not only of a person, but a world: one that was once secure enough to relax and just be, in a world that was once good enough to want to live in. Coming to terms with such losses is subtle and complex work, in large measure because for some of the most catastrophic losses, there is no one to forgive.

WHAT IS GIVEN UP IN FORGIVENESS?

Most serious people who write about forgiveness (those for whom forgiveness is not merely a form of therapy on the cheap), secular and sacred alike, pay a great deal of attention to the question of *who* deserves forgiveness. The answer is almost always some version of the one who repents, demonstrating his or her repentance by changing his or her ways. This is expressed in the steps of repentance laid down in the twelfth century by Moses Maimonides, discussed in the previous chapter. Its importance is expressed in the secular vein by Charles Griswold (2007), who makes the telling of an elaborate narrative of one's offense, and its effect on the victim, central to repentance. One of the functions of such a narrative (though perhaps not its leading function, at least for Griswold) is to test the sincerity of the offender.

Most secular accounts of forgiveness stress the value of viewing repentance as a step-by-step process, each party participating in making the other better. Griswold, Paul Hughes, and Robert Roberts are exemplary. I draw from the psychoanalyst D. W. Winnicott to make a somewhat different argument. Forgiveness need not involve this particular relationship with the offender. Instead, it is about a different relationship with the world, out of which forgiveness may just happen. Forgiveness remains a relationship, but a more complex relationship, one not quite so dependent on the offender. One could argue that forgiveness becomes a relationship with one's internal objects, à la Melanie Klein. That, though, is no explanation, at least not by itself, and in any case, that is not my argument. Not intra-psychic space, but the space that constitutes the interperson, transitional space, is the space I am interested in.

The last two chapters assumed that forgiveness is not just a psychological but also a normative relationship. It might be more accurate to state that forgiveness is a psychological achievement that should not be at liberty to ignore certain normative constraints. Forgiveness was a normative ideal long before it was the subject of psychological study, even though those who developed the normative ideal often possessed keen psychological insight, as Maimonides did. As examples of acts of forgiveness that are beyond the normative pale, I may not forgive simply in order to feel better about myself, to empower myself, or to diminish the offender in some way by demonstrating my moral superiority. Many of those who responded to Wiesenthal's question in *The Sunflower* failed to understand these basic points.

Forgiveness has recently been the subject of considerable philosophical study. For the most part, this study has borrowed those aspects of the religious heritage of forgiveness that are readily rendered mundane, such as the way in which forgiveness restores damaged relationships, bringing the angry and alienated parties into renewed concord. In *The Stanford Encyclopedia of Philosophy*, Hughes (2010) states that the standard definition of forgiveness reveals its main purpose to be the reestablishment or resumption of a relationship broken by wrongdoing. Many contemporary philosophers argue that the resumption of relationships disrupted by wrongdoing requires a moral reassessment of the wrongdoer by the victim.

Robert Roberts (1995) makes, as we have seen, about the sharpest statement of the aims and achievement of forgiveness: "Forgiveness is virtuous because one's anger is given up without abandoning correct judgment about the severity of the offense and the culpability of the offender" (289). It is, Roberts continues, mildly controversial just which emotion is characteristically overcome in forgiveness, though it is widely agreed to be something akin to anger. Bishop Butler (2009: sermons viii, ix) seems to hold that it is resentment, understood as moral indignation. Jean Hampton (1988: 79–87) suggests that forgiveness annuls "moral hatred." Roberts settles on the term "anger" as precise enough, but that does not really seem to be the emotion he intends. Says Roberts (1995: 293):

> I propose, then, that the emotion "overcome" in forgiveness is anger, and that the facet of anger that makes it important sometimes to overcome it, even in its morally purest forms, is the "view" of the offender as bad, alien, guilty, worthy of suffering, unwelcome, offensive, an enemy, etc.[2]

Rather than anger, the devaluation of the offender as unworthy of human respect comes closer to the mark. "Devaluing, dehumanizing hatred or loathing" might be a better, if clumsier, term to characterize what Roberts is asking the one who forgives to give up.

While hatred is given up in forgiveness, the correct judgment that one has been harmed in some morally unjustified way is maintained. Forgiveness is not denial, not even of the fact that the offender's act caused outrage and hatred. Forgiveness rediscovers the human value of the person and the relationship behind the often-righteous anger that devalues the person who has done wrong. Such anger, it turns out, is often rewarding to the victim and by no means easy to abandon, especially when this anger has solidified into the satisfactions of hate (Hampton 1988). This is one reason Winnicott turns out to be such a useful guide, telling us how we might let go of righteous anger, or rather, how to live in the world so that righteous anger and hatred lose their value, indeed their meaning and purpose.

The leading status of repentance as a reason for forgiveness suggests that the aim of reconciliation is basic to the experience of forgiveness, a return to the status of being fellow humans together in a shared world. This requires, as Roberts (1995: 295) states, a sense of self as both member of a community and individual responsible actor, one who can accept and bear the responsibility of doing wrong.

> Forgivingness and the practice of forgiveness are at home in an ethic of community or friendship, one underlain by a sense of belonging to one another. But they [forgivingness and forgiveness] require that there be a strong differentiation of individuals as well, so that the one can bear responsibility for offending the other, and the other can choose to forgive. (290)

In *Before Forgiveness: The Origins of a Moral Idea*, David Konstan (2010) argues that this sense of individuality was largely absent before the eighteenth and nineteenth centuries, even as it made sporadic appearances centuries earlier, as in the work of Maimonides.

Interesting about Winnicott's account is its more subtle depiction of individuality, especially in what he calls transitional space, where the usual distinction between self and other does not apply, lest the creativity, freedom, and security found there be lost. It is from this space that forgiveness happens. Robert's and Konstan's straightforward distinctions between self and other are insufficiently complex to capture what is happening in this space, a claim that applies to almost all who write about forgiveness.

WHOLENESS AND HOLDING

Wholeness doesn't have a good reputation these days, particularly when it is expressed as a metanarrative; that is, a grand narrative purporting to explain all that we experience. Judaism and Christianity are metanarratives. So are some versions of psychoanalysis, such as Freud's. Metanarratives need not be told out loud; they may be implicit in the culture, such as the belief in progress through reason (Lyotard 1984). The trouble with metanarratives is their tendency to drive underground or erase all that does not fit the big story.

Certainly wholeness is not as frequently and as explicitly the goal of forgiveness in the secular treatment of the subject, even as the religious and secular approaches tend to mirror one another, Griswold being a prime example. While some Christian approaches, particularly those with strong links to the Protestant Reformation, write more explicitly about wholeness, it is implicit in the ideals of reunion and concord, "a sense of belonging to one another," as Roberts (1995: 290) put it in discussing both the goal and the framework for forgiveness.

Winnicott's way of thinking about transitional space and transitional relationships allows us to think about wholeness in new terms, ones too fluid to make a good metanarrative. Winnicott's terms are not only especially suited for the concept of forgiveness. They have consequences for the concept, leading to the surprisingly fruitful result of rendering forgiveness less personal, less dependent on the offender and his or her remorse, while not allowing the concept to become a mere means. It would be an exaggeration to say that for Winnicott, forgiveness happens when we no longer have a compelling need to forgive. Nonetheless, the exaggeration would betray a truth.

Consider what D. W. Winnicott (1971a: 1–25) calls transitional space, discussed in Chapter 3. Transitional space is first experienced when the child is held by its mother or other caretaker. If mother is in tune with her child, which means that she neither crushes the child with her anxiety, nor drops the child with her distraction and mental absence, the child does not have to even think "I feel held." Instead, the child is free to be, which means free to begin to explore his or her environment, free to begin to experience him or herself as unique and yet connected to another. The capacity to think of oneself as both unique yet connected serves the individual his or her whole life long, making it possible to live in a community without feeling like a drone.

Seen from this perspective, wholeness need not be that imperialistic state that leads to the search for dominion, resulting in the exclusion of all that does not fit. Wholeness need not be about the elimination or homogenization of otherness. On the contrary, it is the absence of experiences of holding that lead to the intolerance of otherness, difference, and ambiguity. Why? Because in the absence of an experience of holding (originally the holding by parents, later by loved ones, communities, and even ideas and ideals), one tries to create its simulacrum, a wholeness that never was, a wholeness in which there is no otherness; that is, no tolerance of otherness. Totalitarianism is the great and terrible example of what holding in the absence of community looks like; George Orwell's *Nineteen Eighty-Four* is its great literary representation.

One reason the intellectual representation of wholeness leads to intolerance is because it is a creation of the mind, a mind that has had to take over the function of holding, which means it can never let reality just be (Winnicott 1992a: 245–248). The parallel between failed human holding of the child, in which the child must use its mind to hold itself together, and intellectual holding, which has no place for otherness and difference, is not merely coincidental. In both, the mind is doing the work of stringently ordering and categorizing the flow of experience, rather than letting it be; that is, rather than letting oneself experience the world in its rich diversity.

Winnicott refers to experiences of separation, experiences of individuation and loss, in terms of the "I AM" moment, a raw moment in which:

> The new individual feels infinitely exposed. Only if someone has
> her arms around the infant at this time can the I AM moment be
> endured, or rather, perhaps, risked.
>
> *(Winnicott 1965a: 155)*

For adults, cultural forms such as religion can take on this holding
function, containing the individual so that he or she does not feel
infinitely exposed when confronted with a world not made for the
human being. For the fundamental claim of religion, in defiance of
Albert Camus's definition of absurdity, is that the universe is not
mindless of us, that we have a place here.

It is in this context that we should consider one of Winnicott's
comments about religious belief.

> To the child who develops "belief in" can be handed the god of the
> household or of the society ... But to the child with no "belief in"
> god is at best a pedagogue's gimmick, and at worst ... evidence ...
> that the parent-figures are lacking in confidence in the processes of
> human nature and are frightened of the unknown.
>
> *(Winnicott 1965b: 93)*

For Winnicott, belief in God is not so much a matter of whether or not
God exists, but whether or not humans can let themselves go enough to
imagine that He might. One is reminded of a comment Winnicott made
about the child's original transitional object, such as a teddy bear.

> Of the transitional object it can be said that it is a matter of
> agreement between us ... that we will never ask the question
> "Did you conceive of this or was it presented to you from
> without?" The important point is that no decision on this point is
> expected. The decision is not to be formulated. (1971a: 12, original
> in italics)

To compare belief in God to how the young child experiences his or
her teddy bear is not to diminish belief in God. It is rather to say that
all our important beliefs, the beliefs that really matter, the beliefs
that make a culture real, and not just a dead set of rituals, must have

this quality. Belief is not a matter of belief in the sheer (and mere) reality of an external object, but in the reality of an experience because one continually participates with others in creating the experience, and so knows that it is real.[3] One knows without having to constantly ask, "But are we making this up?"

The act of creation is an act of hope. Dare we imagine that this world might (in some way, difficult to envision, given its apparent indifference to human hopes and dreams) be a place that holds us too? Is this an impossible idea to contemplate? Were it an easy idea to contemplate, what would it matter? And so we let our imaginations wander, further perhaps than a rigorous grasp on reality would allow. But holding onto reality too tightly is not the best way of being held. In fact, it is the opposite of being held. It is the way we hold ourselves when there is no one left to hold us, when we face that "I am" moment alone.

The claim that something is religious is the opposite of Albert Camus's claim of absurdity. Religion says that the world is finally hospitable to our deepest human needs, that the world was in some way made with the human being and his or her needs in mind. Contrast this view with Camus's (1955: 28) definition of the absurd. "The absurd is born of this confrontation between the human need and the unreasonable silence of the world." We should not, however, take the term "unreasonable silence of the world" as a condemnation, any more than it is reasonable condemnation to call a rock stupid because it does not speak. The world just is, and because it just is, it would make no sense to call the world absurd.

Nor is human life absurd. Humans make plans, dream dreams, dominate others, fall in love, and die. That's not absurd either, but merely human, all too human. What is absurd is the conjunction – or better, disjunction – between world and humanity. Humans long for the world to participate in some way in their hopes and dreams, to share in their lives, to acknowledge their existence. It is the incommensurability between the world's mere being and humanity's terrible longing for a reply that generates the experience of absurdity.[4]

Camus (1955: 28) calls this longing "nostalgia" (*nostalgie*), and that is a perfectly good word, as long as we understand that one can experience nostalgia, perhaps the strongest and most persistent nostalgia of all, for that which never was. For we live here for a brief while not as the world's guests, but as transients, before moving on into that endless night.

FORGIVENESS WITHOUT REPENTANCE?

Sometimes hate and resentment seem as though they are the only secure things to hold onto in all the world, the only things we can control. When one is in a transitional relationship to the world, then one need not hold on so tightly. Forgiveness is easier as letting go becomes easier: we can let go of our hatred without fear of disintegrating or endlessly falling.

The ability to remain within a transitional relationship, a transitional space, is not just about the ability to avoid grasping onto rage and resentment, hatred and contempt, it is also about avoiding (or rather, not needing) the purity that obsession and ritual seek. In transitional space, there is no purity to be found, and no need to find it. The search for purity is another version of the quest for wholeness. One finds this quest in surprising places, such as Derrida's (2001) claim that true forgiveness can only forgive the unforgivable. Purity binds us to a world of absolutes, which can never have the qualities of a transitional relationship. Purity represents a world of all or nothing at all. Derrida's search for the purity of forgiveness, unsullied by the spirit of exchange, is the opposite of a transitional relationship to the world.

From this perspective, an interesting possibility emerges. Jews, many Christians, and most serious thinkers on the subject, such as Griswold, insist that forgiveness be bound to repentance. One does not forgive an offender who has not asked sincerely, and shown signs of repentance.[5] Maimonides' four steps of forgiveness, outlined in the previous chapter, are all concerned with the ritual of asking for forgiveness. Conversely, much that is wrong with the theory and practice of forgiveness today has to do with people granting forgiveness in the absence of its being properly asked for, as though forgiveness were therapy for the victim. We forgive, according to Smedes (1984: 12–13), "for our own sakes," in order to "heal ourselves" of hurt and hate. But perhaps it is not so simple as yes or no, "don't forgive unless sincerely asked."

Another possibility is suggested by Winnicott. We forgive not when the other has performed the proper ritualized steps of repentance, and not in order to heal or empower ourselves, but when we have reached that transitional space where we no longer need to hold onto our anger, our hatred, and our hurt. *Forgiveness, from this perspective, is something that happens to us at a certain point almost as a by-product of living in the world in a certain way.* In other words, the repentance of the other may not be all that important, but not for the reason suggested by Smedes and others: to regain one's sense of power. Rather, forgiveness just happens when one is in a certain transitional state. It is not a matter of *realizing* that that anger and hatred are no longer central to our lives. Cognitive and emotional insight aren't as important as the state of one's being.

Transitional experience is an internal process within the individual. Transitional experience is not about either/or but about being in a place in which many possibilities exist, so that one can come to imagine oneself as an inhabitant of ever-larger worlds. Where does this transitional state come from? From someone having had his or her arms around us during the "I AM" moments that impose themselves on adults, such as the death of a spouse, or child, or the transgression that is experienced as unbearable and unforgivable.

While transitional experience is intrapsychic, Winnicott was keenly aware that the distinction between internal and external, private and social, becomes problematic under transitional experience. Indeed, this is the point. And yet one must be careful not to simplify Winnicott here. In transitional experience, the boundaries of the self expand to include parts of the external world. If this expansion does not occur, then culture could never become a living experience that can hold us when we are faced with the trauma of everyday life, from illness, to old age to death, to all the other heartaches that confront us, such as the death of a spouse. On the other hand, Winnicott remained committed to the idea that a portion of the self must remain incommunicado, hidden deep inside, so that the self need not be devoted to its protection. When it is, the self cannot use the culture because he or she is too busy protecting him or herself from the intrusions of culture into the self.

While transitional experience is an internal process, it is conceptualized by Winnicott as a relationship in which at least one of the parties is unaware of the relationship, or rather, finds it unnecessary to be constantly aware. One might call this lack of awareness "security." Transitional experience may take place in a variety of settings, from mother's lap to the concert hall to a regular encounter with the community volunteer who brings the homebound man or woman a hot meal. Otherwise expressed, the "I AM" moment that allows us to feel separate is enabled only by the holding that keeps this separateness within bounds. "Within bounds" means that the experience of separateness does not devolve into feelings of disintegration, chaos, and endless falling. This holding may be individual, a mother's or lover's arms, or communal, such as a sense of confidence that there is some place I can go if I become hungry, sick, or terrified. It is from this perspective that one may speak of being in a transitional relationship to the world, even if transitional experience remains strictly intrapsychic.

Though community is no replacement for the loving care and concern shown by individuals, loving care and concern are much more likely to be forthcoming in a coherent community. This is the key point, and no single point stands out more clearly in Kai Erikson's (1976; 1994) study of man-made disasters. Destroy the community, and you make it much more difficult for individuals in these communities to care for each other. Communities hold the people who hold each other when things go wrong.

Forgiveness is supposed to be about a relationship. In Judaism, forgiveness is primarily a two-way relationship: human to human when the offense is one human against another; human to God, when the offense involves an offense against God, such as those declared in the first four Commandments. Emmanuel Levinas (1990: 20) takes this position to an extreme, arguing that not even God can forgive a crime committed by one man against another. Only the victim can do that. "No one, not even God, can ... pardon the crime that man commits against man ... The world in which pardon is all-powerful becomes inhuman."

In Christianity, the relationship is primarily between man or woman and God, though Jesus was clear that mending your relationship with your brother takes precedence to making a sacrifice to God (Matthew 5:23–24; Mark 11:25). From a philosophical perspective, such as the three surveyed at the beginning of this chapter (Griswold, Hughes, Roberts), the relationship is also interpersonal, always about the restoration of a wounded relationship. An object relations approach in psychoanalysis, of which Winnicott is exemplary, must make a similar claim: forgiveness is about the relationship between the offender and the victim. Conversely, most of the troubling and unsatisfactory accounts of forgiveness make it "all about me and my feelings about myself."

Suddenly I claim that Winnicott's view suggests that forgiveness happens when the victim comes to abandon hatred, rage, and resentment, a consequence of his or her having come to reside in transitional space. The offender becomes less important. The other's offense is no longer the center of the victim's world. This too is an object relational (that is, interpersonal) perspective on forgiveness. Only now the "person" in question is not just, or even primarily, the offender, but the relationship between the victim and the larger community in which he or she lives, the holding community, one that begins with family, and includes as many people, practices, artifacts, and ideas as the victim can imaginatively allow to populate his or her world.

In "Forgiveness as a Process of Change in Individual Psychotherapy," Malcolm and Greenberg (2000) compare forgiving clients with unforgiving ones. At issue were serious offenses such as the sexual abuse of a student by his teacher. Though they draw from a few cases, their conclusion is that resolution without forgiveness does not prevent a person from overcoming trauma and getting on with his or her life. The difference is that "when forgiveness is not offered, anger is not followed by an expression of sadness, fear, or vulnerability (which are highly attachment-related emotions that indicate an action tendency toward comfort and/or moving closer)" (198). In other words, forgiveness is how we move closer to the other person, toward whom we feel both attachment and betrayal. Those who did not forgive tended not to have considered forgiveness as an option. Rather, they achieve resolution by moving away from the offender, and toward deeper involvement in other relationships within the community.

Forgiveness seeks closeness to the offender, often the reparation and restoration of actual relationships, as the philosophers considered at the beginning of this essay suggest. Non-forgiveness seeks to regain a sense of one's lost place in, and value to, the community. Actual relationships are no less important; less important is only the relationship to the offender. Both strategies have their place, depending on the extent of the harm, but also on the previous relationship to the offender, as well as the willingness of the offender to repent. One problem with forgiveness today is the tendency to confuse these two goals, using forgiveness to seek power instead of reunion, either with the offender or the holding community.

Winnicott reveals that achieving a transitional position from which forgiveness happens does not, and should not, mean that forgiveness must happen, or even should happen. Transitional space is its own reward. While genuine forgiveness is easier to grant from this space, whether it will be should depend on the values of the victim, as well as the circumstances, such as those studied by more traditional approaches to forgiveness. These include the willingness of the offender to act with repentance, as well as the desire of the victim for a restored relationship, which will depend, in good measure, on the previous relationship. Winnicott reveals sources of forgiveness deeper than the rituals of forgiveness, sources upon which the rituals depend, sources of experience that lead to or are the experience of transitional space.

VICAR JULIE NICHOLSON

An intriguing example of transitional space being its own reward is the case of Julie Nicholson, an Anglican vicar whose daughter, Jenny, 24, was blown up in the Al-Qaeda-led bombings of London subways and buses on July 7, 2005. Shortly after her daughter's death, Nicholson resigned her parish priesthood because she could not forgive the men who murdered her daughter. The tabloid press labeled her the "Vicar who can't forgive."[6] Says Julie Nicholson, "I've preached so many sermons on forgiveness. It's essential to human beings, but in some situations ..." Her voice trails off. She says she will never forget when a parishioner asked, "'You're a priest; do you feel you have a duty to forgive?' It was like a bolt out of the blue, and I thought, 'No, actually I don't,'" replies the vicar with a sad smile. "It doesn't matter to me whether people feel that according to the tenets of the Christian faith I have a duty to forgive. Maybe so. But the reality is I don't."

A disturbing aspect of the interview with Vicar Nicholson is that she seems as lost and unsure about forgiveness as any parishioner. "What are we talking about with forgiveness? What does the word really mean?" The Vicar continues. "When I look at the tunnel at Edgware Road tube station [closest to where the Vicar's daughter was blown up], I feel absolutely full of anger and rage that this happened ... I don't feel that I'm a person consumed with anger and bitterness. But I can get angry over what happened. And for goodness sake why shouldn't I? This shouldn't be happening. To forgive Mohammad Sidique Khan [the lead bomber] on one level is condoning, or at least saying it's not quite as bad as it really is" (Nicholson 2011: 149).

While Vicar Nicholson won't forgive, she is not stuck in a place of rage and hate, but has resumed her spiritual journey in another direction (her interview took place less than two years after her daughter's death). "A thought occurred to me quite recently. [On the day Jenny was killed] I was up in Wales setting table for breakfast, thinking about what we were to be doing on this first sunny day in five days, and already the shadow was cast in London, and I didn't know it yet, but my daughter had been blown to pieces. I found that a really disturbing concept, but also full of hope in a strange way. It just shows us that nothing stops, the world keeps turning, the sun keeps shining ... that although the shadow passes over us, it doesn't stay there."[7]

One might argue that the vicar is trying to put her daughter's death behind her, to move on, as the jargon of popular psychology would have it. But it's not so simple. For, just a few minutes later, the vicar says, "I've taken her back into myself, this seed, this essence, that I sent into the world I've drawn back into myself. I hope that all that she was will give me a richness, and that I'll use that richness to contribute something to the world."

The vicar has found a transitional place, somewhere between letting her dead daughter go into the rhythms of the continuing world, and taking her daughter back inside her, so that she will never have to let her go, but that she can become part of her in some way. Jenny exists somewhere between inside and outside, belonging to the vicar's womb, to the world, to history, to the shadows and the sun, and to the community, which the vicar hopes to reenter enriched by Jenny's presence within. As Vicar Nicholson (2011: 148) puts it:

> since the moment Jenny was missing I have needed my sister and my cousins and they have been with me all the way. These three people from my childhood represent a time of safety and security, I know that now. I also know that I have not only retreated to a place of safety, but I have retreated to a people of safety. *We all need each other and each one of us makes a difference.*

Her last statement refers to the kindnesses she encountered during her journey from Wales to London to identify her daughter's body, and return it for burial during the days after 7/7.

The vicar has done much of the work of mourning. The rest will take a lifetime. Forgiveness would have helped no one, least of all the vicar. Transitional space may result in forgiveness. It need not, and forgiveness is not its goal, but only one possibility. But if transitional space does need not require forgiveness, transitional space seems to have requirements of its own. The most important of these is community, whose elements are both imaginary and real. If real community is not present, the person filled with rage and grief is unlikely to let go of these emotions long enough to learn how to live with them.

FORGIVENESS, HOPE, AND A GOOD ENOUGH WORLD

Hope is an important, and infrequently commented-upon, aspect of Winnicott's work. Hope is most clearly seen, says Winnicott, in anti-social behavior, and even wickedness. (Winnicott is thinking of the wickedness of the child and early adolescent, not the cold, hate-filled wickedness of the adult terrorist or killer.) Anti-social behavior and wickedness reflect an inability to symbolize distress; the need to act it out instead. These acts remain a sign of hope, for they signify that the offender has not given up on the possibility that he or she can communicate his or her despair to someone who can crack the code and understand. Hope is locked up in wickedness, while hopelessness is marked by compliance and false socialization (Abram 1996: 42; Winnicott 1965b: 103–104). Hope is the not-yet-forsaken belief that a person can find someone to hold him while he faces that "I AM" moment, hope that he will not be dropped again as he was once before, at a time before he was able to stand on his own.

Hope as it is expressed in forgiveness is not just the hope that an individual is worth forgiving, that he or she will not betray one's trust again. Forgiveness expresses the hope that the world itself is worth taking a chance on, that the world of family, friends, culture, and community can hold us from cradle to grave, the alpha and omega of holding. Hope trusts that this world is a good enough place in which to live and die. Forgiveness bridges the gap in trust in the world, the gap opened up by absurdity, much as adult forms of holding, such as culture and religion, do. Only whereas culture and religion bridge this gap with stories that tell us that we belong here, forgiveness bridges the gap by saying that even though I may be victimized by particular human relationships, the world is a good enough place to be. Forgiveness overcomes the strictly human absurdity, the unnecessary or surplus absurdity, it might be called, created by wanton aggression and lack of caring.

For the world to be trustworthy requires that the world be worthy of trust, and under certain conditions – hardly limited to genocide – this may not be true. Worthy of trust does not mean "good." It simply means good enough to live in, good enough so that one does not constantly have to be on guard, good enough to sometimes just be. Today this hope is possible in large parts of the world; in larger parts it is probably not, which is likely more difficult to determine than one might first imagine. It is not as simple as drawing boundaries on a map. Some traditional societies (depending upon the pressures they are under) are likely easier places to just be than many modern societies.

Psychological boundaries will also need to be taken into account. The world can seem worthy of trust one day, unworthy the next, depending on intervening experiences. Trauma can change everything in an instant, and change it forever. Trauma can transform a trustworthy world into a world with no place to stand, and no place to just be. Whether the world can ever become a safe enough place to be depends both on the extent of the trauma and the resources available to the traumatized. Narrative resources are important, as discussed in the chapters on trauma. So too are those wordless holding resources that so often go unnoticed, such as the way a secure community finds a place for the traumatized one to be, long before he or she is capable of putting words to his or her experience. Actually, this is not quite right. A secure community provides a holding environment secure enough for the traumatized one to sometimes not be, and so find respite from the terrible burden of self-holding.

Earlier, Smith was quoted as saying that the adhesiveness of forgiveness had to do with the terrible persistence of trauma, and its resistance to therapy. The temptation to be avoided is substituting forgiveness for the long, slow work of mourning. Smith's is a good critique of popular forgiveness, but it's not the only psychoanalytic critique. Almost as common is the argument that even the sincerely held wish to forgive, even forgiveness given, cannot overcome the aggression and anger that remain.

> However much we reify it as an entity, what we call forgiveness
> is part of an ongoing dynamic process that involves continuing input
> from aggressive ... wishes ... It is precisely this aggressive
> component that tends to be avoided when the concept of forgiveness
> is featured too prominently in the [psychoanalytic] work.
>
> *(Smith 2008)*

For Smith, as for many psychoanalysts, it is the aggression still felt against the forgiven one that needs to be worked through, and cannot be when forgiveness is given too readily, when forgiveness is seen as a solution, rather than as one possible outcome of therapy.

Seen from the perspective of Winnicott, the problem is both similar and different. Above all, it is more poignant. Many people, including those who want to offer forgiveness, will never find themselves in transitional space, where they can just be. It is a state, perhaps more than any other, that cannot be willed. Though he is not referring to transitional space, Thomas Moore, psychotherapist and contemporary American spiritual writer, puts it well when he says:

> Forgiveness comes in its own time. Forgiveness comes from some
> other place. We can create the conditions under which we hope it
> will appear. We may feel good that it has appeared. But we can't
> control the whole thing.
>
> *(Doblmeier 2007)*

We must, I think, recognize as legitimate two types of forgiveness. One is willed, and ideally stems from a conscious recognition that the offender has made atonement and demonstrated a continuing commitment to self-transformation. The term "willed" refers, of course, not to the wilfulness of caprice, but the will expressed by developed character. The second type of forgiveness is less thoughtful, more conducive to the soul of forgiveness; that is, the mental and emotional state from which forgiveness is most freely given, that state that has been called transitional space. Of this second type of forgiveness, all we may ask is that it remembers that forgiveness is also a normative ideal, holding the forgiven to proper standards of conduct.

A certain level of trauma is going to make only willed forgiveness possible if there is to be any forgiveness at all. Furthermore, there is no reason to think that willed forgiveness will one day make transitional forgiveness possible. On the contrary, the work of willed forgiveness will make transitional forgiveness less likely; but it was probably unlikely all along. This does not mean that the traumatized person cannot genuinely forgive. If we have learned nothing else from the discussion of forgiveness, we have learned that it has different dimensions, different meanings. Some meanings are antithetical to any true understanding of forgiveness, such as, "I forgive you in order to feel better about myself," or "I forgive you in order to feel empowered." However, other meanings of forgiveness remain intact, such as, "I forgive you because you have revealed through your words and deeds that you understand why your acts hurt, feel remorse for having done them, and are trying to change your life."

Nevertheless, a certain experience of forgiveness, the experience implicit in a Winnicottian understanding of forgiveness, will remain unavailable to those still traumatized by the acts that have victimized them. This is the sad way of the world, and the best thing to be done is to acknowledge it, while appreciating how important social holding – what Erikson calls community – is in fostering not just relief from trauma, but the possibility of a particular type of forgiveness; not forgiveness more genuine than any other, but possibly more satisfying, or rather, the result of a more satisfying experience of life. At the same time, one must recognize the limits of social holding.

For many, not forgiveness, not transitional space, but the lessening of trauma over time in a community of others who can offer social, economic, and moral support seems the most reasonable goal, and one often within reach.

VOICES OF FORGIVENESS: TERRI JENTZ

Nineteen at the time she was attacked, Terri Jentz and her roommate from Yale were bicycling across the country in the summer of 1977. Not far into their journey, they camped for the night in Cline Falls Park, near Redmond, Oregon.[8] Asleep in their tent, they were run over by a pickup truck. At first Terri thought the driver was a drunken fool who somehow didn't see the tent. Next thing she knew, the driver was taking an ax to her roommate. Her roommate was struck in the head, and still suffers from a partial loss of vision and other neurological deficits; she has no memory of the attack. Terri was axed in the arm. Her shoulder, half her ribcage, and one lung had been crushed by the weight of the truck. As the ax man was bringing the ax down a second time over her chest, Terri felt hypnotized by how slowly the ax moved. Evidently Terri was not experiencing an illusion. Reaching up, Terri caught the blade in her hands, just above her chest. "Please, take anything you want, just leave us alone," she cried. Slowly her attacker turned, got back into his truck and left. During the entire attack he had not uttered a word (Whitney 2011b: 37).

Jentz has written a 729-page book about her experience, *Strange Piece of Paradise* (2006), and she tells her story to the video camera with the experience of a writer for whom what is remembered is not so much the event itself, but the subsequent narration of the event. This is not bad. There is no more reason to distrust narrative memory, as it might be called, as opposed to spontaneous memory. One must simply be aware that narrators who have written at length about their experiences talk differently about them. Many of the markers of trauma, such as difficulty with tenses, as well as the usual hesitations and infelicities, are missing. Narrators who have written about their experiences tell stories that conform to the expectations of narrative;

above all, that the story have a beginning, middle, and end. Real life is seldom this neat. Nevertheless, even those who have not written about their lives tend to make the telling conform to the expectations of narrative convention. As Barbara Hardy (1968: 5) remarks, "We dream in narrative, daydream in narrative, remember, anticipate, hope, despair, believe, doubt, plan, revise, criticize, construct, gossip, learn, hate and love by narrative." Some are just more practiced at it than others, and about that we need to be aware.

Jentz opens her interview by saying that because her attacker committed such an extreme transgression in a community unfamiliar with such grave brutality, she believes that members of the community had no way to make sense of the offense, no category in which to put such wanton violence, no good way to talk about it. The result is that "this event had traumatized these people as deeply as it had traumatized me" (Whitney 2011b: 46).

The last statement is untrue, of course. "These people" hadn't spent the last twenty years of their lives obsessed with the attack and their attacker, unable to work for long periods of time. They had not been terrified of crossing the street for fear of being hit and crushed by a car, as Jentz was for several years. They had not been immobilized by hopelessness and panic. At one level, Jentz is trying to realize in fantasy something akin to what Jean Améry upholds as an unrealizable utopian standard of forgiveness: that the offender, including bystanders who knew and did nothing, would wish as intensely as he that reality had been otherwise, that time could be erased and history suspended. In Jentz's case, her wish is that the bystanders be as traumatized as she.

Like Améry, Jentz too was faced with bystanders who did nothing. Not with bystanders who could have prevented the attack, but with many citizens who had a very good idea indeed of the man who committed the attack, and said nothing. They said nothing about the same man who publicly almost killed his girl-friend the day after he attacked Jentz and her roommate – a man who owned a truck like the one Jentz described, a man who was fascinated with axes and hatchets, a man who had a reputation for beating and torturing women, a man whose unusual tire tracks matched those on Jentz's body (Jentz 2006: 622).

While Jentz is simply wrong to equate her trauma with that of the community, it turns out that she was pursuing a subtle and clever strategy, one perhaps unknown even to herself: she would forgive the community so that it might hold, contain, and comfort her twenty years later in the way it failed to do at the time of the original attack. What such a strategy requires, if it is not to be a mere fantasy, is that some members of the community be willing to play their part. Not necessarily to ask for forgiveness, though some did, but that they are willing to be fully present at that delicate "I AM" moment, as Winnicott calls it, when the self is exposed in a new way for the first time. If Jentz and some members of the community play their parts well, then the fantasy of a loving, caring community strong enough to care for Jentz's "wounded, injured, animal self," as she puts it, can finally become real. Real in that inner, living way that the most real things come to exist for us: real because we have created them, while knowing at the same time that they live a life of their own. As Winnicott teaches, we grow up when we consciously realize that no resolution of this apparent conflict is necessary.

Fifteen years after the attack, in 1992, Terri began returning to Redmond on her own to try to find some answers. For years she had been able to tell her story to her friends, but when her friends asked the obvious question, "Well, what happened to the guy who did it?" she had no answer, and had felt no need for an answer. He was never caught, and Jentz had always been taught to move on (Whitney 2011b: 40). Only she couldn't. Returning to Redmond, she lay on the ground where she was attacked, as though she could reabsorb her own blood that had been spilled, as though she could reabsorb her own lost life force (Whitney 2011b: 42).

Within days of her return to Redmond, she learned that the three-year statute of limitations on attempted murder had expired (the Oregon law has since been changed, in part due to Jentz's efforts). No one could be prosecuted for her assault, even should her attacker be found. At that, Terri says, "I started feeling a righteous anger about going after the truth about what happened" (Whitney 2011b: 42). Whether or not he could be punished by the law, Terri was determined to discover the identity of her attacker, and it is this that brought her back to life. Not, Terri is quick to reassure the interviewer, in order to wreak vengeance, and perhaps not simply the abstract desire to know the truth, but because she was able to connect her anger to action that was not self-destructive.

Anger directed outward invigorated Terri Jentz, giving her a sense of power and agency in almost exactly the same way that forgiveness invigorated Eva Kor. Are anger and forgiveness two sides of the same coin, and if so, what would that mean? One thing it might mean is that both anger and forgiveness know and accept the truth of what happened. Though she does not belabor the point, Terri is clear that she does not seek revenge, but justice. One obvious difference between Kor and Jentz is that Jentz believes in an evil that is beyond atonement. Says Jentz, "I think people refuse to understand the bad news of human nature. People commit evil out of the sheer joy of doing it" (Whitney 2011b: 45, 48). Her attacker had attacked, tormented, tortured, and possibly killed other women before being jailed for an unrelated assault against another man. He had made his ex-wife dig her own grave and lie in it night after night. The categories of evil and atonement play no role in Kor's world; only forgiveness. Still, not even Jentz can live without forgiveness; she has to forgive someone. It turns out to be the citizens of Redmond.

For eight years, through all the seasons, Terri returned to Redmond, creating the community that would hold her. It was not, she said, just a matter of finding the perpetrator.

> I began to recognize the outlines of a less obvious motivation
> compelling me to return to the western desert community.
> On some subterranean level, we were all waiting to reconnect, to

bring together our searing memories, to imbue them with meaning and a historical context, to integrate them into a larger, shared narrative.

(Jentz 2006: 246)

Jentz will come to terms with her trauma by making it the community's trauma. Not only that, she will make it herself, not the community, that rejected the original connection fifteen years ago. "The umbilical connection that I denied then was still waiting for me. Just that week, one Redmond resident told me, 'We would have loved to have known you. There was so much sorrow. It would really have been good for us if we could have seen you'" (Jentz 2006: 355).

The central image that Terri uses to refer to her connection is blood. "It felt like the community had given me a transfusion" (Jentz 2006: 590–91). She and her friend had bled so profusely on the night of the attack that the man who carried her to the hospital in the back of his pickup truck had to hose it down the next day with a fire hose (the front seat was occupied by the driver, his wife, and Jentz's more seriously injured companion). And just as one begins to think that Terri is creating an illusory community to care for her, one that didn't care then, and still doesn't, one comes across people like the nurses who cared for Terri and her friend in the weeks following the attack in the surprisingly modern and well-equipped local hospital. This is confirmed in the video testimony of the nurses. To be sure, Terri may have taught the nurses her bloody language of caring, but it hardly matters. They have become part of her blood sisterhood.

Says nurse Kathy Devlin, "When you were attacked and injured so badly, it was 'like you were part of our community. You lived so far away ... I think from my standpoint, you did leave a part of yourself with us'" (Jentz 2006: 616). Ms. Devlin continues:

> I became you. I became Shayna [Terri's gravely injured traveling companion]. There is a time when you're such a part of the patient and the patient is such a part of you. We're the same person. You are at your most vulnerable, and will give me anything. You will be

anything I want you to be at that moment. I'm your lifeline. I'm
your lifesaver. If you can reach out and touch me, everything is ok.
What would I want done for me? I'd want to be safe. I'd want to be
warm. I'd want someone to think of me in those terms. How would
we have wanted to be treated. (616)[9]

Though it may sound strange to say, Ms. Devlin thinks like the
torturer. Only she thinks like the torturer in the name of goodness.
You will do anything for me to save you. So how can I put myself in
your position and give you what you want and need? That is
Ms. Devlin's question. What she shares with the torturer is the awareness of the utter dependence of the victim, the victim's willingness to
do anything to be saved. Nurse Devlin uses this knowledge to identify
with victim and help, the torturer to identify with victim and harm, in
order to extract from the victim either information or more pain.

Terri meets enough people like Kathy Devlin, people who seem
willing to share her pain, inasmuch as humans are willing and able to
do so, while recognizing that what is needed is not two people
writhing in pain, but a fusion that is also a distance, so that one can
minister to the other's pain. In any case, it seems fair to say that
Terri's Aristophanic fantasy (the Aristophanes of Plato's *Symposium)*
of being joined with her nurses via a single beating heart, is not simply
a private fantasy or delusion.

Back in the summer of '77, in July, Shayna and I, and the sisters
of mercy [the three nurses] parted from one another, falling back
into our separate skins. But for those of us with the memory of
the traumatized tissue, who found ourselves running wet with
lifeblood – it was as though we had met in the infinite waterways
of one pumping heart. We, the sisters of mercy and I, who had
experienced this mysterious breakthrough, were left with the
longing for that fluid state of living without finite contours, for
this form of love we had discovered – as though, when
confined to our separate selves again, a part of ourselves had
gone missing. (626)

The fantasy of fusion (though not its full blown, single-beating-heart version) is shared by at least two of the three nurses, and by several other people in the community who strongly identify with Terri's fate; above all, her terrible vulnerability. It is this, it seems, that leads people, especially women, to imagine how easily they could share her fate. Only this time, they do not turn away from her in denial of this knowledge, perhaps because they see she survived, even prospered.

One of the interesting questions raised by Jentz's story is whether, for those who have been severely traumatized, the metaphysical can ever be anything more than the expression of the physical. Jean Améry (1980: 100–101) is contemptuous of the metaphysics he still longs for, arguing that for those who have been tortured, only the physical reality of the body is truly real. Perhaps this is the special knowledge of trauma to which Kai Erikson refers: that in the end, metaphysics is but a detour, or rather an expression in a more abstract language, of the truth of the body. Plato's *Timaeus* would support this interpretation.

Jentz encountered her three nurses relatively late in her eight-year series of pilgrimages to Redmond, and the question nurse Kathy Devlin, Jentz, and several other community members raise vis-à-vis Winnicott, is whether these at least partially shared fantasies of fusion are equivalent to holding. They are. These fantasies, recognized by adults as fantasies, adults who have, in Terri's case, done decades of work coming to terms with their traumatic experience, are themselves the intersubjectively created symbolic expression of holding – not just the fantasies, of course, but the social relationships that go with the fantasies.

The video concludes with Terri Jentz, Kathy Devlin, and another woman who had been helpful to Jentz over the years squeezed together on a not-very-large porch swing. They are looking not just content, but pleased with themselves. They are acting for the camera, of course, but it doesn't seem put on. Terri has forgiven the community for dropping her: dropping her case, not pursuing her attacker, not wanting to know. And the community, or rather, certain members of the community, have used Terri to rid themselves of a residual guilt, and perhaps even a feeling of abandonment by Terri. Terri's parents whisked her away to Chicago as soon as she was stable enough to fly. As Robyn Edy put it years later, "What she really needed to hear from us was that we were sorry. We're sorry it happened. We're sorry we bred such an animal in our midst and did nothing about it" (Whitney 2011b: 45).

In some ways, it is not just Jentz's sudden reappearance after twenty years (no one in the community knew if she was alive or dead), but that she did not look deformed or physically damaged (all her wounds were covered by normal clothing), or act as wounded as she felt when she first arrived, that allowed members of the community to approach her. This is fortunate for Jentz, unfortunate for those who are deeply traumatized and show it, perhaps in that thousand-yard stare, or in the way they hold themselves, as though waiting for the next blow to fall. For Jentz's experience suggests that these people are less likely to be reabsorbed into the community.

JENTZ ON THE BANALITY OF EVIL

Along the way, Terri is given a box of her assailant's most precious possessions, hidden from him by a recent girlfriend, one woman who physically fought back against the Ax man and won (Jentz 2006: 513–515). Terribly excited, Terri thought she might finally gain a glimpse into the Ax man's dark soul. Instead, the box was filled with scraps of paper bearing banalities:

> rituals to conjure strength and a higher power under a full moon. Quasi-mystic ramblings, joining words that looked impressive into sentences that had no meaning. Song lyrics on homiletic themes … Photocopies of crude sayings and jokes and cartoons, such as "Wood and paper products no longer available – wipe your ass with a spotted owl." A crude drawing of a flying saucer.
>
> (Jentz 2006: 511–512)

Jentz is disappointed, referring to how shocked Albert Speer was to find Hitler "lazing away his days, screening Hollywood fluff like *Snow White and the Seven Dwarfs* in his private quarters" (512). Here Jentz follows Jean Améry's (1980) line of thinking when he writes that:

> there is no "banality of evil," and Arendt, who wrote about it in her Eichmann book, knew the enemy of humanity only from hearsay, saw him only through the glass cage. When an event places the most extreme demands on us, one ought not to speak of banality. For at this point there is no longer any abstraction, and never an imaginative power that could approach its reality ... Only in rare moments in life ... and it does not have to be something as extreme as torture ... do we truly stand face to face with the event, and with it, reality.
>
> *(Améry 1980: 25–26)*

Améry (26) assumes that "even in direct experience everyday reality is nothing but codified abstraction." Only in rare moments, such as torture experienced, do we confront reality head-on. Such moments have more the quality of an evil immanence (sharing the quality of transcendence while remaining supremely material and real), and that is surely not banal.

Jentz comes at the argument a little differently, suggesting that while evil is not banal, those who commit it may be. There is a reason. It requires "startlingly little effort" to destroy things. And those who thrive at the task of destruction generally "don't do well with the subtler pursuits of building, creating something positive and enduring, because these pursuits require ... faith and humility" on a daily basis over time (Jentz 2006: 512). Destruction is quick and easy, requiring no great creative intelligence. It is building, creating, what Arendt calls "natality," that requires creativity and focused effort over time.

How much ink has been spilled on the banality of evil that might have been saved for more worthy pursuits had both Arendt and her critics made this simple distinction between the banality of an evil man and the immanent reality of the evil inflicted. As Améry might say, only a scholar looking at the world through a wall of glass (Eichmann was in a bullet-proof glass booth whenever he appeared in the courtroom) could fail to make that distinction, one that would have saved us all a good deal of trouble. While it makes no sense to write about the "banality of evil," sometimes it makes sense to write about the banality of particular evil men and women. Especially since Jentz's explanation fits Arendt's purpose well: to strip evil of its creative power, and so prevent the architects of the Holocaust from coming to be seen as evil demiurges (Elshtain 1995: 84–85). Jentz is no great philosopher, but in turning to Améry for inspiration, she made a wise choice.

This section is concerned with the voices of those who choose to forgive, and at first Jentz turns out to be an odd choice, an odd voice. She forgives, but not the violent offender, whom she regards as evil incarnate. Instead, she forgives the community of bystanders, many of whom knew her attacker, but did not inform or pressure the police. Furthermore, she forgives only by an act of creative imagination, in which she creates a community worth forgiving, one that will hold her, and so help heal her. Beyond this, she turns out to possess a theoretical turn of mind, interested in why people like to kill, as well as Améry's reflections on the banality of evil. In trying to explain the pleasures of evil, Jentz includes this quote from Améry:

> With heart and soul they went about their business and the
> name of it was power, dominion over spirit and flesh, orgy of
> unchecked self-expansion. I also have not forgotten that there
> were moments when I felt a kind of wretched admiration for
> the agonizing sovereignty they exercised over me. For is not the
> one who can reduce a person so entirely to a body and a
> whimpering prey of death a god, or at least a demigod?
>
> *(Améry 1980: 36; Jentz 2006: 212)*

Jentz admits that she felt something of the god-like power of her attacker. "I can still remember the rush of that night – something about the radiation he emitted, the dark charisma during the explosion of power on the brink of murder." In fact, she can identify with it. "Isn't part of the allure (let's come clean) to be on the side of power, on the side of those who dare to tear the fabric of normal existence, to force their will on the world...?" (Jentz 2006: 213). Jentz is an honest woman with access to her inner world. She would immediately grasp Blake's remark that Satan gets all the best lines in *Paradise Lost*.

It is surprising to find so much insight in what is essentially a memoir of trauma and recovery by a woman unschooled in the ways of academic philosophy or psychoanalysis. But, there is no point in assuming that people are less intelligent than they are. If Jentz can feel as well as think as deeply as she does, then hers is a particularly deep voice we are privileged to listen to.

NOTES

1 In addition to the authors cited previously, Akhtar (2002), Frommer (2005), Siassi (2004), and Smith (2008), there is at least one special edition of a psychoanalytic journal devoted to forgiveness (*Psychoanalytic Inquiry* 29 2009, no. 5).

2 Robert's use of quotation marks is puzzling.

3 Unlike Winnicott's story (1986: 133, and Chapter 3) about going to the theater, and each having a different experience of the same play, in many cultural activities such as religion, we are all actors on the same stage. We still have different experiences of the same activity, but since we are not just watching, but doing, the overlap and sense of shared experience may be greater. But perhaps after a certain point of overlap has been achieved, it does not matter.

4 Anyone familiar with the last lines of Camus's *The Stranger* (1988), where Meursault says, "I opened myself to the gentle indifference of the world," knows that Camus's attitude toward the absurdity of the world does not come down to a few lines from *The Myth of Sisyphus*.

5 As the discussion of Wisenthal's *The Sunflower* (1997) revealed, other Christians would, it seems, follow the example of Theodore Hesburgh, who said, "If asked to forgive, by anyone for anything, I would forgive because God would forgive" (164). One hopes that all Christians would remember Dietrich Bonhoeffer's (1963: 47, 54) warnings about cheap grace.

6 Most of the information about Julie Nicholson, and many of the quotations, come from a book written by Nicholson, *A Song for Jenny: A Mother's Story of Love and Loss* (2011). The rest are from a documentary movie, "Forgiveness: Stories for Our Time" (Lunn 2007), in which Nicholson speaks on camera at some length.

7 At the time she learned of the London bombings, Vicar Nicholson (2011, 1–3) was on vacation at her family's home on a small island in Northern Wales. Her bunk bed from her own childhood was where she slept the night before she learned of her daughter's death.

8 Though I originally experienced the testimony of Jentz in the documentary movie, "Forgiveness" (Whitney, 2011a), the book by the same name, *Forgiveness* (2011b), is a virtual transcript of the documentary movie. A few quotations are in the movie that are not in the book, and the book contains extended versions of several quotations from the movie. In addition, Jentz wrote a well-received book of her own about her experience, *Strange Piece of Paradise* (2006). A number of quotations are from this book.

9 Kathy Devlin says that all nurses were taught this in her day, and recognizes this is generally not how nursing is taught or practiced today.

7 Jean Améry: resentment, loneliness, and aging

The most obvious thing to say about the voices of forgiveness is that no one simply forgives or is forgiven according to the standard script. Eva Kor uses forgiveness to seek something else. Whatever it may be, however much we may admire Kor's resilience, she is not granting forgiveness. Katherine Ann Power, alone of all the voices, seeks atonement, using a public ritual, the refusal of parole, for private purposes. Claire Schroeder explicitly refuses to grant Power forgiveness, but displays a good will toward Power that seems at least as valuable. Liesbeth Gerritsen does not seem to truly understand the forgiveness that she is seeking. Vicar Julie Nicholson seems to have entered the place that Winnicott calls transitional space, a place from which she is free to offer forgiveness, and equally free, we discover, to refuse it. Terri Jentz grants forgiveness in a remarkably creative way, creating a community she can implicitly forgive in lieu of the man she cannot.

There is hardly enough evidence here to draw any but the most hypothetical and preliminary conclusions. One suspects, however, that a great deal of forgiveness has this quality. It just doesn't fit the steps laid out by Moses Maimonides, contemporary forgiveness theorists such as Griswold, or anyone else. Human relations and practices are simply more complicated than forgiveness theory.

There is something about Power that is especially impressive. She didn't expect anything in return. I've written about forgiveness as a pas de deux, suggesting this should be understood not so much as a personal relationship as role playing, in which offender and victim play their parts in a drama whose outcome may be forgiveness. One might argue that what Power receives is mental peace or harmony, and evidently she does, but it is not clear that is what she aims at.

She seeks to come to terms with her deed, to make sense of her responsibility, to live with her guilt, not just to be free of her guilt, but to place her guilt in context of all the other guilty parties involved in the Vietnam War. Like Robert McNamara and the generals who prosecuted the war, her hands were bloody too. All could be forgiven, for all were caught up in a moment in history not of their own making, but for Power, this meant not a free pass, but an obligation to suffer publically over an extended period of time.

JEAN AMÉRY

Though the psychoanalytic concepts of Klein and Winnicott organize much of this manuscript's study of trauma and forgiveness, it is Jean Améry's thinking that best reflects the leading themes of this manuscript. Included in the category "Améry's thinking" are those places where he goes wrong. Améry is never more fascinating, or instructive, than when mistaken for the right (that is, an interesting) reason.

Améry's virtues are several. Above all, he is honest and down to earth, reminding us of trauma's overwhelming physical reality. His unrest, he tells us, is not because he is oppressed by some vague metaphysical distress, whether it is called Being, or Nothingness, or God, or the Absence of God. It comes from the numbers on his arm, and his awareness that under certain circumstances it could all happen again (1980: 99–100). Before this reality, every theory pales. At the same time, Améry would not reduce us to our bodies, for he is also the great utopian thinker who would reverse time, holding history at a standstill, so that perpetrator and victim alike might return to a time and place before the offense. Sometimes it is good to wish for the impossible. Améry states that it is this impossible wish that is the foundation of ethics. It is a wish that any ethics of forgiveness must confront, even if it is a wish at once magnificent and perilous.

Améry keeps us honest about one more thing, or at least he comes closer than almost anyone else. Trauma and forgiveness are both about rage, a subject that gets mentioned infrequently when talking about either. Yet, in the end, Améry fails to understand something terribly important about humans: that we live our lives as links in a chain of generations. This does not invalidate his conclusions, but without grasping this about Améry, we will not know how to value him; that is, how to put his conclusions about trauma and forgiveness in context.

In describing a passport picture of herself taken a few years after her assault, Terri Jentz (2006: 476) writes about covering up different parts of the picture until suddenly she could see the rage in her forehead and brows. Why is this rage so difficult to know? Because coming too close to this rage seems to risk self-destruction. Though the sources of Améry's suicide were complex, seeming to have much to do with despair and illness, the lesson learned by many was that he was consumed by his rage. As Cynthia Ozick wrote about Primo Levi's suicide:

> And since "the rage of resentment is somehow linked to self-
> destruction" – as Levi himself had pointed out analyzing the suicide
> of Jean Améry, another writer who survived Auschwitz – his
> [Levi's] final book on the camp should be seen "as the bitterest of
> suicide notes."
>
> (Ozick 1989: 36–37)[1]

My primary source is *At the Mind's Limits: Contemplations by a Survivor on Auschwitz and its Realities*, which, as previously mentioned, was originally titled *Jenseits Von Schuld und Sühne: Bewältigungsversuche eines Überwältigten*. The first part of the title, "Beyond Guilt and Atonement," is easily read as Améry's ironic evocation of Nietzsche. The subtitle presents a problem in translation. The most direct translation would have the subtitle referring to the author himself, *The Attempts of an Overwhelmed Man to Come to Terms*. But the content of the book suggests a second way to read the subtitle as referring to German attempts to overcome or overthrow the Nazi past. I prefer to read it both ways, emphasizing the second.

The title in English, *At the Mind's Limits*, is one of those rare cases where the title of the translation is a better, or at least a more subtle title, capturing the essence of Améry's project. It does not refer to an event that is almost unimaginable, the Holocaust. It refers to the way in which the mind, Améry's mind, could no longer transcend its circumstances. For this is what intellectual life was about for Améry, and perhaps it was even more important for him than most, for he was an autodidact and exile who found in literature a new home. Améry (1980: 7) tells the story about dragging himself back from the I. G. Farben factory in the Auschwitz complex after a grueling day. A flag waving in front of a half-finished building reminded him of a line from a Hölderlin poem. He tried to recite the poem, to somehow let the poem possess him, to enter the world of the poem, if only for a moment, but it didn't work. "The poem no longer transcended reality." This is what *At the Mind's Limit* is about, the ultimate dominance of the material over the spiritual, about how relatively easy it is to crush the spiritual, particularly in men who lack religious or ideological commitments. In the end, the mind is so terribly, frighteningly embodied. Winnicott would agree.

The tacit player in this drama is Primo Levi (1996), whose book, known in its American translation as *Survival in Auschwitz* (and in Britain as *If This is a Man*), was published a couple of years before Améry's. The books have quite a different structure. Levi's is a narrative, Améry's a series of thematically connected essays. However, Levi (1989: 146) agrees with Améry that those with spiritual or ideological armor did best in Auschwitz. Where they differ is on the possibility of transcendence. In a well-known chapter in *Survival in Auschwitz*, Levi spontaneously translates a portion of Dante's *Divine Comedy* into French as he and his friend Jean (Pikolo) tramp through the snow carrying a heavy caldron of thin soup to feed the hungry men they are working with (Levi 1996: 109–115). For Améry, the real truth of the camps is that it made such glorious moments impossible.

RESENTMENT

Améry (1980: 68) writes that "it did not escape me that *ressentiment* is not only an unnatural but also a logically inconsistent condition [*Zustand*]. It nails everyone of us onto the cross of his ruined past." Sometimes called the *Zustand* passage, it reveals *ressentiment* to be a violent occupation of the will and the time sense of the person. The result is to so preoccupy Améry with the wish to undo the past, and the equally impossible wish that his tormentors would wish this as much as he, that there is no exit to the future, a future that Améry calls the "genuine human dimension" (68).

Before continuing, a word needs to be said about the term *ressentiment*, which figures so heavily in Améry's argument. Writing in German, Améry uses the same French term, *ressentiment*, as Nietzsche did. Améry intends us to see the connection. What does not seem to matter is whether one uses the terms resentment or *ressentiment*, *Verstimmung* or *Groll*. The French term possesses no subtle connotations lost when its English or German translations are used. Writing about Nietzsche, Arthur Danto considers some possible distinctions between the French, English, and German terms before concluding that "it may have been one of those expressions that civilized people simply used" (Solomon 1994: 103).[2] Whatever is decided about Améry's use of the term *ressentiment*, and the not-very-subtly implied critique of Nietzsche, does not depend on hidden subtleties of the term itself.

The *Zustand* passage sounds like a definition of trauma. It is, but we need to be careful, for it reveals that the experience of trauma may itself have ethical import. It does, and its import resides in its answer to the question asked by Kai Erikson: "... to what extent does it make sense to conclude that the traumatized view of the world conveys a wisdom that ought to be heard in its own terms?" (Erikson 1995: 198). A key aspect of this wisdom is now apparent: that the twisted sense of time, the inability to be free of time past so characteristic of trauma, is not just a neurological or psychological phenomenon. It is also an ethical demand: "that the irreversible be turned around, that the event be undone" (Améry 1980: 68).

One might simply argue that the demand is absurd, impossible; there is no choice but to move on. But consider what Herbert Marcuse called the *"promesse de Bonheur,"* the promise of utopian happiness, the demand for joy, peace, and contentment, even the freedom from time, all of which become ever-more important even as they seem ever-more impossible. Referring to the images of Orpheus and Narcissus, Marcuse (1962: 162) wrote:

> They have not become the culture-heroes of the Western world: theirs is the image of joy and fulfillment; the voice which does not command but sings; the gesture which offers and receives; the deed which is peace and ends the labor of conquest; the liberation from time which unites man with god, man with nature. Literature has preserved their image. In the *Sonnets to Orpheus*, Rilke writes:
>
> She made herself a bed within my ear
> And slept in me. All things were in her sleep ...
> Within her slept the world. You singing god, o how
> Did you perfect her so she did not long
> To be awake. She rose and slept.
> Where is her death?   *(I,2)*

It is of course ironic that Améry is talking about dystopia, in which the promise of happiness is reversed. But the promise remains: the hopeless hope that one could return to a time before the horror and set it right. Or as Améry (1980: 72) puts it:

> What happened happened. This sentence is just as true as it is hostile to morals and intellect. The moral power to resist contains the protest, the revolt against reality, which is rational only as long as it is moral. The moral person demands annulment of time.

Améry is not writing about some abstract utopia. In this particular context, he is writing about capital punishment of the mass murderer, no matter how much time has passed since his deeds. "Thereby, and through a moral turning-back of the clock, the latter can join his victim as a fellow human being." But Améry is also writing about something more general: how morality must stand against nature; in this case, the "biological healing that time brings about" (72).

A well-known Kantian (1960: 46) maxim about morality states that "ought implies can" (*"sollen impliziert können"*). One should not make ethical demands of people that are impossible to fulfill. An ethical system that assumes that people have the potential to be morally perfect would violate this demand. Entirely aside from whether this dictum about morality deserves to be enshrined as it has, Améry's ethics do not contradict it. Améry is not asking that people reverse time – an impossibility. He is asking that people wish that time could be reversed, and to base their morality on the hypothetical demand that it could be. To ask that offenders and bystanders *wish* as strongly as he that it never happened, that history could be done over, is idealistic but not impossible. Certainly no more impossible than asking that everyone consider what would happen if the principle by which he or she were about to act were to become a universal law (Kant 1993: 30). Whether Améry's is the best ethical system is another question, but do not be misled because Améry's version of the categorical imperative is extraordinary.

For Améry, morality becomes the science of the impossible, as impossible as the utopia that Marcuse is writing about in the context of what he calls the Great Refusal, the refusal to go along with a world ruled by what he calls surplus repression, repression that preserves privilege, not civilization. We should read Améry in this same vein, as a utopian, writing about an impossibility, the reversal of time, in the hope that those living would come to see how the Hell that was made just a generation or two ago lives on in the tortured bodies and minds of survivors, some of whom seem to have made a decision to hold onto the reality of their experience, with all its pain, rather than to offer cheap forgiveness. For most, of course, holding onto the pain is no choice.

Thomas Brudholm (2008: 110) comes close to capturing aspects of Améry's moral ideal when he writes that:

> One can say that to move on is – in fact – possible, but ethically it is "impossible." To undo what has been done is in fact impossible, but wanting to do so saves the ethical possibility – that is, the possibility of relating with moral sensibility to what has been done.

Relating with a moral sensibility in an entirely new way, one might add.

But hasn't Nietzsche shown us that all resentment is bad, the morality of the weak, the last man, one whose soul squints? (Nietzsche, *Gay Science* sec. 276; *Ecce Homo*, sec. 10). Perhaps not. Recall Theodor Adorno's (1974: 97–98) startling assertion that Nietzsche's wish to love his fate, *amor fati*, is little more than "ignominious adaptation" to one's prison. Or as Améry (1980: 68) puts it:

> Thus spake the man who dreamed of the synthesis of the brute with the superman. He must be answered by those who witnessed the union of the brute with the subhuman; they were present when a certain humankind joyously celebrated a festival of cruelty, as Nietzsche himself expressed it.

About cruelty it is best to be deadly serious. If one has difficulty being deadly serious, it helps to keep Irving Greenberg's (1977: 23) statement in mind. "No statement, theological or otherwise, should be made that would not be credible in the presence of burning children." Or more realistically, millions of burning children.

One might argue, with good cause, that whatever Améry means with the term "resentment," he is not writing about the petit bourgeois man cataloguing all the snubs he has received in the course of his daily life, and plotting his little paybacks. We are talking about the proper attitude in the face of horror, such as the torture, torment, and mass murder of millions. Or as Giorgio Agamben (1999: 100) puts it,

"Jean Améry was thus led to formulate a genuine anti-Nietzschean ethics of resentment that simply refuses to accept that 'what happened, happened.'"

In fact, Nietzsche's concept of resentment needs to be examined more carefully before reaching this conclusion, for, with the concept, Nietzsche was referring to more than the bile of the bourgeois. First, however, a more basic reckoning with Nietzsche is needed. Améry goes too far in suggesting that Nietzsche provided intellectual support for Nazi cruelty. For that is precisely what Améry believed, at least in his earliest postwar works.[3] Since Walter Kaufmann (1975) first wrote about and translated Nietzsche into English after the War, the interpretation of Nietzsche as inspiration for the Führerstadt has been shown to be a sham. Nevertheless, one cannot lightly dismiss Thomas Mann's (1970) comment in 1947 about "how bound in time, how theoretical too, how inexperienced does Nietzsche's romanticizing about wickedness appear today! We have learned to know it in all its miserableness." Mann's comment is particularly significant since before the war, Mann wrote about Nietzsche in terms both respectful and admiring. About Mann's 1947 comment, Philippa Foot (1994: 7) asks simply, wasn't he "right in saying that Nietzsche had not faced the reality of evil?"

World War I, World War II, the Holocaust, Hiroshima – the century of atrocity had not yet begun when Nietzsche went insane, even if its outlines were visible in German militarism and nationalism, which Nietzsche held in contempt. Nietzsche plays with cruelty and evil in a way that is simply no longer tolerable, even if today it is not intellectually fashionable to call Nietzsche out on this topic. Nevertheless, one must also say that, for the most part, Nietzsche was clear that the superior man sublimates his cruelty, directing it toward himself, making himself hard and strong. Cruelty may also be sublimated through the *agon*, the contest with an opponent of equal worth. Always a theorist of the self as composed of a multiplicity of selves, a society of selves, Nietzsche saw cruelty as best deployed against the weak-willed self in oneself. It is not the superior man, but the last man, who feels powerful only when he has given himself up to the hatreds of the dominant group (*Beyond Good and Evil*, first essay).

While Améry has much of value to say about resentment, do not be mislead by his anti-Nietzschean project. Améry's contribution has little to do with Nietzsche, and much to do with his rejection of time. Nietzsche too rejected time. The difference is that while the eternal return imagines that the events of one's life repeat themselves over and over, Améry imagines that we might return to a time before the Holocaust and set things right, do history over.

Nietzsche wished that everything – above all, one's worst moments – return again and again exactly as before, all in order to prove the strength of one's will (*Gay Science*, sec. 341). Clever as Adorno's riposte was, is not the eternal return truly the nightmare that defines trauma, one in which one cannot escape the dread from which one longs to be free? Only Nietzsche would idealize that nightmare and call it "will." Améry, on the other hand, would go back in time to set things right. More precisely put, Améry holds that to act as though one wished this above all else is the only ethical stance. But perhaps their views on time have more in common than first appear.

SOURCES AND CONSEQUENCES OF RESENTMENT

The sources of resentment for Améry are not entirely clear. Sometimes Améry writes as if his resentment began only a couple of years after the war, when he became aware that the Germans were trying to overcome their past by ignoring it, forgiving themselves, and moving on, looking only to the future. His resentment, a clinging to the insults and injuries of the past (more precisely put, the atrocity that was the recent past), was a protest against a new Germany that acted as if the Holocaust did not happen, or it happened a long time ago, and it was time to move on. Germans called this *Vergangenheitsbewälti-gung*, an overcoming of the past, though the connotation is stronger, as in forcefully overcoming or overthrowing the past (Améry 1980: 66–67). This does not seem an entirely adequate explanation of the sources of Améry's resentment, and yet one hesitates to go along with Brudholm's (2008: 98–100) psychological explanation that Améry's resentment is so strong because as a prisoner he could not express his anger and outrage, or feel his horror. Resentment is the result of rage and horror that were repressed in the name of survival at the time they were originally experienced.

This could be true, but it seems unnecessary to explain Améry's resentment. About his experience, Améry (1980: 34) wrote that the survivor of torture can no longer feel at home in the world. "Whoever was tortured, stays tortured. Torture is ineradicably burned into him, even when no clinically objective traces can be detected." One result is a strange and totally undeserved shame at being so weak, exposed, and vulnerable. Another is a loss of trust in humanity that can never be regained, such as the knowledge that the lovely lady next door who greets you every morning would likely turn her head and look away as you are led off to the concentration camp. Undeniable is the knowledge that you live in a world inhabited by fellow men, some of whom are really "antimen," torturers and tormenters who would cause you endless pain before going home to dinner with their families. As for the rest of those among whom you live, hardly a one would lift a finger were you to be hauled away again tomorrow. There are exceptions, and Améry names some of them, but he does not draw the line between the SS and the rest, or Nazis and the rest. It is the vast majority of Germans, and French, including neighbors and clerks, versus the very few (Améry 1980: 40, 72–76, 94–96).

To know this now about the world, the world as it was then – and that under certain unique but hardly unimaginable conditions, the world as it could become again – is to live in a different world forever. It is "knowledge as disaster," as Blanchot (1995: ix) puts it. One consequence of having become wise through knowledge as disaster may be to become *aidos*, that marvellous ancient Greek word meaning blessed and cursed at the same time. There are, however, certain experiences that so exceed the normal, experiences by virtue of which the victim does not become *aidos*, but *oulomenos*; that is, simply cursed with knowledge. As Améry puts it:

> Trust in the world includes all sorts of things ... the certainty
> that by reason of written or unwritten social contracts the other
> person will spare me – more precisely stated, that he will respect
> my physical, and with it also my metaphysical being. The
> boundaries of my body are also the boundaries of my self. My
> skin surface shields me against the external world. If I am to
> have trust, I must feel on it only what I want to feel. At the first
> blow, however, this trust in the world breaks down ... The other
> person ... forces his own corporeality on me with the first blow.
> He is on me and thereby destroys me. It is like a rape.
>
> (Améry 1980: 28)

Améry certainly writes about his torture as though it were a rape, a violation of the intimate boundaries of his own person. Contained within this violation is a terrible knowledge from which he will never be free, a knowledge that will undermine his ability to naively trust in the world as he once did.

One might argue that this account of Améry's resentment is not so different from Brudholm's psychological interpretation: then he couldn't express his anger, outrage, and horror; now he can. As far as whether Brudholm's is a valid psychological interpretation, the question is not whether Améry could *express* his anger, outrage, and horror, but whether he could *know* them. He was in no position to write a contemporaneous diary, and so we look to his writings for evidence. Later writings are not the best evidence of earlier psychological states. Nevertheless, I know of no other essayist (certainly not Primo Levi) who writes with a harder edge about the reality of the Holocaust, particularly his experience as victim of torture, an experience he recounts in excruciating detail. "Torture is the most horrible event a human being can retain within himself" (Améry 1980: 22). One might ask if there were not some way to share this experience. Améry answers that the only way to share the experience would be to inflict it on another, to in effect become a torturer, and that is a moral impossibility (33). If Améry is correct, the problem is not his repressed outrage and horror, but the nature of torture itself – that the experience cannot be shared but must be contained within one's body and soul forever. Even projective identification, the psychological projection of the experience into another in order to share it, would be evil. This Améry seems to believe, even if some people would, in fact, be able to psychologically share the experience without being overwhelmed, for this is what good therapists, and occasionally friends and lovers, do.

Améry's postwar resentment makes a claim about reality, about the tenuousness of the civilized bond, that one can only truly know from the other side, when the bond has been broken, and one is among the victims. His is a truth claim. Améry's everlasting resentment is how he lives with this truth, protesting against it, much as Job protested his innocence against the Lord (Job 9–10). Only this time, there was no Lord of the Whirlwind appearing to Améry to explain that on God's timetable, the timetable of eternity, it all makes sense (Job 38–42.6). And so all Améry could do was hold onto his resentment, his protest in the name of life in the face of horror.

If Améry could respond, he would argue that the term "trauma" is at once too abstract and too clinical. All he is doing is responding to reality in a world in which the bond of civilization can no longer be counted on.

> I ... am not "traumatized," but rather my spiritual and psychic condition corresponds completely to reality. The consciousness of my being a Holocaust Jew is not an ideology. It may be compared to the class consciousness that Marx tried to reveal to the proletarians of the nineteenth century.
>
> *(Améry 1980: 99)*

Améry (1980) considers survivors who do not pursue retribution the true conformists; they lack the Holocaust equivalent of class-consciousness. Consider, he says, the man who willingly "submerges his individuality in society and is able to comprehend himself only as a function of the social ... He calmly allows what happened to remain what it was." Implicitly, at least, he forgives, for he does not demand recompense. He appears normal. "His time-sense is not dis-ordered, that is to say, it has not moved out of the biological and social sphere into the moral sphere. As a deindividualized, interchangeable part of the social mechanism, he lives with it consentingly" (71). In effect, he treats the Germans as children. Punishing the child long after his misdeed is senseless, for the child cannot make the connection between distant deed and punishment. But are the citizens of Germany really children, or is it just easier to act as though they are, and so avoid the responsibility of resentment?

Any reader familiar with Nietzsche will immediately say to him or herself that here is where the resentment that Améry writes about truly resides, with the man who does not pursue recompense. The resentment with which Nietzsche is concerned is a story of people who are unhappy, who wish to improve their lot, but can't, and so "invent a story according to which they are really well off" (Bittner 1994: 130). Is this not the story of the man or woman who forgives too easily, as though to say, "My soul was not really destroyed. I'm still a productive member of society. Look at me, I flourish almost as much as those who tormented me." Though Nietzsche plays with cruelty and evil in ways that are, let us say, adolescent, his teachings on resentment apply almost perfectly to those whom Améry would *also* spurn: the man or woman afraid to stand out from the crowd, the man or woman who finds comforting anonymity in forgiveness or its simulacrum, acceptance, as though one did not have to take the past as seriously as all that. If one takes the lesson of Nietzsche's eternal return as meaning that every moment in the past matters infinitely (for it will repeat itself infinitely), then the past that Améry seeks to rescind and Nietzsche's eternal return both share an appreciation for the everlasting importance of every past deed.

TO BE HATED: RESENTMENT AND RECONCILIATION

Jean Améry, it seems, would hold onto his resentment forever. He could never see the world as good, not even good enough. Given the torture and torment to which he was subjected, this is understandable. Indeed, perhaps the simplest and most important thing Améry has to teach is the experience of what it is to live daily with those who would annihilate one's being.

All trauma is not, of course, the result of the will to annihilation. The drunk driver who smashes into my car and kills my child is not acting out of hatred. Or at least not out of a particular hatred of me and my kind. The antiman, as Améry calls him, embodies hatred, for he wishes to annihilate Améry and his kind. To live with this knowledge, not only for the duration of the war, but forever, is knowledge as disaster of a particular sort: that there are humans on this planet who only appear human; in fact, they are antihuman, the enemies of life. This is what Améry means when he argues that torture was the essence of National Socialism.

> Torture becomes the total inversion of the social world, in which we can live only if we grant our fellow man life, ease his suffering, bridle the desire of our ego to expand. But in the world of torture man exists only by ruining the other person who stands before him.
>
> *(1980: 35)*

For the Nazis, sovereignty required the physical expansion of so-called Aryan man into everyman, beginning with the ruination of Jews, Romani, and others. For the antiman to exist as he will, you may not exist at all. But first you must be made to suffer so much that you do not care to exist.

It is hard to imagine worse, unless worse is living with this knowledge. Nevertheless, if one reads the essay on "Resentments" in *At the Mind's Limits* closely, it becomes apparent that Améry too seeks a type of reconciliation with his tormentors (1980: 62–81). What, he implicitly asks, would lead him to abandon his resentment? If his tormentors, as well as those Germans who came after, wished as much as he that which is impossible: that the Holocaust and all that went with it never happened, that time could be erased, that the past could be unmade, remade, done over. If what were impossible were to be wished as deeply by offenders and bystanders, then there would be no need for resentment (1980: 78).

In Améry's history of victims and executioners, there is a moment in which a tiny utopian crack opens, and the light of reparation comes through. It is a light of an impossible wholeness. Not just because time can never be erased, but because even when they both deeply regret the past, victims and offenders can never see the world, and want the same thing in the same way. Still, it is intriguing that even in the midst of Améry's dark vision there is a glimpse of utopian wholeness, evocative of Walter Benjamin's angel of history who "would like to stay, awaken the dead, and make whole what has been smashed," only to be swept up in the violent storm of progress.[4] The moment does not last. Améry's essay and his book closes in darkness, in which he fears that Hitler's Reich will come to be regarded as no better or worse than any other historical epoch, a little bloodier perhaps, but that's all.[5] Nonetheless, the fleeting utopian moment speaks to the strength of the ideals of wholeness and reparation that remain in *At the Mind's Limits*. A strength that make Améry's *On Aging* (1994), published only a couple of years later, especially discouraging.

Améry's resentment is a measure of his longing for a relationship with his tormentors and their successors, including those who want to overcome the past (*Vergangenheitsbewältigung*). Améry wants not permanent and unrelenting resentment, but that the perpetrators and those who stood by doing nothing wish as strongly as he that it had never happened. If this were so, then the objective ground of resentment would have disappeared. At one point, Améry imagines that this would be most likely to happen when the antiman finally stood before the firing squad.

> When SS-man Wajs stood before the firing squad, he experienced the moral truth of his crimes. At that moment, he was with

me – and I was no longer alone . . . I would like to believe that at the instant of his execution he wanted exactly as much as I to turn back time, to undo what had been done. When they led him to the place of execution, the antiman had once again become a fellow man.

(Améry 1980: 70, author's emphasis)

Like romantics of old, Améry seeks union in death. Unfortunately, there is no reunion to be had there either. Of course the SS man wishes to turn back time, to undo the past. At the moment of his execution, he probably wishes it as strongly as Améry. But he wishes it for his own selfish reasons: not because he sees the wrongness of his deeds (or at least there is no reason to think so), but because the SS man does not want to die the death he has inflicted so many times on others. If Améry thinks this creates the possibility of some reunion between them, so be it, but it is a reunion of the lowest common denominator, between animals who wish to live. Torture reduces its victims to this status, the status of squealing animals, as Améry puts it, but this is hardly the plane on which to seek reunion.

In fact, torture, including the torture that was the concentration camps, does more than reduce a man or woman to a squealing animal. It isolates its victim forever. "The experience of persecution was, at the very bottom, that of an extreme *loneliness*. At stake for me is the release from the abandonment that has persisted from that time until today" (Améry 1980, 70, author's emphasis). Consider Améry's utopian dream, that he and his persecutors could be reunited, whether in life or death (for some such as Wajs, it could only be death), as long as they wish as strongly as he that history be rerun, that the past be done over. This fantasy is familiar from our study of forgiveness, for it is a fantasy of fusion, of the reunion of lost souls, satisfying what Griswold (2007: 193) refers to as the "soul's deepest yearnings," by which he means "deep reunion, love, and harmony."

Ultimately, Améry realizes that a reunion among humans can never happen. *At the Mind's Limits* ends in a tone of deep resignation. Unable to persuade the world to help him force yesterday's murderers "to recognize the moral truth of their crimes," Améry is "alone, as I was when they tortured me" (Améry 1980: 95–96). One might argue that Améry is hopeless, but that is not quite correct. Resentment – the animating spirit of *At the Mind's Limits*, is subtended by a quest for attachment and understanding in the face of loneliness. Resentment, the dream that time could be reversed so that it would no longer be necessary to live in a world of antimen, their apologists, and successors – makes no sense except as hope that men and women could one day live together in a world worthy of human beings.

Edith P. (T-107), an articulate and thoughtful survivor, struggled with how to confront the Germans. Unlike Améry, hers was primarily a mental and emotional exercise. She lives in the United States and has little to do with actual Germans. She was trying to come to terms with how to think about them, particularly her tormentors.

> As I get older my children are no longer at home. There isn't even a [parents'] grave to go cry to. I have given a great deal of thought to how to conduct myself with Germans. I don't hate Germans. I feel I would waste a lot of time. But sometimes I wish in my darkest hours they would feel what we feel when uprooted ... when there is nobody to share your sorrow or your greatest happiness.

Edith wanted, I believe, that her tormentors understand her suffering as she understood it, and the only way that could happen is if they felt the same thing, for hers was a suffering beyond words.

This is what Améry meant when he said he couldn't explain the experience of torture without inflicting it on others, which would be immoral. This is what Améry wanted when SS-man Wajs faced the firing squad. Both Améry and Edith allowed themselves to imagine that they could inflict upon their tormentors what they themselves felt, a punishing explanatory fusion that lessened their loneliness via bodily (ex)communication. *Lex talionis* as communion.

Yet, Edith is different. Edith has not just the comfort of her family (her "native American" husband, by which she means native born), her three daughters, her grandchildren, but perhaps even more important, the pain of losing her parents, a pain that she holds dear, as the only way of holding onto them. This is the same way Anita Epstein, the woman who writes about Eva Kor, holds onto her parents. These categories do not enter into Améry's thought. So what is an important, recurring but nonetheless secondary theme in Edith's life, a desire for communication with her tormentors that is at the same time a desire to inflict her suffering on them, became central to Améry.

This does not make Améry wrong. We (but not he) are fortunate in what his life lacked, for it rendered his intellectual focus intense. For Améry, resentment remained forgiveness that has not yet found a worthy object, for its standards are impossibly high. The term "impossibly high" is not a criticism. Utopian ideals often help us better understand what we can, can't, and shouldn't demand of each other in the real world.

Though Améry sometimes writes as if he is only concerned with the generation that perpetrated and suffered the Holocaust, generally he assumes that subsequent generations of Germans inherited their parents' history, if not their guilt. This includes an inherited responsibility for the deeds of previous generations (1980: 76). The question is not so much how far such responsibility goes, for it goes some way, but whether it even makes sense to ask of subsequent generations of Germans that they wish it had never happened with the same fervor as ... whom, the children and grandchildren of survivors? It seems as if the morality of resentment, understood as a refusal to accept the past, coupled with the hope that one's persecutors do so with the same fervor, is confined to a single generation. Indeed, there is very little in Améry that connects the generations.

ON AGING

Améry's On Aging (1994) would seem to be about another topic. In fact, it illuminates his perspective on trauma and history. Both books were published within a couple of years of each other.[6] Perhaps Améry's (1994: 116) most puzzling comment is that he found the terror of his experience at Auschwitz more bearable, less filled with the horror and anguish than the experience of aging. In Auschwitz, clambering over dead bodies, hearing people shot, "I was spared from fear." But now, old and tired:

> fear is with me, a deaf feeling that never makes me tremble, just an extremely persistent one, which in a slow kind of way becomes part of my person, so much so that I can no longer say that I *have* any fear. Instead, I say that I *am* fear.
>
> *(1994: 117)*

Add to this that *On Aging* contains not one word about the experience of torture that Améry underwent as a member of the resistance before being sent to a series of concentration camps, and one wonders what has happened. For it is the experience of torture that is the central horror of *At the Mind's Limits*.

The simplest thing to say about *On Aging* is that for Améry, his body itself became a death camp. More generally, while an ethically based revolt and resistance against any forgiveness and moving on from the Nazi horror makes sense, this same revolt and resistance directed at death itself (for that is the theme of *On Aging*) makes no sense. "Since the contradiction of death overshadowing our entire life makes all logic – which is surely always the logic of life – and all positive thinking invalid, ideas of death have to take their shape in opposition to logic" (Améry 1994: 115). What made sense in *At the Mind's Limit* as an ethical refusal to accept reality no longer makes sense as an ontological refusal to accept reality; not death, but an individual's death before his or her time, a death inflicted by hate, or by carelessness, selfish inequality, lack of imagination and empathy: a death from any of these sources contradicts life. But not a death that comes in its own time, in its own way. That is life.

It is difficult to make sense of what happened to Améry, and perhaps it is unnecessary to know. *At the Mind's Limit* makes a valid claim for an ethical refusal to accept the reality of time: time passing, time healing, time leading to what passes for forgetting. *On Aging* is notable for the way it is frozen in static time. This is particularly apparent when one notices the complete absence of generations. *On Aging* is populated by single bodies. There are no children, no families, no marriages, no legacies, no patrimonies, nothing that connects this generation with subsequent (or previous) generations. Death is entropy of the individual body, but without death, the world would be trapped in a downward spiral of entropy, as there would be no place for anyone or anything new. Out of death, a natural death, death in its own time, comes life.

Even Auschwitz loses something of its salience for the relatives of survivors, as well as the rest of us, as one generation succeeds another. In some ways this is bad, which is why history of the horror must always be taught. But this too is the way in which the world renews itself.

One must imagine that the terrible trauma suffered by Améry, trauma that he was able to fight in the form of an ethical refusal to accept reality, came back to haunt him as he became aware of his loss of vital powers, the death that he could see coming toward him (but still years away; he would not die until ten years after the publication of *On Aging*, and then by his own hand). This return of the trauma of Auschwitz to take its revenge on the aging body has by now almost become a theme of Holocaust literature, Primo Levi and Jean Améry its leading lights. Sociological research supports this observation (Botwinick 2000),[7] as does my own research in the Fortunoff Video Archive. Abe L. (T-1394) puts it this way:

> I thought that when the years go by, the Holocaust would go further away ... I dream about it. I can't get something like that out of my system. All gone now, especially the children. You can't get that out of your mind. The hole in your heart gets bigger. The Holocaust is getting closer not farther.

It is by no means obvious why this occurs, though many survivors refer to the increasing power of Holocaust memories in their later years (Fred E., T-664; Sara F., T-3022; Simon R., T-987; Edith

P., 107, 974) Robert Kraft (2002) studied the testimony of 125 survivors, concluding that memories of extreme trauma don't change, whereas most memories do. The result is that the context of the traumatic memory changes, as aging survivors lack the distractions of rebuilding a life, raising children, and so forth. As Kraft puts it, "The power of distraction is most evident when it diminishes ... a fading happier childhood, a decrease in worldly distraction, and the constant, laser clarity of the remembered horror combine to worsen the torment of traumatic memory" (43–45). Eva L. (T-71) puts it more simply when she says, "When I was younger it was easier. I was busier." To this I would add diminishing physical powers, increasing dependency, closeness to death and annihilation – all this intensifies the original trauma, which evoked similar experiences, albeit at the hand of man, not nature.

Whether this conclusion applies to traumas less overwhelming than the Holocaust is unclear, but it is a sobering reminder, in this case of how easily Améry's ethics of resentment can become a terror of death. One might speculate that Améry's ethics of resentment was always a defense against the terror of death, but doing so is unnecessary. Améry's ethics of resentment is justified on its own ethical grounds; grounds that fail – or rather, make no sense – when transformed into resentment against a natural death. The ethics of resentment become the ontology of resentment only at the cost of a denial of the legitimate claims of life, which include a natural death.

Consider Edith M. (T-4298), who brought with her seven worn black and white photos, which she holds quietly in her lap until the very end of a fairly long (over two hours) interview. Finally, in what seems to be a ceremonial moment arranged beforehand with the interviewer, she calls the roll of the dead, simply stating for the camera who each person in each photo is. The camera lingers on each photo for a long moment.

Her father, a handsome man with fedora and pipe, who perished (her term) while in the resistance in Bucharest.

Her mother, who perished at Auschwitz.

Her sister, who perished in the ghetto.

Two aunts who survived, along with their husbands and children,
    pictured with them, all of whom perished in concentration camps.

Joseph, a first cousin, who perished in a concentration camp.

Her mother's brother, who perished in a concentration camp.

Several cousins and their spouses, who all perished in concentration
    camps.

Her life seems one of unremitting loss. And yet the interview
that leads up to this recitation renders this conclusion more complex,
for it is the same Edith M. who at the time of the interview (2004)
had recently retired from her job in New York City and built a house
on her younger daughter's property. Her elder daughter lives eight
houses away, close enough so they can all walk to see each other
on Shabbos, the Jewish Sabbath. Born in a *shtetl* whose Jewish population was destroyed, Edith will (if she is reasonably fortunate)
die surrounded by her children and half a dozen grandchildren in a
Jewish community where all live within walking distance, about
as close to life in the shtetl as one is likely to find in the twenty-
first century in the suburbs of Atlanta, Georgia, a major city in the
American South.

Edith is unusual, but it is common to hear survivors say that
their children and grandchildren are their greatest satisfaction. For
many, this claim takes on added poignancy when one learns that they
are often referring to second families, the first having all been
murdered in the Holocaust. I often felt awkward hearing survivors,
predominantly men, refer to their families as their "revenge" against
Hitler and his minions, a not-uncommon sentiment. In context, it
makes sense.

Survivors understand that the Nazis were not out to murder
them as individuals. The Nazis were out to exterminate the Jewish
people. To survive long enough to bring children into the world, to see
them raised in the practice of the faith, to marry other Jews, and bring

yet another generation into the world – what affirms the continuity of life more than this; not just individual life, but the life of the Jewish people? It is (at least from my perspective as an outsider) not merely the fact that the Jewish individual is a member of the Jewish people, but that he or she understands him or her self as a member of a community in time that brings meaning to life, and to death. For then one is not merely a social atom fleeting through time and space.

Can the reader imagine surviving Hitler's mad dream to die as an old man or woman after having brought forth new generations? Would one not feel that one had achieved a small victory over the senselessness of death? Not, of course, against the senselessness of the ontological death that faces us all, but the death that would come too soon, inflicted by those humans Améry calls "antimen." I conducted few interviews myself. One was with an old and dying man who had survived Auschwitz-Birkenau. Having lived a remarkably adventurous life, surviving by dint of boldness and resourcefulness time and again, he said simply, "I know there is no way out of this corner, but I have held my grandchildren ..."[8] I was puzzled by his statement at the time, at its apparent lack of context, but after having viewed almost 200 videotaped testimonies, its context is now clear.

Améry's problem isn't that he didn't marry and have lots of children. Many survivors didn't. Many couples remained childless. Améry's problem is that the category of children, generations, and patrimony play no role in his thinking about aging and death. The equation by which he lived and died has too few elements: the individual = death. "The ontic density of my existence gets thin and the fear of dying fills up the empty space as pure negativity" (117). No wonder he was terrified. Who could face death so all alone? Many survivors do, of course. Most poignant of all, perhaps, are those survivors who speak of never feeling more alone then when surrounded by family (Eva L., T-71). There is something about the horror of the experience of the Holocaust that never goes away.

DOUBLING AND WRITING

One might imagine that writing about the Holocaust – indeed, writing about old age, writing about virtually anything that terrifies us – would be therapeutic, or cathartic. At least these are terms in common use to refer to the benefits of writing about such terrible experiences. My hypothesis, which is hardly proven by two cases, is that it doesn't work that way at all; quite the opposite is the case. Consider how most survivors cope. They cope by doubling, as discussed in Chapter 2. The trouble with writing so much about trauma is that it interferes with doubling. Writing isn't cathartic. The *katharsis* about which Aristotle famously wrote (*Poetics*, c. 6) concerns the experience of *watching* a Greek tragedy, not suffering an atrocity and writing about it over the next few decades. The novelist Philip Roth (an author who interviewed Primo Levi, and later became his friend) has a character in a recent novel say:

> When Primo Levi killed himself everyone said it was because of his having been an inmate at Auschwitz. I thought it was because of his writing about Auschwitz, the labor of his last book [*The Drowned and the Saved*], contemplating the horror with all that clarity. Getting up every morning to write that book would have killed anyone.
>
> *(Roth 2007: 151)*

Surely it is not so simple. Many survivors write about their experiences. Some presumably find catharsis in doing so. But for Levi and Améry, the Holocaust became a life's work. Each struggled mightily to come to terms with the experience. Levi struggled for intellectual clarity: clarity of expression, of description, of understanding. Only the last eluded him. Améry struggled for moral clarity: how to be true to his experience of torture and torment, and yet find some way to imagine the conditions of genuine forgiveness. He found them in the denial of time; above all, the refusal to let time heal his wounds, any wounds. He found these conditions in the refusal to let time, ethical time, move forward from where it had stopped in Hell. Whatever else one may think of such a strategy, it is a full-time occupation, not one to encourage doubling. On the contrary, it leaves its practitioner daily confronted with an experience that cannot be mastered; indeed, can hardly be lived with, except by living beside it. This, his art, his philosophy, would not allow, though one should not imagine that he lived the life of a hermit or a saint.

According to his biographer, Améry married a woman who truly loved him. He had affairs, traveled (generally to speak about the Holocaust, frequently on the radio), but, again, he seems never to have encountered a child (Heidelberger-Leonard 2010). Though I have not speculated about the source of the absence of generations in Améry's work, Heidelberger-Leonard does, going back to an early unpublished novel, *Die Schiffbrüchigen* [*The Shipwreck*], where Améry has the female protagonist recoil in disgust at her pregnancy. Generalizing perhaps a little too freely, his biographer says that "irrespective of his experience of Auschwitz, the idea of procreating was appalling: the mere thought of a pregnant woman disgusted him" (38). Be that as it may, one can readily see how making a career of the Holocaust (a characterization Améry would have likely detested), while a public service, would interfere with the doubling that allows life to continue for so many Holocaust survivors. The absence of children, his own or others, in Améry's work, and with it the absence of generations, may have intensified his isolation.

AND WHAT NOW?

It would be easy to say that relationship between *At the Mind's Limit* and *On Aging* is one in which Améry creates a misleading parallel structure between the ethics of resentment and aging. Since there is no logical relationship between the two, the argumentative flaws in *On Aging* do not and should not affect the ethical argument in *At The Mind's Limit*. While there is some value in separating the works in this way, the relationship is more complex. Améry's claim that survivors must preserve their resentment until the Germans long for the annulment of time as strongly as do thoughtful survivors is a valid ethical stance, a stance that refuses to let history heal old wounds. However mistaken Améry is about applying that same attitude toward aging, his ethics of resentful refusal have their own merit.

Trouble is, the merit of resentful refusal is limited to a single generation. The ethics of the annulment of time provide no guidance for subsequent generations in dealing with Germans, collaborators, and bystanders. This becomes more true every day. The resentment to which Améry refers can make no sense, or at least nothing like the original sense, when applied to the children of survivors, let alone their age cohort, which includes the children of perpetrators, the rest of us, and subsequent generations. Indeed, it hardly makes sense when applied to anyone but a survivor. To be sure, one can draw some general guidelines – such as, don't forget history, don't forgive too easily or too readily – but there is nothing special or particular about Améry's approach in this regard.

Améry's ethics of resentful refusal fails to offer any guidance for subsequent generations because he doesn't seem to believe in subsequent generations. He doesn't deny them, or disbelieve in them. Subsequent generations rarely enter into his calculations. Even as he expresses concern about younger Germans, he cannot demand of them what he plausibly demands of the generation that committed, collaborated, or tolerated mass murder. If subsequent generations cannot be held responsible in the same way, surely it cannot be expected that they wish to undo the past with the same fervor as the Holocaust's victims. This is what the succession of generations means.

Sadly, Améry did not live to see many members of still-younger generations demand a reckoning with the Holocaust. Many younger Germans were extraordinarily responsive to Daniel Goldhagen's *Hitler's Willing Executioners: Ordinary Germans and the Holocaust* (1996). The book appeared in 1996, at just that point when a new generation of Germans seemed finally ready to take on the subject in the face of their elders' reticence. Jürgen Habermas' defense of

Goldhagen against an older generation of German historians is a particularly fascinating moment in that encounter.[9]

Améry's *On Aging* is a brave confrontation with death. *At the Mind's Limits* is a brave refusal to forgive and forget, or so it might seem in the lands of liberalism triumphant, no longer confined to the West. However, when one recalls that the mark of the Holocaust is that it was not directed at individuals, but a *genos* (an ethnic group *is* an extended kinship group), and that aging only makes sense in terms of the succession of generations, then one realizes that the central flaw in both books is the same. Améry does not see that if the Holocaust was a crime against generations (indeed, the very existence of generations), then the death that is the result of natural aging is proper and necessary so that the generations continue. To resist the genocides of yesterday and today, it is necessary to continually assert the power of life over death. This is not the same thing as locating all value in the individual.

THE FUTURE OF MELANCHOLY

Although Améry's argument is flawed, it is not without its virtues, particularly when compared with certain postmodern tropes or tendencies in the study of melancholy. Améry is melancholic, almost by definition, or so I will argue. What makes Améry's melancholy unique is his demand that others feel it with him. Indeed, this is what he means by resentment, or rather, what the resolution of resentment would look like: that Germans and their conspirators feel the same melancholy that he feels. This would be at some remove from the ordinary definition of melancholy, which makes of frozen grief an affair so private it is unknown even to the conscious self.

In *The Ego and the Id*, Freud (1923) wrote that the ego seems to be formed by a process identical to that of the melancholic loss of an object, in which the lost object is set up inside "the ego, as it [also] occurs in melancholia." What changed from "Mourning and Melancholia" (1917) to "The Ego and the Id" was Freud's recognition that the process by which the ego comes to terms with loss in melancholia is the process by which the ego comes to terms with all loss in virtually all circumstances: by internalizing the lost object. What was once seen strictly as an illness, melancholy understood as a grief that could not be worked through became the way we all learn to live with life and loss. Identification with the object, the lost person, is not how we keep the object; it is how we let the object go, probably the only way.

> We did not appreciate the full significance of this process and did not know how common and how typical it is ... When a person has to give up an object, it may be that this identification is the sole condition under which the id can give up its objects ... it makes it possible to suppose that the character of the ego is a precipitate of abandoned object-cathexes and that it contains the history of those object choices.
>
> (Freud 1923: 28–29)[10]

With the term "character of the ego" – the sedimentation of objects loved and lost – Freud refers to the unique pattern by which each individual organizes his or her identifications. It is these identifications that make up the character of the person, the closest Freud ever comes to characterizing the self as distinct from the ego.

It is this insight that sets the path taken by the psychoanalytic theory that has come to be known, in all its variations, as object relations theory. We identify with others in order to let them go, and grief over this loss is the central experience in emotional development. Melanie Klein (1940) is the theorist who began this development, but it has gone off in a dozen different directions. Post-Freudians are fond of this turn in Freudian theory, for it connects the ego more directly to its objects. For the risk was always that the object was merely "soldered" to the instinct (Phillips 1997: 152).

Identification makes the ego moral. Rather than simply using objects to satisfy its desire, the ego becomes so attached to its objects that their precipitate (the idea the ego has of them after they are no longer present) is constitutive of the ego. Without such identifications, the ego would be bereft. With this turn, the ego becomes genuinely loving and moral, committed to those it desires. Indeed, in some deep sense, the ego is made up of those it desires, particularly those it has loved and lost. As Adam Phillips (1997: 153) puts it, "Partly through the work of Klein, mourning has provided the foundation for development, in most versions of psychoanalysis." About this development, he is ambivalent, lest it downplay the rage at the object that we have lost. For in the unconscious, loss is experienced as abandonment.

In melancholy, the rage is intense, and the psyche is divided against itself, the ego identifying with the object. The superego is left with the ego's disowned rage at the object that has departed, now directed at the ego. This split characterizes ordinary identification and loss as well. What marks melancholy is the intensity of the rage, so much so that the ego is diminished rather than enhanced by its identification with an object under such intense assault. It is in this sense that Freud (1917: 249) is best understood when he writes that in melancholy, the "shadow of the object falls upon the ego." In melancholy, rage against the abandoning object diminishes the ego.

AMÉRY AND MELANCHOLY

Jean Améry was an advocate of melancholy. Though he never used the term, the sense he intended came close to Freud's (1917: 248) understanding of melancholy as revolt against loss. Only in Améry's case, he demanded that his melancholy be shared. The shadow of the Holocaust had fallen upon an entire nation. Neither Améry nor the German nation would be free until the citizens of Germany (and their collaborators) judged themselves by the standards of what they have caused to be lost. As in melancholy, the citizens of Germany must think of themselves as both the lost object as well as the cause of its destruction.

Resentment is not the same as the revolt that Freud wrote of, but it is similar in that it turns the self from the world to the losses of the past. Améry would explicitly transform resentment into an ethic that is not only devoted to the past, but demands, as discussed, "the annulment of time." About melancholic time, Judith Butler (1997: 182) writes:

> the melancholic seeks not only to reverse time, reinstating the imaginary past as the present, but to occupy every position [self, object, and in Améry's case German], and thereby to preclude the loss of the addressee ... Vainly the melancholic now says what he or she would have said, addressed only to himself, as one who is already split off from himself, but whose power of self-address depends upon this self-forfeiture.

Améry was unlike the usual melancholic, for he made his loss known.[11] Améry addresses others; he made of his loss a public demand. The self-denigration of the melancholic, brought on by abandonment, is turned outward, where it properly belongs: on the Germans who caused his loss. From this will to inflict his melancholy on others, Améry created a new morality, a new categorical imperative.

In demanding melancholy of the Germans, one sees the rage behind melancholy – and why not? It is what kept Améry alive, turning the otherwise "merciless violence of conscience" (Freud 1923: 53) holding sway in the superego outward. If the Germans too were melancholic, then they would share Améry's melancholy, and he would not be so terribly alone. Améry himself suggests this line of reasoning, but first a point of clarification. From a strictly theoretical perspective (the theory of mourning and melancholy), one would have to say that Améry also raged at the dead who abandoned him. However, from a moral perspective, this is impossible; the dead are the victims of the Germans. And so Améry rages against the Germans, while identifying in some way with them; not, however, in the usual way, the way that has come to be known as "identification with the aggressor," Anna Freud's (1966) term. With this term, Anna Freud referred to the tendency to identify with the one who has the power to destroy the victim. One does so because the powerlessness of victimhood is unbearable.

Améry's resentment was in some respects a measure of his longing for a relationship with his tormentors and their successors. As discussed, Améry imagined that this would be most likely to happen when the antiman, as he called him, finally stood before the firing squad. Though of course he did not demand the execution of all (but only a few) Germans, for Améry to find in an SS man's death a site of reunion is to say that Améry found identification easiest at the point of death. He was not asking that Germans merely remember and regret what they had done. He was asking that some suffer as he had suffered, so that in imagining their fear, he might not be so terribly lonely. This might sound sadistic. For Améry, it had more to do with finding someone who understood the fear and isolation he lived with every day. For in the end, this was the most terrible legacy of torture, to be left "alone, as I was when they tortured me" (Améry 1980: 96). Who better to understand than the one who had inflicted the torture? Not when the torturer was comfortably back home, but in the moments before his execution.

LOSS AND CLOSURE

Judith Butler suggests that both grief and melancholy can be a playful, or at least a sensuous surprise, like the silk lining of a rough coat suddenly felt against the skin (Butler 2003: 470). While recognizing that our losses may not be representable according to narrative explanations that would make sense of history, she resists the conclusion that even the worst losses can ruin us. She equivocates.

> The rituals of mourning are sites of merriment; [Walter] Benjamin knew this well, but as his text effectively shows, it is not always possible to keep the dance alive. If suffering, if damage, produces its own pleasure and persistence, it is one that takes place against a history that is over, that takes place now as a setting, a configuration of bodies that move in pleasure or fail to move, that move and fail to move at the same time.
>
> (Butler 2003: 472)[12]

The editors of the volume *Loss: The Politics of Mourning*, in which Butler's essay appears, Eng and Kazanjian (2003: ix), write that they seek to produce "a counterintuitive understanding of lost bodies, spaces, and ideals by configuring absence as a potential presence." Whatever this means exactly depends on the particular historical loss in question, not loss in general, which does not exist. One of the essays is on the Armenian genocide. None of the essays refers to the Holocaust. One could argue that the Holocaust has been intensively studied; that it need not be included in every collection devoted to historical loss. More interesting is the impasse reached in the question-and-answer between Marc Nichanian, author of "Catastrophic Mourning," on an aspect of the Armenian genocide, and David Kazanjian, one of the book's editors (Kazanjian and Nichanian 2003). Over and over, Kazanjian tries to find an "affirmative engagement with history" stemming from the genocide, loss as a new beginning. Over and over Nichanian denies it. "The Catastrophe is the end of all history and all politics. Minerva's bird has sung long ago. The only thing that remains to do is understand what happened ... There is no remainder" (142). Finally Nichanian terminates the (email) exchange, restating that against the "will to extermination," there is no affirmation. The annihilatory will must be destroyed, victims mourned, but one can never begin anew.

Nichanian is right. Or if he is not, then Améry has shown what it would take for him to be wrong, a utopian ideal of shared melancholy (melancholy unto death, in some cases) that can serve as a standard, but not as a practice. Butler would resist premature closure. The most terrible losses, and the melancholy that goes with them, carry within them the potential for new life, new dances, new pleasures, even if they are apparently frozen in grief. But sometimes it's just not true. Why not say so? To comprehend Lawrence Langer's *Holocaust Testimonies: The Ruins of Memory* (1991), is to understand that some losses are so catastrophic that they contain no new lives beneath the ruins, no bodies waiting to be revived from apparently dead but only stunned corpses. The survivors whose testimonies

I viewed found not new beginnings, but new ways of surviving. Some were more successful than others.

Generalizations about closure and history are not very helpful. In any case, while this is not strictly an empirical question, it is not one in which ontological, or even anti-ontological, pronouncements are helpful, no matter how open-ended. "In describing melancholia as a confrontation with loss through the adamant refusal of closure, Freud also provides another method of interpreting loss as a creative process" (Eng and Kazanjian 2003: 3). Keeping Nichanian's refusal of affirmation in mind, what if we read Améry in this fashion? Améry's melancholy refuses closure, having nothing but disdain for those who would bring the Holocaust to conclusion. The difference is that Améry's refusal of closure opens him not to the future, but commits him to keeping the past alive. Not only can the Holocaust never be forgiven, but resentment toward its perpetrators can never be abandoned until they wish as much as Améry that it never happened, even – or especially – if this takes place on the march to the perpetrator's place of execution.

Keeping the past alive, cultivating resentment and all that goes with it, including the everlasting memory of hurt, pain, and loneliness, is not what is usually meant by an "affirmative engagement with history." Yet, for some losses it is the most authentic engagement. Closure is a gate that swings open and shut in both directions. It opens to the past so that it can one day be opened to the future. About some losses our task is to take as much care as we can to respect the past: mourn its victims, understand the causes of their victimhood, being clear on what reparation would require, while being equally clear on why that is virtually impossible.

This should not, of course, foreclose genuine attempts at partial and incomplete recompense. Add to this the task of making "never again" more than just a slogan, and incomplete closure is no longer an attempt to make life out of death, but to preserve the life that remains. Is that not enough?

NOTES

1 Ozick is quoted in Diego Gambetta, "Primo Levi's Last Moments" (1999). Gambetta argues against Levi's death being a suicide. He is interesting but not persuasive.

2 Robert Solomon cites personal correspondence as the source of this quotation from Danto, reflecting a position with which Solomon concurs.

3 Améry's position on Nietzsche is actually quite complex, evolving over the years, as Irène Heidelberger-Leonard (2010: 80–81, 271–272) demonstrates in her biography of Améry. Shortly after the war, Améry held that when Nietzsche wrote that "one should strive 'not for contentment but for power, not for peace but for war' . . . he means exactly what he says. There can be no clearer way of expressing it, and the leading German clique acted in precise accordance with those maxims . . . For that reason, this man's books should be banned" (*Zur psychologie des deutschen Volkes* [1945, vol. 2, 508]). However, in one of his last works, "Nietzsche-der Zeitgenosse" (Nietzsche—Our Contemporary), Améry (1975) appreciates Nietzsche as rightly in revolt against the masses.

4 At: walterbenjamin.ominiverdi.org/wp-content/walterbenjamin_concept history.pdf. No translator given. *On the Concept of History*, original 1940, thesis 9. The connection to Walter Benjamin's angel of history is suggested by Thomas Brudholm in *Resentment's Virtue* (2008: 109, 115).

5 Améry 1980: 70. "Resentments" was originally the last essay of *At the Mind's Limits*. "On the Necessity and Impossibility of Being a Jew" was added to later editions. It too closes on a note of deep resignation.

6 *On Aging* was first published in 1968, two years after *Jenseits Von Schuld Und Sühne*. *Jenseits* (*At the Mind's Limits*) was a collection of essays originally published over a period of time.

7 Among 921 elderly patients admitted to a psychiatric hospital in Israel during a five-year period, Holocaust survivors had a significantly higher rate of attempted suicide (Barak et al. 2005). Whether this research can be generalized to the survivor population at large, and what this might mean, remain a question.

8 I interviewed this survivor in 2006. Details are withheld at the request of the family.

9 A fascinating account of Goldhagen's reception in Germany can be found in Michael Zank's "Goldhagen in Germany: Historians' Nightmare & Popular Hero" (2008).

10 In Freudian psychoanalysis, a cathexis (plural cathexes) is the investment of mental or emotional energy in a person, object, or idea.

11 Freud (1917: 245) defines melancholy "in contradistinction to mourning, in which there is nothing about the loss that is unconscious."

12 The work by Walter Benjamin to which Butler refers is *The Origin of German Tragic Drama*.

8 Conclusion: trauma as knowledge

Is there anything to be learned about trauma from where Améry went wrong? He was right, it seems, in holding on to his resentment; right in the sense that his is a coherent and defensible ethical position, though certainly not the only valid position. He was wrong in turning that resentment toward the natural process of aging and death, even though aging and death bring with them their own share of trauma. In other words, some trauma – above all, the trauma of aging and death – has to be accepted as part of the bargain of life. Best, said the ancient Greeks, never to have been born; second best to go back quickly from whence one came (Sophocles, *Oedipus at Colonus* 1211–1227). Yet, somehow one suspects the Greeks never believed this; they loved life too much, even its pain. The wages of life are death.

I have argued that Améry's view was distorted by his isolation. He had no sense of himself as part of a larger family, community, society. His was a single body under siege, even as he lived with and among others. He was not socially isolated. Rather, the trauma of the Holocaust – and above all, the trauma of torture – made his life unbearably lonely, though one suspects that he was vulnerable in this regard. But perhaps this is to say that he was no more than human. In any case, for Améry, fantasies of forgiveness, fusion, and revenge became inseparable.

Yet, this is not the whole story. Had Améry not been outraged at death, unwilling to accept life on the terms it is offered, with death its final payment, it seems less likely that he would have held to the utopian proposition that Germans and others should not be forgiven until they wished as much as he that the Holocaust had never happened. There is a symmetry here too. To not accept what must be accepted, death coming in its own time in its own way was not a logical, but perhaps a psychological, precondition for Améry's version of the categorical imperative. Only it is really a categorical aporia: you may be forgiven only if you do not need forgiveness, because you wish as strongly as I that it had never happened.

But perhaps this proposition too misunderstands forgiveness. Perhaps the Holocaust, for those who perpetrated it, is simply unforgivable. Améry's search for an alternative to forgiveness in a shared desire that it never happened comes too close to a desire to share too much with the perpetrators, who will always be antimen. In other words, Améry will never share a moment with SS man Wajs, a moment in which "he was with *me* – and I was no longer alone" (Améry 1980: 70). It may sound anticlimactic, but aloneness is the greatest and longest-lasting legacy of the Holocaust for so many survivors. One suspects this is the case for many victims of severe trauma.

What do we learn from Améry, among all the others who suffered trauma and are able to share their experience? We learn that trauma is not just an affliction; trauma is a form of knowledge. Traumatic knowledge is ethical knowledge. The inability to move forward, the inability to let go of the past and live in the present tense, serves vividly to embody the memory of what must not be forgotten. Most who suffer trauma would presumably be better served by finding other, more abstract, less physically embodied and embedded forms of memory and expression, but this requires people to pay attention, to listen, to really hear. It also requires the type of holding that Winnicott tells us is needed at that delicate "I AM" moment of infinite exposure, when the traumatized self listens to itself speak, and feels what it has to hear. To hear and to hold, to hold and to hear. Both are needed.

Sometimes hearing and holding are the same; someone to listen is enough. Sometimes not. Terri Jentz seemed to have needed a type of physical holding: by the natural environment of Redmond, and by the women who originally cared for her the night she was run over and axed, women who years later were willing to play a role in her fantasies of fusion. In my opinion, the successful treatment of severe trauma (which is never complete) requires someone to reciprocate the victim's fantasies of fusion, while remaining steadfast should individual boundaries threaten to collapse completely. This need not be the same person who listens.

In the end, this is Caruth's most significant failure as a trauma theorist. Not that she conceptualizes trauma as an experience that lacks psychological depth, not even that its victims must be spoken for, but that her account leaves no place and has no room for the practice of holding. How could holding matter in such a text-based, literary account of trauma, in which the bodies of the traumatized are almost completely absent? And yet, even as this is theoretically true, the counter-example of *Hiroshima mon amour* comes to mind. Caruth's (1996: 25–26) critique opens with a description of the film's opening scene, a twinning of bodies. Two interlaced bodies covered with sparkling ash, evidently victims of the atomic bombing of Hiroshima, segue into two interlaced bodies, first smooth, then sweaty, making love, the French woman and Japanese man. Though Caruth does not mention it, if one watches the haunting opening of the film, in neither case is it entirely clear whose body parts belong to whom, reflecting perhaps the French woman's fusion with her dead German lover.[1] It seems as if every generalization I make about Caruth, about trauma, about forgiveness, must be taken back, qualified. But how could it be any other way when writing about complex concepts and authors?

FORGIVENESS IS A VIRTUE

Forgiveness is a virtue, but like all virtues, it becomes one only when applied to the right people at the right time in the right circumstances. This is, of course, Aristotle's teaching about the mean (*N. Ethics* 1109a: 25–30). Forgiveness is often irrelevant, frequently undesirable. Many accommodations are possible between offender and victim. Améry (1980: 77) argues as explicitly against postwar revenge as he does against forgiveness. Yet, in Améry's desire, what he calls his moral desire, to annul time, one sees even more clearly what so much forgiveness seeks – what Griswold (2007: 193) refers to as the "soul's deepest yearnings," by which he means "deep reunion, love, and harmony."

Améry rejects atonement. At least that is the implication of the German title of his book, *Jenseits Von Schuld und Sühne*, which readily translates as "Beyond Guilt and Atonement." But perhaps he, and we, should not be so quick to dismiss atonement. The single most powerful act relating to forgiveness I encountered was Katherine Ann Power's refusal to accept parole because she understood that no one would believe her remorse and regret as long as she had something to gain from acting contrite. On the contrary, "I had to suffer, and I had to be seen to suffer." Without this public sacrifice, her atonement would be merely personal.

Atonement is particularly appropriate for public acts of wrong-doing, such as Power's. Furthermore, there is no reason that atonement necessarily be connected to forgiveness. Power did not expect forgiveness and did not receive it. As she said, she had no right to expect anything. Power made atonement because she had come to that place where she could stop blaming everyone else and include herself among those who had shed blood during the Vietnam War. She seems to have forgiven herself, but to put it that way cheapens the experience. Rather, she saw herself as an actor caught up in history in much the same way as McNamara and the generals, which, far from lessening her guilt, only made her need for expiation through atonement stronger – an atonement in which her suffering must be both public and extended.

It seems as if this is precisely what Améry should want. Instead of demanding the impossible as an ethical standard – that Germans wish or want that the Holocaust never happened as much as he – why does Améry not wish that Germans make sincere atonement in the manner of Power? That is, that they accept that they were caught up in a unique time in history, *and for this reason* must make acts of public atonement requiring enormous sacrifice, such as years of prison freely undertaken. Is this any more utopian than Améry's ideal? I surmise that Améry rejected atonement in part because it would separate him from the war criminals with whom he longed for a reunion. A reunion in an alternative history, a history in which fusion and revenge are almost the same. Atonement separates the wrongdoer, making his or her crimes forever real, forever inscribed in time.

Earlier, the utopian aspect of Améry's time annulled was praised by noting its ironic similarity to Marcuse's *promesse de Bonheur*. Now it is time to return to earth, and remember that it is impossible. The pain of the past cannot be shared; there will be no recompense; others will never truly understand no matter how hard they try. Most don't try very hard to begin with. It is said that upon finally coming to accept this fact, Améry committed suicide (Reiter 2005: 220–223). Perhaps, but the same author who reaches this conclusion also reports that "in an interview that he gave when *Hand an sich legen* [translated as *On Suicide*] was published, Améry describes himself as having been suicidal since childhood" (220).[2] These things are always complicated. A single case proves nothing, especially when it is impossible to know enough about this single case to say anything definitive.

What is the case, what must be accepted, are the limits of recompense, of understanding, of what may be accomplished by forgiveness, or similar ways of thinking. Forgiveness cannot heal trauma. Forgiveness has a relatively small but significant role to play. Only in the hands of an imaginative master, such as Terri Jentz, and a willing community, Redmond and environs, can forgiveness create an ex post facto holding community adequate to allow Jentz to relive her "I AM" experience of being a living, breathing open wound. The experience was healing for Jentz, and evidently for some members of the community, and that is about as good as it gets. Usually it doesn't get as good, particularly among strangers and the truly guilty.

Trauma and forgiveness are related in a more abstract and subtle way than may first appear. Forgiveness, asked for in the right way and at the right time, sincerely asked for, roughly following a modern version of the steps laid down by Maimonides (Chapter 5), can help overcome trauma. Forgiveness can help liberate us from "simultaneity ... the dream time of vengeance," as Ignatieff puts it (Griswold 2007: 192). Given at the right time, forgiveness can help move the past into the past tense. Nevertheless, even forgiveness sincerely asked and sincerely given is no cure for trauma; nor should we expect it to be.

From trauma to forgiveness, the key question seems to be that raised by Winnicott: can one change the quality of one's attachments so as to spend time in transitional space, where one no longer needs to hold on to one's attachments in quite the same way? This includes the attachments to one's traumas that seem so central to almost any account of traumatic disorder. By "attachment," I do not mean, of course, affectionate bonding, but attachments that have more the quality of a repetition compulsion, the inability to let go of something from which one longs to be free. From Freud's (1920) account of trauma as repetition compulsion, to Caruth to Klein to Winnicott to Kai Erikson, this unwanted attachment seems central to almost any understanding of trauma. Indeed, Ruth Leys makes repetition key to the mimetic and the anti-mimetic accounts of trauma, the two schools of thought she employs to organize her genealogy of trauma theory, as discussed in Chapter 3.

Recall Winnicott's distinction (Chapter 3) between "subjective objects" and "objective objects." Subjective objects are those things we believe exist for us, mirroring our needs and wishes. Objective objects are things that exist external to us, without reference to us and our needs. We invest tradition, the objective object, with something of the subjective object, and bring it to life. The tradition becomes personal, and the personal takes on an existence beyond me. It is in this way that religion becomes subjectively real and true, not merely subjective, and not merely a fact in the world either, for I have had a role in creating my religion and my God. But only a role. Were I the sole creator, I would be insane.

How does Winnicott's psychoanalytic view, a view that is friendly to religion, as shown in Chapter 6, influence the view of forgiveness inspired by Winnicott in that same chapter? All the information required to answer this question is found in the answer to another. How much does Winnicott's view require the cooperation of the universe, the universe that is deaf to our pleas, according to Camus? Not much cooperation, it seems. We (not you or me, but we as a community) can speak for the mute universe, a purely objective object, and so invest even the universe with subjectivity. This is what the authors and editors of the Bible did. This is what humans did thousands of years before the first book of the Hebrew Bible was written, presumably before anything was written, and humans have been doing it ever since. Humans who write about God do this in a more self-conscious way, perhaps, but all who write explicitly or implicitly about humanity's place in the universe do this, novelists and poets included. Indeed, about this topic, the line between fiction and nonfiction is about as fuzzy as it gets.

If we humans can make the universe live with human meaning, then there is no reason to think that humans cannot make communities good enough and strong enough to hold traumatized men and women, so they might begin to heal – communities like those discussed in Chapters 5 and 6, communities like those assumed by Moses Maimonides, even communities like the one constructed by Terri Jentz and her supporters. Holding communities hold the people who hold the traumatized, and so help liberate them from the eternal return of trauma.

If my language here seems a little redundant, it is necessary. Transitional experience is intrapsychic. Traumatic experience at the level it has been discussed in this manuscript is so devastating that there is no reason to think that living in a supportive community will, by itself, be sufficient to aid recovery, though some traumatized people, as we have seen, are remarkably inventive in finding sources of support. Generally, however, these sources of support will be particular other people who love, care for, or befriend the traumatized. These supportive people are more likely to be found in what I have called "holding communities," but might just as well be called "communities," were the term not so corrupted ("the business community," "the legal community").

The subjective creation of objective reality does not require much help from the cosmos, but certain social conditions make it almost impossible.[3] Among these are the social conditions are the obvious ones: the Holocaust, famine in the Horn of Africa, genocide in Darfur, and mass rape in the Congo. Also included are the lesser chronic traumas suffered by marginalized populations every day, such as those written about by Kai Erikson (1976; 1994). At some point, it becomes impossible for humans to invest the world with subjectivity. The result is psychological death, unremitting trauma that destroys an individual's ability to participate in transitional experience; that is, to just be. These individuals may belong to groups we call "the marginalized," but it happens to them one by one.

For Winnicott (1992c: 99), the mother acts as the young child's second skin, so that the child does not have to live too much on the surface, always responding, never just being. Trauma is capable of destroying a vulnerable community's ability to protect its members from bodily and psychological insult (the skin function). For Améry, torture forever destroyed his confidence in any human community's skin function. This is what he means when he says, "Whoever has succumbed to torture can no longer feel at home in the world" (1980: 40). Since humans need not just protection, but meaning, they also require a rich culture. More than this, they must be psychologically able to participate in its creation, which means they must be free to be, the first freedom. Trauma renders a vulnerable community unable to provide its members the security to participate in this freedom.

Bad in itself, life in a state of chronic trauma makes both the granting and acceptance of forgiveness almost impossible. This is unfortunate not because forgiveness is a great act of healing, it is not; though forgiveness has its role to play. Rather, forgiveness is a virtue, calling forth some of the most fully developed human capabilities in both offender and victim. Prime among these is the acceptance of human vulnerability and all that goes with it. If there were no other reason to read Améry but to learn this lesson, that would be reason enough. I may be readily harmed by another, and I may harm another. If this were not true, forgiveness would be unnecessary. Furthermore, forgiveness leads me to recognize that even my moral goodness requires the cooperation of others. This is the pas de deux quality of forgiveness, a claim that remains valid even if these others are not the original offenders, but those who help to make this a good enough world to live in. This was the point of Chapter 6. In the experience of forgiveness, perhaps more than any other experience of virtue, one recognizes the power of others to allow one to practice the virtue.

Under the right circumstances, forgiveness recognizes our flawed humanity, how readily and easily we hurt each other, and how difficult it often is to let go of hatred, rancor, and resentment. Even in Améry's creative deployment of resentment, one sees the way in which it serves to connect him to those who would destroy him, holding out the hopeless hope of reconciliation and union. Most who hold onto their hatred and rancor do so with far less moral creativity, but with the same desire to hold onto the hurt, as though hurt and hate had become their most reliable companions.

To forgive is to be twice vulnerable: the first time when we are hurt, the second time when we say that we were hurt, recognize that the one who has hurt us has made amends, and so no longer cling to the righteousness of our rancor. It feels (at least for a little while) as if we are left with nothing at all, nothing but friends, lovers, and the holding community. Often this is enough; usually we don't have all three. Sometimes we don't have anyone. When one forgives, one says, at least in the extreme case, "You hurt me, and you meant to hurt me. But I can see that you are intent on making amends, and I believe from your story and your actions that you are a changed person, and so I am going to give you another chance to hurt me by resuming my relationship with you. I am going to do this even though I realize that you will never really understand how much you hurt me. No matter how hard you try, you will never get it." Most people don't put it this way, but this is what forgiveness often means.

Forgiveness is a virtue, but it is not the sum of all virtues. Forgiveness is not all powerful; it will not make you, me, or us whole. Moreover, forgiveness is often unsuitable. To learn when forgiveness is appropriate is itself a virtue. Because forgiveness is a preeminently social virtue, it is good to live in a community that encourages individuals to practice forgiveness. Communities do this not by preaching forgiveness, but by providing a holding environment suitable for its various members: children, adults, the aged, the infirm, the afflicted, and the unfortunate. When human communities fail to do this, they fail in their most basic responsibility.

NOTES

1 The famous opening scene is readily available on the Internet.
2 The original source is *Die Zeit, 8/13/76.* Though the interview reads a little ambiguously, with Améry actually saying that suicide had been his preferred manner of death "since childhood." Not the same thing, but how many children actually think about this? Maybe more than we know.
3 Regarding help from the cosmos, recall Camus's *The Plague* (1972), in which the community of Oran became stronger under the assault of an epidemic, not only for the leading characters, such as Dr. Rieux, Jean Tarrou, and Monsieur Grand, but for many (certainly not all) citizens, who organize themselves into various brigades. On the other hand, Thucydides' (II.7) account of the plague that decimated Athens in 430 BCE finds only the dissolution of community.

References

Classical works cited in the text in the form that is usual in classical studies, such as Plato's *Symposium*, and Milton's *Paradise Lost*, are not repeated here. Nor are citations to Nietzsche, when they are given by book, chapter, and section number. Citations to the Bible are given in the conventional form in the text by chapter and verse.

Abram, Jan. 1996. *The Language of Winnicott*. Northvale, NJ: Jason Aronson.

Adorno, Theodor. 1974. *Minima Moralia: Reflections from Damaged Life*, trans. E. F. N. Jephcott. London: New Left Books.

Agamben, Giorgio. 1999. *Remnants of Auschwitz*, trans. D. Heller-Roazen. New York: Zone Books.

Akhtar, Salman. 2002. "Forgiveness: Origins, Dynamics, Psychopathology and Technical Relevance," *Psychoanalytic Quarterly* 71: 175–212.

Alford, C. F. 1989. *Melanie Klein and Critical Social Theory*. New Haven, CT: Yale University Press.

Alford, C. F. 1990. "Melanie Klein and the *Oresteia* Complex," *Cultural Critique*, no. 15: 167–190.

Alford, C. F. 2006. *Psychology and the Natural Law of Reparation*. New York and Cambridge, UK: Cambridge University Press.

Alford, C. F. 2009a. *After the Holocaust: The Book of Job, Primo Levi, and the Path to Affliction*. New York and Cambridge, UK: Cambridge University Press.

Alford, C. F. 2009b. "What if the Holocaust Had No Name?" *Holocaust Studies: A Journal of Culture and History* 15 (3): 71–94.

Alford, C. F. 2012. "Jean Améry: Resentment as Ethic and Ontology," *Topoi* 31 (2): 229–240.

American Psychiatric Association. 2000. *Diagnostic and Statistical Manual of Mental Disorders*, 4th edn, text revision. Washington, DC: American Psychiatric Publishing.

Améry, Jean. 1966. *Jenseits von Schuld und Sühne: Bewältigungsversuche Eines Überwältigten*. Munich: Szczesny. [German original of *At the Mind's Limits*]

Améry, Jean. 1975. "Nietzsche-der Zeitgenosse," *Merkur* 29 (no. 331): 1141–1149.

Améry, Jean. 1980. *At the Mind's Limits: Contemplations by a Survivor on Auschwitz and its Realities*, trans. Sidney Rosenfeld and Stella P. Rosenfeld. Bloomington, IN: Indiana University Press.

Améry, Jean. 1994. *On Aging: Revolt and Resignation*, trans. John D. Barlow. Bloomington, IN: Indiana University Press.

Améry, Jean. 1999. *Suicide: A Discourse on Voluntary Death*, trans. John D. Barlow. Bloomington, IN: Indiana University Press.

Arendt, Hannah. 1958. *The Human Condition*. University of Chicago Press.

Arendt, Hannah. 1964. *Eichmann in Jerusalem: A Report on the Banality of Evil*. New York: Viking Press.

Arendt, Hannah. 2003. "Response to Gershom Scholem." In P. Baehr (ed.), *The Portable Hannah Arendt*, New York: Penguin, pp. 391–396.

Barak, Yoram, Aizenberg, Dov, Szor, Henry, Swartz, Marnina, Maor, Rachel, and Knobler, Haim Y. 2005. "Increased Risk of Attempted Suicide Among Aging Holocaust Survivors," *American Journal of Geriatric Psychiatry* 13 (8): 701–704.

Benjamin, Walter. 1940. *On the Concept of History*. walterbenjamin.ominiverdi. org/wp-content/walterbenjamin_concepthistory.pdf. [No translator given.]

Bergson, Henri. 1998. *Creative Evolution*, trans. Arthur Mitchell. Mineola, NY: Dover. [original 1911]

Bergson, Henri. 2007. *The Creative Mind: An Introduction to Metaphysics*, trans. Mabelle Andison. Mineola, NY: Dover. [original 1936]

Bittner, Rüdiger. 1994. "Ressentiment." In R. Schacht (ed.), *Nietzsche, Genealogy, Morality: Essays on Nietzsche's On the Genealogy of Morality*, Berkeley, CA: University of California Press, pp. 127–138.

Blanchot, Maurice. 1995. *The Writing of the Disaster*, trans. Ann Smock. Lincoln: University of Nebraska Press.

Blumenthal, David. nd. "Repentance and Forgiveness." www.crosscurrents.org/ blumenthal.htm.

Bonhoeffer, Dietrich. 1963. *The Cost of Discipleship*. New York: Macmillan.

Botwinick, Sara. 2000. "Aging After Surviving: How Religious Holocaust Survivors Cope with their Trauma," *Journal of Jewish Communal Service* 76: 228–235.

Brodbeck, May. 1958. "Methodological Individualisms: Definition and Reduction." *Philosophy of Science* 25: 1–22. Also at: www.jstor.org/stable/185333.

Brudholm, Thomas. 2008. *Resentment's Virtue: Jean Améry and the Refusal to Forgive*. Philadelphia, PA: Temple University Press.

Butler, Joseph [Bishop]. 2009. *Fifteen Sermons Preached at the Rolls Chapel*. Gloucestershire, UK: Dodo Press. [original 1726]

Butler, Judith. 1997. *The Psychic Life of Power*. Stanford, CA: Stanford University Press.

Butler, Judith. 2003. "Afterword: After Loss, What Then?" In D. Eng and D. Kazanjian (eds.), *Loss: The Politics of Mourning*. Berkeley, CA: University of California Press, pp. 467–473.

Butler, Judith. 2004. "Violence, Mourning, Politics." In *Precarious Life: The Powers of Mourning and Violence.* London: Verso, pp. 19–49.

Camus, Albert. 1955. *The Myth of Sisyphus and Other Essays,* trans. Justin O'Brien. New York: Vintage Books.

Camus, Albert. 1972. *The Plague,* trans. Stuart Gilbert. New York: Vintage Books.

Camus, Albert. 1988. *The Stranger,* trans. Matthew Ward. New York: Vintage Books.

Caruth, Cathy. 1995. "Introduction." In C. Caruth (ed.), *Trauma: Explorations in Memory,* Baltimore, MD: Johns Hopkins University Press, pp. 3–12, 151–157.

Caruth, Cathy. 1996. *Unclaimed Experience: Trauma, Narrative, and History.* Baltimore, MD: Johns Hopkins University Press.

Defoe, Daniel. 1953. *Robinson Crusoe and the Further Adventures.* London: Collins.

Delbo, Charlotte. 1995. *Auschwitz and After,* trans. Rosette Lamont. New Haven, CT: Yale University Press.

Delbo, Charlotte. 2001. *Days and Memory,* trans. Rosette Lamont. Evanston, IL: Marlboro Press/Northwestern University Press.

Derrida, Jacques. 1999. "Le siècle et le pardon." *Le Monde des Débats,* no 9, Décembre: 10–17.

Derrida, Jacques. 2001. *On Cosmopolitanism and Forgiveness,* trans. Mark Dooley and Michael Hughes. London: Routledge.

Dilthey, William. 1988. *Introduction to the Human Sciences: An Attempt to Lay a Foundation for the Study of Society and History,* trans. Ramon Betanzos. Detroit, MI: Wayne State University Press. [original 1883]

Doblmeier, Martin. 2007. *The Power of Forgiveness.* Alexandria, VA: Journey Films. [documentary film]

Elshtain, J. B. 1995. *Augustine and the Limits of Politics.* Notre Dame, IN: University of Notre Dame Press.

Eng, David and Kazanjian, David. 2003. "Introduction: Mourning Remains." In D. Eng and D. Kazanjian (eds.), *Loss: The Politics of Mourning.* Berkeley, CA: University of California Press, pp. 1–27.

Epstein, Anita. 2010. "Can a Holocaust Survivor ever Forgive the Germans?" At: www.haaretz.com/jewish-world/can-a-holocaust-survivor-ever-forgive-the-germans-1.296163. [original June 14, 2010]

Erikson, Kai. 1976. *Everything in its Path: Destruction of Community in the Buffalo Creek Flood.* New York: Simon and Schuster.

Erikson, Kai. 1994. *A New Species of Trouble: The Human Experience of Modern Disasters.* New York: W. W. Norton.

Erikson, Kai. 1995. "Notes on Trauma and Community." In C. Caruth (ed.), *Trauma: Explorations in Memory.* Baltimore, MD: Johns Hopkins University Press, pp. 183–199.

Felman, Shoshana. 1992. "Education and Crisis, or the Vicissitudes of Teaching." In S. Felman and D. Laub (eds.), *Testimony: Crises of Witnessing in Literature, Psychoanalysis, and History*. New York: Routledge, pp. 1–52.

Felman, Shoshana and Laub, Dori. 1992. *Testimony: Crises of Witnessing in Literature, Psychoanalysis, and History*. New York: Routledge.

Ferenczi, Sándor. 1988. *The Clinical Diary of Sándor Ferenczi*, J. Dupont (ed.). Cambridge, MA: Harvard University Press. [original 1932]

Ferenczi, Sándor. 1994. *Final Contributions to the Problems and Methods of Psychoanalysis*. London: Karnac Books. [original 1955]

Foot, Philippa. 1994. "Nietzsche's Immoralism." In R. Schacht (ed.), *Nietzsche, Genealogy, Morality: Essays on Nietzsche's On the Genealogy of Morality*, Berkeley, CA: University of California Press, pp. 3–14.

Foucault, Michel. 1994. *The Birth of the Clinic: An Archaeology of Medical Perception*, trans. Alan Sheridan. New York: Vintage.

Freud, Anna. 1966. *The Ego and the Mechanisms of Defense*, rev. ed., trans. Cecil Baines. New York: International Universities Press, pp. 109–121. [vol. 2 of *The Writings of Anna Freud*].

Freud, Sigmund. 1898. "Sexuality in the Aetiology of the Neuroses." In James Strachey (ed.), *The Standard Edition of the Complete Psychological Works of Sigmund Freud*, 24 vols, vol. 3: 261–286. London: Hogarth Press, 1953–1974 [*The Standard Edition* is hereafter cited as SE.]

Freud, Sigmund. 1909. Analysis of a Phobia in a Five-Year Old Boy. *SE* 10: 22–152.

Freud, Sigmund. 1913. Totem and Taboo. *SE* 13: 1–163.

Freud, Sigmund. 1914. Remembering, Repeating, and Working-Through. *SE* 12: 145–156.

Freud, Sigmund. 1915. The Instincts and their Vicissitudes. *SE* 14: 109–140.

Freud, Sigmund. 1917. Mourning and Melancholia. *SE*: 14: 243–258.

Freud, Sigmund. 1920. Beyond the Pleasure Principle. *SE* 18: 3–64.

Freud, Sigmund. 1921. Group Psychology and the Analysis of the Ego. *SE* 18: 67–144.

Freud, Sigmund. 1923. The Ego and the Id. *SE*, vol. 19: 1–66.

Freud, Sigmund. 1930. Civilization and its Discontents. *SE* 21: 59–148.

Freud, Sigmund. 1938. Splitting of the Ego in the Process of Defense. *SE* 23: 271–278.

Frommer, Martin S. 2005. "Thinking Relationally about Forgiveness." *Psychoanalytic Dialogues* 15: 33–45.

Gambetta, Diego. 1999. "Primo Levi's Last Moments: A New Look at the Italian Author's Tragic Death Twelve Years Ago." At: www.bostonreview.net/BR24.3/gambetta.html.

Girard, René. 1977. *Violence and the Sacred*, trans. Patrick Gregory. Baltimore, MD: Johns Hopkins University Press.

Gobodo-Madikizela, Pumla. 2003. *A Human Being Died that Night: A South African Story of Forgiveness*. New York: Houghton Mifflin.

Goldhagen, Daniel Jonah. *Hitler's Willing Executioners: Ordinary Germans and the Holocaust*. New York: Knopf.

Greenberg, Irving. 1977. "Cloud of Smoke, Pillar of Fire: Judaism, Christianity, and Modernity after the Holocaust." In E. Fleischner (ed.), *Auschwitz: Beginning of a New Era?* New York: KTAV Publishing House.

Greenspan, Henry. 1998. *On Listening to Holocaust Survivors: Recounting and Life History*. Westport, CT: Praeger.

Griswold, Charles. 2007. *Forgiveness: A Philosophical Exploration*. Cambridge University Press.

Hampton, Jean. 1988. "Forgiveness, Resentment and Hatred." In Jeffrie Murphy and Jean Hampton, *Forgiveness and Mercy*. Cambridge, UK: Cambridge University Press, pp. 35–87.

Hardy, Barbara. 1968. "Towards a Poetics of Fiction: An Approach through Narrative." *Novel: A Forum on Fiction* 2 (1): 5–14.

Hart, H. L. A. 1994. *The Concept of Law*, 2nd edn. Oxford University Press.

Heidelberger-Leonard, Irène. 2010. *The Philosopher of Auschwitz: Jean Améry and Living with the Holocaust*. London: I. B. Tauris.

Hercules, Bob and Pugh, Cheri. nd. *Forgiving Dr. Mengele*. First Run Features. [documentary film].

Hughes, Paul. 2010. "Forgiveness." In *Stanford Encyclopedia of Philosophy*. http://plato.stanford.edu/entries/forgiveness/

Jentz, Terri. 2006. *Strange Piece of Paradise*. New York: Farrar, Straus and Giroux.

Jones, L. Gregory. 1995. *Embodying Forgiveness*. Grand Rapids, MI: William B. Eerdmans.

Kant, Immanuel. 1960. *Religion within the Limits of Reason Alone*, trans. Theodore Greene and Hoyt Hudson. New York: Harper Torchbooks.

Kant, Immanuel. 1993. *Grounding for the Metaphysics of Morals*, trans. James Ellington, Indianapolis, IN: Hackett.

Kaufmann, Walter. 1975. *Nietzsche: Philosopher, Psychologist, Antichrist*, 4th edn. Princeton, NJ: Princeton University Press. [original 1950]

Kazanjian, David and Nichanian, Marc. 2003. "Between Genocide and Catastrophe." In D. Eng and D. Kazanjian (eds.), *Loss: The Politics of Mourning*. Berkeley, CA: University of California Press, pp. 125–147.

Khan, Masud. 1963. "The Concept of Cumulative Trauma." *The Psychoanalytic Study of the Child* 18: 286–306.

Kierkegaard, Søren. 1980. *The Concept of Anxiety*, trans. Reidar Thomte. Princeton University Press.

Klein, Melanie. 1928. "Early Stages of the Oedipus Complex." In *Love, Guilt, and Reparation and Other Works 1921–1945*. New York: The Free Press, 1975, pp. 186–198. [volume 1 of *The Writings of Melanie Klein*, ed. R. E. Money-Kyrle]

Klein, Melanie. 1940. "Mourning and its Relation to Manic-Depressive States." In *Love, Guilt and Reparation and Other Works 1921–1945*, pp. 344–368.

Klein, Melanie. 1946. "Notes on Some Schizoid Mechanisms." In *Envy and Gratitude and Other Works, 1946–1963*. New York: The Free Press, pp. 1–24. [volume 3 of *The Writings of Melanie Klein*, ed. R. E. Money-Kyrle]

Klein, Melanie. 1948. "On the Theory of Anxiety and Guilt." In *Envy and Gratitude and Other Works, 1946–1963*, pp. 25–42.

Klein, Melanie. 1957. "Envy and Gratitude." In *Envy and Gratitude and Other Works 1946–1963*, pp. 176–235.

Klein, Melanie. 1963. "Some Reflections on 'The Oresteia.'" In *Envy and Gratitude and Other Works 1946–1963*, pp. 276–299.

Klein, Melanie. 1964. "Love, Guilt and Reparation." In Klein and Joan Riviere, *Love, Hate and Reparation*. New York: W. W. Norton, pp. 57–119.

Konstan, David. 2010. *Before Forgiveness: The Origins of a Moral Idea*. New York: Cambridge University Press.

Kor, Eva Mozes. 1995. In M. Wright (ed.), *Echoes from Auschwitz: Dr. Mengele's Twins, The Story of Eva and Miriam Mozes*. Terre Haute, IN: CANDLES, Inc.

Kraft, Robert. 2002. *Memory Perceived: Recalling the Holocaust*. Westport, CT: Praeger.

Kristeva, Julia. 2001. *Hannah Arendt*, trans. Ross Guberman. New York: Columbia University Press.

Kushner, Harold. 2004. *When Bad Things Happen to Good People*. New York: Anchor. [reprint edition]

Lacan, Jacques. 1977. *Écrits: A Selection*, trans. Alan Sheridan. New York: W. W. Norton.

LaCapra, Dominick. 1998. *History and Memory after Auschwitz*. Ithaca, NY: Cornell University Press.

Lang, Berel. 1994. "Forgiveness." *American Philosophical Quarterly* 31: 105–115.

Lang, Berel. 2000. *Holocaust Representation: Art Within the Limits of History and Ethics*. Baltimore, MD: Johns Hopkins University Press.

Langer, Lawrence. 1978. *The Age of Atrocity: Death in Modern Literature*. Boston, MA: Beacon Press.

Langer, Lawrence. 1991. *Holocaust Testimonies: The Ruins of Memory*. New Haven, CT: Yale University Press.

Laub, Dori. 1995. "Truth and Testimony: The Process and the Struggle." In C. Caruth, (ed.), *Trauma: Explorations in Memory*. Baltimore, MD: Johns Hopkins University Press, pp. 61–75.

Levi, Primo. 1989. *The Drowned and the Saved*, trans. Raymond Rosenthal. New York: Vintage International.

Levi, Primo. 1996. *Survival in Auschwitz: The Nazi Assault on Humanity*, trans. Stuart Woolf. New York: Touchstone Books. [published in England as *If This Is a Man*]

Levinas, Emmanuel. 1990. *Difficult Freedom: Essays on Judaism*, trans. Sean Hand. Baltimore, MD: Johns Hopkins University Press.

Leys, Ruth. 2000. *Trauma: A Genealogy*. University of Chicago Press.

Lifton, Robert J. 1986. *The Nazi Doctors: Medical Killing and the Psychology of Genocide*. New York: Basic Books.

Likierman, Meira. 2001. *Melanie Klein: Her Work in Context*. London: Continuum.

Lunn, Johanna. 2007. *Forgiveness: Stories for Our Time*. Montreal, Quebec: National Film Board of Canada. [documentary film]

Lyotard, Jean-François. 1984. *The Postmodern Condition: A Report on Knowledge*, trans. G. Bennington and B. Massumi. Minneapolis, MI: University of Minnesota Press.

Maimonides, Moses. 1983. *The Book of Knowledge: From the Mishneh Torah of Maimonides*, trans. H. M. Russell and J. Weinberg. New York: KTAV Publishing House. Also at: www.torahlab.org/download/rambam_sourcesheet.pdf [original twelfth century BCE]

Malcolm, W. and Greenberg, L. 2000. "Forgiveness as a Process of Change in Individual Psychotherapy." In M. McCullough, K. Pargament, and C. Thoresen (eds.), *Forgiveness: Theory, Research, and Practice*. New York: The Guilford Press, pp. 179–202.

Mann, Thomas. 1970. "Nietzsche's Philosophy in Light of Recent History." In *Thomas Mann: Last Essays*. New York: Alfred A Knopf.

Marcuse, Herbert. 1962. *Eros and Civilization: A Philosophical Inquiry into Freud*. New York: Vintage Books.

Marcuse, Herbert. 1978. *The Aesthetic Dimension*. Boston: Beacon Press.

Meltzer, Donald. 1981. "The Kleinian Expansion of Freud's Metapsychology." *International Journal of Psycho-Analysis* 62: 177–185.

Michaels, Walter Benn. 1996. "'You Who Never Was There': Slavery and the New Historicism, Deconstruction and the Holocaust." *Narrative* 4 (1): 1–16. Also at: www.jstor.org/stable/20107068.

Miller, James. 1993. *The Passion of Michel Foucault*. New York: Simon and Schuster.

Murdoch, Iris. 1966. *The Time of the Angels*. London: Penguin Books.

Murphy, Jeffrie. 1988. "Forgiveness and Resentment." In Jeffrie G. Murphy and Jean Hampton, *Forgiveness and Mercy*. Cambridge University Press, pp. 14–34.

Murphy, Jeffrie. 2003. *Getting Even: Forgiveness and its Limits*. Oxford and New York: Oxford University Press.

National Council of Churches [NCC]. 2001. *Journey Toward Forgiveness: From Rage to Forgiveness*. Harrisonburg, VA: Mennonite Media for the NCC. [documentary film]

Neisser, Ulric. 1994. "Self-Narratives: True and False." In U. Neisser and R. Fivush (eds.), *The Remembering Self*. New York: Cambridge University Press, pp. 1–18.

Newberry, Paul A. 2001. "Joseph Butler on Forgiveness: A Presupposed Theory of Emotion." *Journal of the History of Ideas* 62 (2): 233–44.

Nicholson, Julie. 2011. *A Song for Jenny: A Mother's Story of Love and Loss*. London: Harper.

Nietzsche, Friedrich. 1968a. *The Birth of Tragedy Out of the Spirit of Music*. In *Basic Writings of Nietzsche*, trans. Walter Kaufmann. New York: Modern Library, pp. 3–144.

Nietzsche, Friedrich. 1968b. "On the Genealogy of Morals." In *Basic Writings of Nietzsche*, trans. Walter Kaufmann, pp. 439–602.

Niewyk, Donald, ed. 1998. *Fresh Wounds: Early Narratives of Holocaust Survivors*. Chapel Hill: University of North Carolina Press. [narratives collected by David Boder]

Nussbaum, Martha. 1986. *The Fragility of Goodness: Luck and Ethics in Greek Tragedy and Philosophy*. Cambridge University Press.

Ogden, Thomas. 1979. "On Projective Identification." *International Journal of Psychoanalysis* 60: 357–373.

Ogden, Thomas. 1989. *The Primitive Edge of Experience*. Northvale, NJ: Jason Aronson.

Ozick, Cynthia. 1989. *Metaphor and Memory*. New York: Knopf.

Pagani, Karen. 2010. "The Uses and Abuses of Joseph Butler's Account of Forgiveness: Between the Passions and the Interests." *South Central Review* 27 (3): 12–33.

Phillips, Adam. 1988. *Winnicott*. Cambridge, MA: Harvard University Press.

Phillips, Adam. 1997. "Keeping it Moving: Commentary on Judith Butler's 'Melancholy Gender/Refused Identification.'" In Judith Butler, *The Psychic Life of Power*. Stanford University Press, pp. 151–159.

Reiter, Andrea Ilse Maria. 2005. *Narrating the Holocaust*, trans. Patrick Camiller. New York: Continuum.

Rice, Alison. 2002. "Forgiveness: An Interview with Julia Kristeva." *PMLA* 117 (2): 278–295. Also at: www.jstor.org/stable/823274.

Ricoeur, Paul. nd. "Memory, History, Forgiveness: A Dialogue Between Paul Ricoeur and Sorin Antohi." At: www.janushead.org/8–1/Ricoeur.pdf.

Ricoeur, Paul. 2004. *Memory, History, Forgetting*, trans. Kathleen Blamey and David Pellauer. University of Chicago Press.

Rilke, Rainer Maria. 1945. *Sonnets to Orpheus*, trans. Jessie Lemont. New York: Fine Editions Press.

Roberts, Robert C. 1995. "Forgivingness." *American Philosophical Quarterly* 32 (4): 289–306.

Roth, Phillip. 2007. *Exit Ghost*. New York: Houghton Mifflin.

Russell, Jesse and Cohn, Ronald. 2012. *Katherine Ann Power*. Stoughton, WI: Books on Demand.

Rustin, Michael. 1982. "A Socialist Consideration of Kleinian Psychoanalysis." *New Left Review*, 131: 71–96.

Said, Edward. 1979. *Orientalism*. New York: Vintage Books.

Scarry, Elaine. 1987. *The Body in Pain: The Making and Unmaking of the World*. New York: Oxford University Press.

Schimmel, Solomon. 2002. *Wounds Not Healed by Time: The Power of Repentance and Forgiveness*. Oxford University Press.

Schwartz, Murray. 2002. "Locating Trauma: A Commentary on Ruth Leys's *Trauma: A Genealogy*." *American Imago* 59 (2): 367–384.

Segal, Hanna. 1952. "A Psycho-Analytical Approach to Aesthetics." *International Journal of Psycho-Analysis* 33: 196–207.

Segal, Hanna. 1997. "Silence is the Real Crime." In *Psychoanalysis, Literature and War: Papers 1972–1995*. London: Routledge, pp. 143–156.

Segal, Hanna. 2007. "Introduction to Bion." In *Yesterday, Today and Tomorrow*. London: Routledge, pp. 211–218.

Siassi, Shahrzad. 2004. "Transcending Bitterness and Early Paternal Loss through Mourning and Forgiveness." *Psychoanalytic Quarterly* 73: 915–937.

Smedes, Lewis. 1984. *Forgive and Forget: Healing the Hurts We Don't Deserve*. New York: Harper and Row.

Smedes, Lewis. 1998. "Stations on the Journey from Forgiveness to Hope." In Everett Worthington Jr. (ed.), *Dimensions of Forgiveness: Psychological Research and Theological Perspectives*. Philadelphia, PA: Templeton Foundation Press, pp. 341–354.

Smith, Henry F. 2008. "Leaps of Faith: Is Forgiveness a Useful Concept?" *International Journal of Psychoanalysis* 89: 919–936. Also at: onlinelibrary.wiley.com/doi/10.1111/j.1745–8315.2008.00082.x/full.

Solomon, Robert. 1994. "One Hundred Years of Ressentiment: Nietzsche's Genealogy of Morals." In Richard Schacht (ed.), *Nietzsche, Genealogy, Morality: Essays on Nietzsche's On the Genealogy of Morality*. Berkeley, CA: University of California Press, pp. 95–126.

Stonebridge, Lyndsey. 2000. "Bombs, Birth, and Trauma: Henry Moore's and D. W. Winnicott's Prehistory Figments." *Cultural Critique* no. 46: 80–101.

Ulanov, Ann Belford. 2001. *Finding Space: Winnicott, God, and Psychic Reality*. Louisville, KY: Westminster John Knox Press.

van der Kolk, Bessel, and van der Hart, Onno. 1995. "The Intrusive Past: The Flexibility of Memory and the Engraving of Trauma." In C. Caruth (ed.), *Trauma: Explorations in Memory*. Baltimore, MD: Johns Hopkins University Press, pp. 158–182.

Weigel, Sigrid. 2002. "Secularization and Sacralization, Normalization and Rupture: Kristeva and Arendt on Forgiveness," trans. Mark Kyburz. *PMLA* 117 (2): 320–323. At: www.jstor.org/stable/823282.

Whitney, Helen. 2011a. *Forgiveness. Helen Whitney Productions, Clear View Productions Foundation, and WETA*, Washington, DC. [documentary film]

Whitney, Helen. 2011b. *Forgiveness: A Time to Love and a Time to Hate*. Campbell, CA: Fastpencil.

Wiesel, Elie. 1982. *The Accident*, trans. Anne Borchardt. New York: Bantam Books

Wiesenthal, Simon. 1997. *The Sunflower: On the Possibilities and Limits of Forgiveness*. New York: Schocken Books.

Winnicott, D. W. 1965a. *The Family and Individual Development*. London: Tavistock.

Winnicott, D. W. 1965b. "Morals and Education." In *The Maturational Processes and the Facilitating Environment*. Madison, CT: International Universities Press, pp. 93–107.

Winnicott, D. W. 1965c. "The Theory of the Parent-Infant Relationship." In *The Maturational Processes and the Facilitating Environment*, pp. 37–55.

Winnicott, D. W. 1965d. "Communicating and Not Communicating Leading to a Study of Certain Opposites." In *The Maturational Processes and the Facilitating Environment*, pp. 179–192.

Winnicott, D. W. 1965e. "Ego Distortion in Terms of True and False Self." In *The Maturational Processes and the Facilitating Environment*, pp. 140–152.

Winnicott, D. W. 1965f. "The Capacity To Be Alone." In *The Maturational Processes and the Facilitating Environment*, pp. 29–36.

Winnicott, D. W. 1971a. "Transitional Objects and Transitional Phenomena." In *Playing and Reality*, New York: Routledge, pp. 1–25.

Winnicott, D. W. 1971b. "The Location of Cultural Experience." In *Playing and Reality*, pp. 95–103.

Winnicott, D. W. 1971c. "Creativity and its Origins." In *Playing and Reality*, pp. 65–85.

Winnicott, D. W. 1986. "The Child in the Family Group." In C. Winnicott, R. Shepherd, and M. Davis (eds.), *Home is Where We Start From: Essays by a Psychoanalyst*. New York: W. W. Norton, pp. 128–141.

Winnicott, D. W. 1989. "The Concept of Trauma in Relation to the Development of the Individual within the Family." In C. Winnicott, R. Shepherd, and M. Davis (eds.), *Psychoanalytic Explorations*. London: Karnac, pp. 130–148.

Winnicott, D. W. 1992a. "Mind and its Relation to the Psyche-Soma." In *Through Paediatrics to Psycho-Analysis*. London: Karnac, pp. 243–254.

Winnicott, D. W. 1992b. "Primary Maternal Preoccupation." In *Through Paediatrics to Psycho-Analysis*, pp. 300–305.

Winnicott, D. W. 1992c. "Anxiety Associated with Insecurity." In *Through Paediatrics to Psycho-Analysis*, pp. 97–100.

Winnicott, D. W. 1992d. "Hate in the Countertransference." In *Through Paediatrics to Psycho-Analysis*, pp. 194–203.

Zank, Michael. 2008. "Goldhagen in Germany: Historians' Nightmare & Popular Hero. An Essay on the Reception of *Hitler's Willing Executioners* in Germany." At: www.bu.edu/mzank/Michael_Zank/gold.html. An earlier version of this essay appeared in *Religious Studies Review* 24 (3) 1998: 231–240.

Žižek, Slavoj. 1989. *The Sublime Object of Ideology*. London: Verso.

Index